Run Grow Transform

Integrating Business and Lean IT

Endorsements

Run Grow Transform takes the next logical step to driving enterprise value by showing how to integrate Lean IT thinking deeply within the business itself—creating a multiplier effect. This could be the game-changing playbook for IT 3.0.

Mark Katz, CIO and Senior Vice President, Esselte Corporation (global leader in office supply products, including Oxford and Pendaflex)

A powerful read detailing how companies can leverage their Lean IT transformation to supercharge the business.

Tom Paider, Associate Vice President, IT Build Capability Leader, Nationwide

What CIO is not under constant pressure to cut costs, increase output, and foster innovation, keeping pace with growth and business transformation? Lean IT is the key set of disciplines to achieve just that. The consistent application of the practices described in this book has enabled Embraer to reap huge gains. They are practice proven, and I recommend this book to all IT professionals as a desktop companion.

Alexandre Baulé, Vice President, Information Systems, Embraer (third largest commercial jet producer in the world)

Provides a superb framework for applying Lean practices to help business and IT work together to get more value from IT capabilities. You can use this book as a guideline for focusing the benefits gained from Lean IT practices to help grow and transform your business.

Thomas Knutilla, IT Group Director, Ryder System Inc.

This book sheds light on the way to the bridge between sister cities of Lean and Innovation. Steve captures today's issues in relatable terms and examples—I felt the pages could have been lifted straight from our own management status reports or project issues meetings.

Melissa Barrett, Enterprise Architecture and IT Strategy, Premera Blue Cross

Good read! The role of IT in enterprise Lean transformation is vital to success. *Run Grow Transform* addresses a much-needed perspective.

Jim Garrick, FedEx Express, Lean Operations

In a time where Business and IT must join hands to reduce waste, drive innovation, and create a competitive advantage, this book presents an inspiring view. It is a must-read for everyone on this journey.

David Bogaerts and Jael Schuyer, Lean-Agile coaches, ING

The "business as usual" scenario is not an option in today's economy and global challenges. A transformation in methods, tools, and frameworks is needed to guide your business decisions. This book is your first step!

Khuloud Odeh, IT Director, Grameen Foundation

Steve Bell has mapped a new trajectory for CIOs seeking to successfully navigate the path of transformation to chief *innovation* officer. For the majority of those stuck expending most of their enterprise resources on "run the business" activities, this book provides a roadmap for operational and innovative excellence. I challenge any CIO to read Chapter 1 of Bell's breakthrough work and not be compelled to start this journey—from run, to growth, to innovation—and in so doing become a transformative leader in the creation of real and sustainable business value.

Jeffrey Barnes, Society for Information Management, Regional Director, Advanced Practices Council

Not just for Lean practitioners, **Run Grow Transform** is a must-have reference for any IT organization, regardless of size, age, or industry, looking to move to the next level of performance.

Sarah Topham, Lean Deployment Leader, Information Technology and Product Management, Paychex, Inc.

The pattern we often see is a high volume of IT investment followed by a disappointing contribution to the business. This book is a must-read for those seeking to break this pattern and transform IT into a source of innovation and value-add for the business.

Bruno Guiçardi, COO, Ci&T

My advice is simple: read, learn, adopt. Steve Bell has hit another home run with this book. Lean is going to affect your organization whether you like it or not. Either your organization will adopt the wisdom contained in this book and thrive or your competitors will do so and put you out of business. Once again: read, learn, adopt.

Scott Ambler, (co)author of twenty books, including *Disciplined Agile Delivery*

With all that has already been written about Lean, it's rare to see truly new insight added to the discussion. Steve Bell does just that by continuing to push the frontiers of Lean thinking into the creative and rapidly evolving world of IT. **Run Grow Transform** is thought provoking, well grounded in research, and a great read for anyone interested in why Lean methods work. Jeff Sutherland and I had a blast exploring the relationship of Lean and Agile/Scrum principles with Steve, and I expect readers will too.

Alexander Brown, COO, Scrum Inc.

Steve has a unique background as an IT professional who has studied Eastern philosophies and immersed himself in a deep understanding of Lean. This book focuses on the most critical and challenging issue for any aspect of the development or use of IT: creating a collaborative learning culture.

Jeffrey Liker, PhD, professor, University of Michigan; author of *The Toyota Way*

This book opens a new chapter in the use of IT systems in a Lean world by its practical, pragmatic, and yet Lean-focused advice to IT people and their managers and—just as important—their customers.

Brian Maskell, coauthor of *Practical Lean Accounting*

The acquisition, processing, and delivery of information are critical to Lean transformations and business excellence in general, yet IT departments are often on the sidelines in such efforts. There is waste and opportunity for improvement in the IT function itself, but perhaps more importantly there is tremendous opportunity with how information is processed and leveraged within the larger organization. In **Run Grow Transform** Steve Bell describes how IT can become a powerful agent supporting organizational improvement.

Kevin Meyer, President, Specialty Silicone Fabricators

All too often the IT organization is viewed as an impediment to Lean transformation, when it truly can be a catalyst. Steve's book sorts out all the noise, the jargon, and the "hero culture," guiding the reader to what is so obvious yet so hard to see: build your culture around your customer!

Josh Rapoza, Director of Web Strategy and Operations, Lean Enterprise Institute

Aligning Lean and IT is a great challenge with a big payoff. We have successfully applied Lean thinking in our supply chain redesign and SAP implementation. This book really shows how Lean and IT can create a strong enterprise; it is a great inspiration.

Klaus Lyck Petersen, Group Process Manager, Solar A/S

With the advent of technologies like 3D printing and cloud computing we are on the verge of a third industrial revolution—one that traditional management paradigms are simply not designed for. *Run Grow Transform* sets out the principles and practices necessary for success in the new economy and is required reading for anybody involved in managing an organization that depends on technology for its success.

Jez Humble, Thoughtworks Studios; author of *Continuous Delivery*

A must-read for any organization that is pursuing a continuous improvement program based on the Lean principles. This book provides the insight to further integrate Lean IT and business process improvement. In today's world, real business improvement cannot be achieved without the IT factor; this book will help any organization achieve the improvement they are seeking.

Barry J. Brunetto, Vice President, Information Systems, Blount International

Twenty years of manufacturing and business process improvement using Lean methodologies, and I never considered applying Lean to IT. I am now inspired to transform my department using Lean IT, and I've already seen significant results in the first ninety days. This book lays a foundation for excellence.

Darren Hogg, IT Director, WIKA Instrument Corporation

Most companies in their Lean journey realize (with a lot of pain) that they must transform their IT processes in order to support their main product and service processes. This book stresses the importance of the complete value stream, which is necessary for enterprise transformation

Flávio A. Picchi, Executive Director, Lean Institute Brasil

Whether you're a leader, an IT professional, or a change agent, you MUST read this book! Steve Bell's refreshing take on how to develop and leverage your IT capabilities to innovate, deliver greater value, and reduce cost will help you gain market share and become a truly outstanding organization.

Karen Martin, author of *The Outstanding Organization*

In thirty years of coaching Lean transformations, the most significant impediments I have encountered are poor-quality information and unresponsive IT groups that resist change. This book provides much-needed guidance to help us surmount these most frustrating obstacles.

Michael Rowney, PhD, Rowney Consulting

Run Grow Transform contains the tools for IT leaders and performers to thrive in the face of the many conflicting demands from their customers, with limited resources. Delivering beyond the helpful folk wisdom and narrow techniques and technologies found elsewhere, Steve Bell and his contributors provide practical full value stream lifecycle methods for continuous improvement using Lean in an IT and customer (business) setting.

Martin Erb, Director of Professional Services, Pink Elephant

Precise, concise, and entertaining, this book provides the reader with crucial tips on how IT can help enterprises survive and thrive in a fast-paced technological and economic environment. This is mandatory reading not only for businesses and IT organizations, but also for universities and policy makers.

Fuat Alican, PhD, Vice President, Central American Scientific Research and Education Center

Run Grow Transform clarifies the eternal quest of IT—simplify "running" the business to eliminate waste of operational resources. Redirect IT spending to create innovative solutions to grow the business and create sustainable competitive advantage to transform the way customers interact with your business before your competitors do. This book offers plain, actionable advice from one who has been on the frontlines.

Tom Foco, Value Stream Solutions

A valuable and much-needed perspective on the integration of business and IT. Provides sound, practical advice and challenges us to think about a central issue of business performance: value stream flow.

Richard Askew, Wipro Consulting Services

It really is all about *process:* Lean IT helps IT professionals view everything they do in a new way. *Run Grow Transform* will help everyone recognize that end-to-end transformation means board room to point of customer delivery, not board room to CIO.

Thomas Jollands, Tata Consultancy Services

This is a long-overdue book that addresses the key challenges for today's IT organization and puts Lean IT into a context that is too often lacking.

James Finister, Tata Consultancy Services

Thought leader Richard Florida has identified the ongoing tension between creativity and organization as the biggest issue at stake in this emerging age. This book proposes a useful framework to address that very problem while leading IT strategy in a twenty-first century organization. If you're a CIO, you cannot afford to miss this thoughtful, knowledgeable, yet very practical read.

Cecil Dijoux, Lean Software Development Manager, Lectra

Run Grow Transform

Integrating Business and Lean IT

Steven Bell

Foreword by Daniel T. Jones

With Charles Betz
Troy DuMoulin
Paul Harmon & Sandra Foster
Mary Poppendieck and
John Schmidt

CRC Press
Taylor & Francis Group
Boca Raton London New York

CRC Press is an imprint of the
Taylor & Francis Group, an **informa** business

A PRODUCTIVITY PRESS BOOK

CRC Press
Taylor & Francis Group
6000 Broken Sound Parkway NW, Suite 300
Boca Raton, FL 33487-2742

First issued in hardback 2017

ISBN-13: 978-1-4665-0449-3 (pbk)
ISBN-13: 978-1-138-44034-0 (hbk)

Library of Congress Cataloging-in-Publication Data

Run grow transform : integrating business and lean IT / edited by Steven C. Bell.
    p. cm.
  Includes bibliographical references and index.
  ISBN 978-1-4665-0449-3 (alk. paper)
  1. Information technology--Management. I. Bell, Steve, 1960 Sept. 30-

HD30.2.R865 2013
658.4'038--dc23   2012031354

Visit the Taylor & Francis Web site at
http://www.taylorandfrancis.com

and the CRC Press Web site at
http://www.crcpress.com

This book is dedicated to humanitarian organizations around the world. May Lean principles and practices help you to develop capability, improve efficiency, create transparency, ensure proper stewardship of scarce resources, and above all, improve the lives of those you serve.

All proceeds from this book will support the development of Lean4NGO—drawing the Lean, nonprofit/NGO, and philanthropic communities together to serve this shared purpose.

Contents

Foreword
Run Grow Transform

Daniel T. Jones

Lean Meets IT

The Evolution of Lean

This book is very timely. The coming together of the Lean, Agile, and information technology (IT) services and operations communities presents some very interesting new challenges and opportunities. This book outlines an ambitious landscape for how Lean thinking can transform IT and brings together the different perspectives of several thought leaders in the field. The big questions it raises are what IT and Lean can learn from one another and what kind of new synthesis might be seen as a result.

Our understanding of Lean has certainly evolved over time. In the past it was used to address very different activities in different sectors. It has also widened to encompass whole value creation systems and deepened through our understanding of what kind of Lean management system is needed to lead and sustain it. The core Lean thought processes have proven to be very robust over time, and Lean has turned out to be the most useful and operational synthesis of the different strands of business improvement practice.

As Lean spread across sectors, we learned that we needed different starting points to design Lean value streams for different kinds of activities. From the automotive industry, we learned the importance of establishing basic stability and standard work to achieve flow. From the construction industry, we learned the importance of correctly defining user needs and specifications up front. From the process industries, we learned to separate the high volume from the long tail of complicated or low-volume work. From retail and distribution, we learned to design rapid-response replenishment systems. From financial services, we learned to eliminate unnecessary demand created by broken processes. From healthcare, we learned the importance of making the plan of work (admission, diagnosis, treatment, and discharge) visible to everyone involved. Every business is in fact a collection of these different types of value streams, and these insights are also relevant for designing and improving IT value streams.

From these many experiences, it is apparent that using Lean tools to make localized improvements within a department is not enough. It is necessary to look end to end at the entire sequence of actions required to create the value for which customers are paying, which usually flows horizontally across many departments and even several organizations. It also involves synchronizing many supporting value streams, including IT product development and service delivery.

The waste you see as you follow these value streams is actually a symptom of much deeper root causes, and unless we correctly diagnose and tackle these root causes we will not improve the performance of the organization as a whole. Diagnosing whole systems led to some surprises. For example, it highlighted that the place to unblock the patient flow through hospitals was by improving the discharge process and that the biggest source of delays and waste in retail distribution is in the information systems passing forecasts and orders upstream.

In addressing these system-level problems, it became apparent that management's job is actually to unblock and enable these streams of value creation to flow in line with customer demand. In fact, a Lean management system needs to be built up from the value creation process itself. This means rethinking the mental models, tasks, and behaviors of leaders at every level in an organization.

Managing Lean

The first task of Lean management is articulating what customers (internal and external) want and what the organization needs to accomplish, focusing improvement activities on the *vital few* performance gaps that would make the biggest difference in meeting these needs. Lean management is about focus and alignment, not command and control. Spending time in a structured dialogue to turn these high-level goals into concrete actions at the frontline is much more productive than gaming targets in a command-and-control environment.

The second task is to deploy the right cross-functional projects to address the root causes of these performance gaps. The related third task is to help frontline staff members to stabilize their processes by making progress visible, by repeated problem solving, and by escalating issues upward to resolve higher-level problems. These tasks are about managing the horizontal flow of value creation as well as the vertical, functional deployment of resources. A *value stream leader* has to be given the end-to-end responsibility for gaining agreement on what needs to be done all along the value stream, for defining the resources necessary to accomplish this, and for managing the improvement activities to deliver the results. This separation of the horizontal responsibility for value creation from the vertical authority over resources is not easy to grasp, but it is fundamental to managing Lean value systems.

The fourth task is to develop the problem-solving capabilities of everyone and to integrate the work through learning by doing. Leaning value streams begins by establishing stability and then, step by step, removing all the buffers. This means that every step becomes more interdependent, which multiplies the probabilities of interruptions to the whole flow. These interruptions, in turn, signal the next step in the never-ending improvement journey to the perfect value stream with no waste, overburden, or system-generated variation. Reducing lead times also makes the value stream much more responsive to changes in customer demand.

Tightening the synchronization of all the steps therefore depends on the problem-solving skills of frontline staff and those supporting them, not on experts far away from the action. This is why Lean thinkers often talk about developing people before making products and why all managers learn the importance of developing and mentoring their subordinates. The need for everyone to see progress against plan in real time and to be able to respond to deviations from the plan as they happen is why Lean thinkers also place so much importance on visual management of progress, problem solving, and improvement projects. This illustrates the fact that the real customer for IT support is the value stream itself. Integration into the value stream team is the most effective way IT support can play its true role in enabling the flow of value creation.

Challenges for IT

The pull that brings Lean thinking into any sector is frustration with the way things work today. That is certainly true with IT.

I have seen many examples of this, e.g., when helping big multination-als to set up Lean programs to realize the performance improvements that were not obtained from their huge investments in enterprise resource plan-ning (ERP) systems based on the mental models of command and control. I have also often been asked how Lean can help to speed up the inordi-nately long time, often as long as a year, it takes to make changes in these systems. Several years ago, much to my surprise, I was asked to launch a series of Lean initiatives at SAP to improve the software development process and customer response systems. More recently we have observed, time and time again, the wisdom of Leaning the core processes or value streams in an organization before and not after deploying a large system such as SAP.

The natural reaction to these challenges is to "fix" current IT systems and modify and rebrand them as Lean. This effort will quickly run into the sand and will not bridge the underlying differences between traditional and Lean approaches to managing complex organizational systems. Resolving these underlying tensions—recognizing the need for flexibility and rapid change and applying Lean not as a collection of tools but rather with an apprecia-tion of Lean as a set of principles—will determine whether IT can, indeed, become Lean and truly serve the organization and the creation of value for customers. In the end, this boils down to the mental models on which tra-ditional IT systems were designed. IT is just at the beginning of the journey to challenge these mental models, spurred on by Lean pioneers looking for very different solutions to their business problems.

For example, I remember the IT director of a global pharmaceutical firm declaring that "all change in this organization is led by IT." This reflects the view that change is driven by technology, designed by experts, and imple-mented from the top through command and control. Lean questions each of these assumptions, reversing the separation of "thinking" by experts and only "doing" on the frontline to engaging everyone at every level in learning by doing as part of their daily work. In this way, change arises from within the value streams, creating new and often innovative value for customers.

And just as IT does not lead the value proposition, automation is not the right solution for every circumstance, particularly not for complex and adap-tive systems in which employees are constantly improving the way work is performed and improving the ability to respond to changes in customer needs. Lean thinkers are always looking for simpler, more flexible forms of automation to help people in control of the process while liberating them from unnecessary burdens.

This reminds me of a professor once telling me that system optimization was "just a math problem." This traditional view of optimization is usually about improving the utilization of assets rather than optimizing end-to-end flows of value creation. Simulating end-to-end systems can be extremely useful in matching capacity with demand and in evaluating different alternatives. But in most complex systems, it is usually impossible to reach the levels of data accuracy needed to also use them to trigger every production batch or shipment along the value stream, particularly when you are trying at the same time to uncover problems instead of buffering and hiding them. The end result is that everyone games the system and creates even more chaos. This is why Lean thinkers often switch off material requirements planning (MRP) systems on the shop floor. This is also why Toyota retains the responsibility for overall system design and does the integration of the IT system components it purchases from IT vendors itself.

I also remember an exasperated manager telling me "We can't change the IT system because the guy who designed the algorithms is no longer here!" Until then, no one had needed to make changes to the system, but as soon as we began redesigning their supply chains, this "invisibility" became a problem. Making everything visual is the essential context for learning by doing. Gaining agreement across functions on what needs to be done is much easier when the value stream and its problems are visible on a wall rather than hidden on a project plan or in a computer. Reviewing performance against plan and spotting and reacting to deviations quickly is also greatly facilitated by visual management. We have also been able to make the status of every step along a supply chain visible at every location across the world. Problem solving using A3 sheets makes the thought process as well as the proposed solutions visible to the mentor. Learning by doing and working together spreads and accelerates when all participants understand and can see how and why their system is not working as well as it could.

The practice of Lean will only be sustained if it helps to solve business problems in a new way to deliver superior performance and if it liberates new energies in frontline staff. We have seen how turning customer support staff into problem solvers reverses the low-wage outsourcing model. I have also seen frontline staff in the back office of a bank demonstrate their ability to simplify, redesign, and automate process after process. Many project teams are freeing up time by using the *Oobeya* visual management rooms pioneered by Toyota. Translating these energies into bottom-line results for the organization as a whole takes a bit longer and requires management to rethink its work and the way it understands and uses IT capabilities.

Toward a New Synthesis?

My hunch, however, is that as the various IT disciplines (development, operations, application support, etc.) continue to embrace Lean within each enterprise and industry, we may see a new synthesis that will inspire other sectors to redouble their Lean efforts. This could be from a combination of Leaning the software development, testing, and continuous delivery processes; new opportunities to do new things opened up by the Internet; and a real focus on working with consumers to create value in their lives—in other words, a step beyond Lean product design and visual project management to a new model of Lean innovation based on very rapid experiment cycles and a rich dialogue and feedback from users. This in fact goes right back to the heart of Lean, deepening learning from very frequent *kaizen* experiments in a visual environment where feedback is immediate and clear.

As the Internet profoundly changes the way every business relates to its suppliers and customers, businesses will be challenged to rethink their products, processes, and business models. We have already seen Lean thinking inspire the Lean startup movement and begin to shift power from providers to users. For startups as well as established businesses, Lean innovation and Lean thinking will be essential in exploiting these new opportunities. This book opens this new door.

Acknowledgments

I want to begin by thanking several pioneers who have been leading the way and from whom I have drawn my inspiration for many years. As Lean thinking tackles systemic and global challenges in financial services, energy management, government, education, healthcare, humanitarian aid, environmental protection, and many other industries and endeavors, IT capabilities must play an essential role. So it is with my profound appreciation for their vision, teaching, and patience that I thank Dan Jones, Jim Womack, John Shook, and H. Thomas Johnson for passing on this vision to a new generation.

I am indebted to an amazing team of collaborators who helped make this book a reality. Not only have they shared insights from their own disciplines, they have also challenged and expanded my thinking about Lean across the many disciplines and communities that, collectively, we have come to call "IT." First of all, I am deeply grateful for Dan Jones, who brought tremendous insight from the journey of many other industries to a fearless exploration of the world of IT. My profound thanks go out to Charles Betz, Troy DuMoulin, Sandra Foster, Paul Harmon, Mary and Tom Poppendieck, and John Schmidt. I also thank the case study contributors for sharing their journeys: Bruno Guicardi (Ci&T), David Bogaerts and Jael Schuyer (ING), and Murat Ihlamur (Netsis).

I want to thank all those who have talked, e-mailed, reviewed drafts, contributed material, offered ideas, and helped me find the essential message of this book:

Juan Abbud, StemCell
Rajeev Agarwal, State Street
Fuat Alican, Central American Scientific Research and Education Center

David Almond, State of Oregon
Shawn Alvey, Nike
Scott Ambler, IBM
Richard Askew, Wipro
Harlan Barcus, Capital Pacific Bank

Jeffrey Barnes, Society for Information Management

Alexandre Baulé, Embraer

John Bicheno, Cardiff University

David Bogaerts, ING

Alex Brown, Scrum, Inc.

Barry Brunetto, Blount International

Richard Carroll, Con-way

Douglas Cooper, Mercy Corps

Susan Cramm, Valuedance

Ward Cunningham, CitizenGlobal

Cecil Dijoux, Lectra

Stephen Dine, Datasource Consulting

Evan Durant, Tektronix/Danaher

Martin Erb, Pink Elephant

Conor Fanning, Bombardier Aerospace

James Finister, Tata Consultancy Services

Olga Flory, Lean Enterprise Institute

Tom Foco, Value Stream Solutions

Bruce Greiner, IBM

Bruno Guicardi, Ci&T

Tim Heller, JP Morgan Chase

Bill Henderson, Perkins Consulting

Scott Heydon, Retail Transformation Group

Jez Humble, ThoughtWorks

Allison Jenkins, McKinsey & Company

H. Thomas Johnson (retired)

Tom Jollands, Tata Consultancy Services

Joseph Junker, IBM

Dave Kelley, Nike

Tom Knutilla, Ryder Systems, Inc.

Rakesh Kumar, Microsoft

Jeffrey Liker, University of Michigan

Jim Luckman, Lean Transformations Group

Brian Maskell, BMA Associates

Kurt Milne, IT Process Institute

Jason Moriber, Waggener Edstrom

Kholoud Odeh, Grameen Foundation

John O'Donnell, Lean Enterprise Institute

Aleksey Osintsev, TEC

Tom Paider, Nationwide

Chris Perretta, State Street

Tom Perry, CyberSource/VISA, Inc.

Klaus Petersen, Solar A/S

Flávio Picchi, Lean Institute Brazil

John Pierce, TripWire

Scott Porritt, Nike

Joshua Rapoza, Lean Enterprise Institute

Linda Ray, W. W. Grainger

Andrew Rome, consultant

Mike Rother, University of Michigan

Michael Rowney, Rowney Consulting

Tim Schipper, Steelcase

Jael Schuyer, ING

Alan Shalloway, NetObjectives

David Soule, Capital One

Mark Striebeck, Google

Jeff Sutherland, Scrum, Inc.

Chris Thompson, Lean Institute Brazil

Sarah Topham, Paychex

Conrad Volkmann, Microsoft

John Watts, Micron Technology

Brian Wellinghoff, Barry-Wehmiller

George Westerman, MIT Sloan CISR/CDB

Doug Younger, Nike

My thanks to Michael Sinocchi, executive editor at Productivity Press, and your hard-working staff for your commitment to advancing the body of Lean knowledge and for your continuing support of my research and publication. Thanks also go to Jennifer Stair and Marc Johnston for a Lean approach to editorial project and production management.

I am profoundly grateful to my wife Karen Whitley Bell. As a hospice and palliative care nurse she has a keen sense for listening to the spoken and the unspoken. And as an award-winning author, her insights, skilled reading, and tenacious editing throughout this process have been so helpful. She is a partner in every sense of the word.

Finally, I want to thank all those in the Lean community who give their time, energy, knowledge, and skill to help those in the nonprofit and NGO community worldwide. I am deeply grateful for your service to others. If you would like to become part of this community of practice, please visit http://www.Lean4NGO.org.

Steve Bell
Portland, Oregon
July 2012

Author and Editor

Steve Bell began his career in the early 1980s as an accountant, where he learned to appreciate the underlying information and systems needed to run a business. When IBM introduced the first PC, he joined the world of IT at the very beginning of the ERP industry evolution.

He first became acquainted with Lean principles and practices in the early 1990s, when he quickly realized that the key to creating effective IT systems was engaging employees in the simplification and continuous improvement of business processes before investing in information systems. He applied this philosophy to ERP and software development projects, which led to his first book, *Lean Enterprise Systems* (Wiley, 2006).

The success of this book led him more deeply into the practice of Lean IT, where he began facilitating *kaizen* events and strategy deployment initiatives, while integrating Agile software development and IT service management with the fundamental Lean principles. This led to his second book, *Lean IT* (Productivity Press, 2010), which received the 2011 Shingo Prize for Operational Excellence research award.

Steve serves on the faculty of the Lean Enterprise Institute. He travels worldwide presenting workshops, leading *gemba* walks, and advising clients on applying Lean IT principles and practices to solve their daily business challenges, including fast and effective governance and portfolio management, continual IT service improvement, end-to-end application development lifecycle management, ERP agility and continuous improvement, and the design of effective quality and measurement systems that help teams focus on the right things.

In addition to his work leading Lean IT transformation, Steve and his wife Karen are actively involved in the nonprofit and nongovernmental organization (NGO) community. As founders of Lean4NGO (http://www.Lean4NGO.org), their mission is to bring Lean practices to humanitarian aid organizations, improving operational efficiency (use of scarce resources) and effectiveness (improved outcomes) to benefit the three billion people living at the bottom of the pyramid on less than $2 a day.

Steve may be reached through his website at http://www.LeanITStrategies.com.

Contributors

Charles Betz is research director for IT Portfolio Management for Enterprise Management Associates. He has eighteen years of IT experience spanning IT support, network administration, IT consulting, technical architecture, software engineering, data management, application management, enterprise architecture, and IT portfolio management. He is author of *Architecture and Patterns for IT: Service Management, Resource Planning, and Governance* (2nd ed., Wathman, MA: Morgan Kaufmann, 2011).

Prior to joining EMA, Charles spent six years with Wells Fargo as senior enterprise architect and ultimately vice president for IT Portfolio Management and Systems Management. He has held positions for Best Buy, Target, and Accenture, specializing in ERP systems architecture, enterprise application integration, data architecture and metadata systems, and configuration management.

Charles is one of the first IT industry analyst bloggers, founding the http://www.erp4it.com weblog in the fall of 2003 to examine the convergence of IT management systems and the influences of industrial theory on IT management.

Troy DuMoulin, Vice President Professional Services, Pink Elephant (http://www.pinkelephant.com), is a leading ITIL and IT governance authority with

a solid and rich background in executive IT management consulting. Troy holds the ITIL Service Manager and Expert certifications and has extensive experience in leading IT service management (ITSM) programs with a regional and global scope. He is a frequent speaker at ITSM events and is a contributing author to multiple ITSM books, papers, and official ITIL publications, including ITIL's *Planning to Implement IT Service Management* (OGC 2002) and *Continual Service Improvement* (OGC 2007). Troy has also worked with ISACA on COBIT 4.0 development and alignment with ITIL.

Sandra Foster spent thirteen years with Digital Equipment Corporation in a variety of sales and marketing roles, including regional manager. Sandra is

 a cofounder of Adaptive, a software company specializing in metadata and enterprise architecture management solutions. Since 1994, Sandra has been helping clients improve business performance by designing and implementing effective, efficient, and adaptable business processes. She has led and participated in many strategic business process improvement projects for private and public sector companies around the globe in all aspects of business from the front office to the back office. She has taught over 5,000 people innovative courses in business process management, business process modeling and analysis, facilitation, and project management. She is a thought leader in ways to improve business performance. Sandra lives in Winnipeg, Manitoba, Canada. See http://www.peopleprocessandtechnology.ca.

Paul Harmon is a cofounder and executive editor at Business Process Trends (http://www.bptrends.com), an internationally popular website that provides a variety of free articles, columns, surveys, and book reviews each month on trends, directions, and best practices in business process management.

Paul is also a cofounder, chief methodologist, and a principal consultant of BPTrends Associates (http://www.bptrendsassociates.com), a professional services company providing executive education, training, and consult-

 ing services for organizations that are interested in understanding and implementing business process management.

Paul has been a senior consultant at Cutter Consortium and edited their *Expert System Strategies*, *CASE*, and *Business Process Reengineering Strategies* newsletters. He has authored or coauthored over twelve other books, including the very popular *Expert Systems: AI for Business* (Wiley, 1983). Paul also writes two short articles each month on current business process management topics, which are mailed to the members of the BPTrends website.

Mary Poppendieck has been in the IT industry for over four decades. She has managed solutions for companies in several disciplines, including supply chain management, manufacturing systems, and digital media. As a seasoned leader in both operations and new product development, she brings a practical, customer-focused approach to software development problems.

A popular writer and speaker, Mary's classes on managing software development offer a fresh perspective on project management. Her book *Lean Software Development: An Agile Toolkit* (Addison-Wesley Professional, 2003) won the Software Development Productivity Award in 2004. She has also published the sequels *Implementing Lean Software Development: From Concept to Cash* (Addison-Wesley Professional, 2006) and *Leading Lean Software Development: Results Are Not the Point* (Addison-Wesley Professional, 2009).

John G. Schmidt is vice president of global integration services at Informatica Corporation, where he advises clients on the business potential of emerging technologies and directs the company's Lean and Agile integration practice. Previous employers include Wells Fargo, Bank of America, Best Buy, American Management Systems, and Digital Equipment Corporation. He has written hundreds of articles on systems integration, Lean and Agile IT practices, enterprise architecture, and program management. He was the first to write a book about how to implement an integration shared-services function in 2005, *Integration Competency Center: An Implementation Methodology* (Informatica), and followed it up in 2010 with *Lean Integration: An Integration Factory Approach to Business Agility*

(Addison-Wesley Professional). He is a frequent speaker at industry conferences and served as director and chairman of the Integration Consortium from 2002 to 2009.

Introduction

Out of clutter find simplicity
From discord find harmony
In the middle of difficulty lies opportunity

Albert Einstein

When IT is done right it's a game changer. But this book is not about IT.

Nor is it about the mission to "align IT with the business" or to "deliver IT value to the business." That mission is over. In fact, it has been misguided from the start. IT and the business are one. There is no "IT value" separate from business value. And in this new and often disruptive information age, there is increasingly limited business value separate from IT.

This book, for leaders and senior managers from all disciplines within the enterprise, is about integrating and leveraging transformative IT capabilities with *every* asset of the enterprise. It offers a framework to facilitate collaboration and stimulate innovation, resulting in new ways to create value for customers, not just once, or now and then, but over and over, every day.

For many enterprises, IT remains the most challenging asset to successfully integrate into its culture, strategy, and flow of value. This disconnect has been vexing CEOs and CIOs for decades. It's expensive, disruptive, and frustrating.

So why have some newly minted enterprises succeeded and completely transformed their industry (think Amazon.com, Expedia, Skype, and many others) while most enterprises expend excessive resources and effort on technology yet still struggle to control costs, produce consistent results, and deliver meaningful business value? It's easy to attribute their success as simple timing; these companies were conceived during the rise of the Internet, so technology is deeply embedded in their business model and DNA.

But the reason for their success is more nuanced. Talk with technologists who work within one of these Web 2.0 companies, and often you'll discover that they don't even think of themselves as an IT organization. They just see themselves as a part of an enterprise that creates technology-enabled things that people will really like and will want more of. That's not timing. That's culture. That's leadership. That's vision. And developing that sort of culture, leadership, and vision is possible even among enterprises that have been around for decades, even a century or more.

How can you become equally creative and fast moving? What is the secret sauce? It is a *singular focus on delivering value to the customer*, where all individuals can clearly see how their work interrelates with others. This, in turn, requires a management system that effectively engages individuals and teams so that their collective work supports enterprise strategy. Such a management system also works as a rapid feedback cycle, quickly informing leadership of daily issues and changes in the marketplace, accelerating decision making, and promoting enterprise agility. Such an approach requires leadership that inspires creativity and enables collaboration, manages risk, and creates a path for innovation and, ultimately, transformation. This approach is embodied in the principles and practices of Lean thinking.

In short, a key aim of Lean is to maximize customer value by reducing waste then investing the gains to create additional value through continuous improvement and innovation. Lean has evolved for decades to many industries beyond manufacturing, including financial services, transportation, healthcare, and the public sector.* Every Lean initiative touches IT in some way, but until recently, IT was often excluded from the team. A common criticism of IT has been that it is inflexible and resists change and continuous improvement. This must change. IT can cease to be an inhibitor and instead become a catalyst for growth and transformation across the enterprise.

I've helped guide numerous enterprises to introduce Lean thinking into their IT organization, creating measurable, sustainable improvements.

---

* Toyota is considered the preeminent example of Lean practice. But over the years, many other companies have applied Lean principles to improve their ability to deliver value to their customers, including Alcoa, Amazon.com, Baxter Healthcare, Beth Israel Deaconess Medical Center, Boeing, Bose, CapitalOne, Cardinal Health, Cessna, Cisco, Cleveland Clinic, Coca-Cola, Danaher, Dell, Denver Health System, E&J Gallo Winery, Esselte, FedEx, Fidelity Investments, Ford, General Electric, W.L. Gore & Associates, Gorton's Seafood, W.W. Grainger, Group Health Cooperative, Hon, ING, Intel, Ingersoll Rand, John Deere, Kimberly-Clark, Lockheed Martin, Mayo Clinic, Medtronic, MillerCoors, Nationwide, Northrup Grumman, Parker Hannifin, Pietro Fiorentini, Pirelli, Pratt & Whitney, Shell Oil, Southwest Airlines, Starbucks, State Street, Steelcase, Tesco, Thedacare, Virginia Mason Hospital, Wells Fargo, WiPro, and many, many more.

I wrote the first book to use the term "Lean IT," *Lean Enterprise Systems, Using IT for Continuous Improvement* (John Wiley & Sons, 2006) and followed it up with the Shingo Prize-winning book, *Lean IT: Enabling and Sustaining Your Lean Transformation* (Productivity Press, 2010). As a member of the Lean Enterprise Institute faculty, and as I teach, coach, and speak around the globe, I am fortunate to meet many remarkable individuals and enterprises who are pushing the envelope of Lean thinking in the world of IT. You will hear many of their stories in this book.

However, Lean IT is still an emerging discipline, and even as *Lean IT* was going to print, I realized something vital was still missing from the body of knowledge. If we're not careful, too much emphasis on Lean IT alone can create a series of sophisticated, high-performance organizational silos. The *real transformative value* is realized when IT is fully integrated into an enterprise-wide Lean practice, enabling the enterprise to run better and invest the gains in growth and transformation.

Is integrating IT capabilities into all aspects of your business important to you? Does this integration—or the lack of it—affect your value proposition? To help you address these questions, let's engage in a short Lean exercise. We start by asking, "What is the problem?" What is the current state? Where would you like to be? What obstacles stand in your way? And how might you overcome them? With these questions we begin the Lean problem-solving process....

What Is the Business Problem?

Consider the experience of PACCAR (PCAR), a heavy truck manufacturer founded in 1906, makers of the Kenworth, Peterbilt, and DAF brands. In 2008 CEO Mark Pigott, great-great grandson of the company's founder, was poised to mark PACCAR's seventy-first straight year of posting a profit. Then, in the fourth quarter of 2008, global markets plunged, and with it, PACCAR's revenues dropped by nearly half. Pigott asked what sort of value proposition would convince PACCAR's customers to invest in new trucks when they could keep the old ones running with a little more maintenance. Pigott and his team understood that they had to offer customers not just new bells and whistles but transformative value if they were going to make the sale.

Delivering superior customer value is the *purpose*, the *true north* of the enterprise and everyone in it. Yet in survey after survey, the majority of business people report that IT does not understand their business and does not deliver value proportional to the investment and effort. Frequent complaints include that the IT organization is slow to respond, engages in projects that rarely finish successfully or on time, creates systems with excessive complexity that are difficult to use and maintain, and is unable to keep up with the rapid pace of business change. These surveys repeatedly show that executives are often "baffled, frustrated, and even angered by their IT organizations."[1]

The impact is difficult to measure. How much of the global IT spend, estimated at US$3.4 trillion in 2010,[2] is waste? 10%? 20%? More? How do you define IT waste in the first place? And beyond dollars and effort wasted on IT consumption and investment, what about the value of lost opportunities and business disruption caused by poor-quality information and ineffective information systems?

Current State

In 2009 *Harvard Business Review* published a survey in which business and IT professionals were asked the same questions (see Figure I.1)[3]. Notice the similarities in responses, especially the last statement: *"The business doesn't understand how to use its systems and technologies."* How would people within your enterprise respond to these questions?

This report shows that both constituencies seem to agree with the basic challenges, but most remain unable to bridge the divide between "the business" and "IT." That leads to a curious question: Just what is IT? We speak of

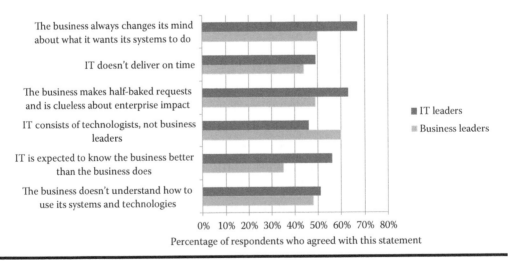

Figure I.1   Same questions, similar answers.

IT as if it were a thing, a renegade entity that must somehow be harnessed. But in fact IT is not homogenous; it is a diverse set of powerful capabilities. Entire subcommunities of technical specialists have formed around various disciplines, such as operations, service management, application development, integration, data management, business intelligence, enterprise architecture, and business process management. Add to this the fact that many enterprises are shifting a significant share of their IT spend to highly skilled (and further specialized) external service providers. This results in greater fragmentation and discord as these various community members compete for attention and funding.

This state of affairs raises another curious question: How can IT "align with the business" unless IT aligns with itself? How can we help such diverse technical communities to collaborate effectively both together and alongside their business colleagues to serve the end customer? Lean thinking has addressed this question before, as it has overcome siloed thinking in many industries and across globe-spanning value streams. Now it is IT's turn.

What Is Our Target State?

Not a week goes by without a new IT-enabled product or service making news for its fascinating new capability, bestowing temporary fame and competitive advantage for the company and unleashing a potentially disruptive force on an industry. Once hidden behind the curtain, IT capability, competency, and agility are now key elements of modern enterprise strategy—not just for Web 2.0 companies, but for all companies.

With jobs and families' livelihoods on the line, PACCAR believed that innovative IT capabilities could create the most compelling value proposition to invest in a new truck. They engaged their IT colleagues and worked in partnership with outside experts, coordinating several competing cellular providers to provide complete and uninterrupted coverage. The result, called TruckerLink, is real-time, online GPS navigation (interfaced with Google Maps), vehicle monitoring, and fleet management services, available both in-cab and remotely to dispatchers and fleet managers. No other truck manufacturer offered anything like it. These capabilities would help optimize fleet performance and reduce maintenance costs. And they would help drivers to make well-informed decisions while on the road. These were all IT-enabled capabilities, but "IT" was not on anyone's mind—teams were too busy asking "What will our customers think is *really* useful?" and aiming for it.

What Are The Root Causes?

It's clear that IT capabilities must be an integral part of enterprise strategy, yet the longstanding business/IT alignment challenge remains unsolved for many, but not for lack of trying. Why is that?

Those on the frontlines, closest to the customer, dealing with daily variation and uncertainty, are in the best position to make improvement and innovation happen. But what if a frontline team doesn't understand the new capabilities that IT can offer? And what if the technologists that can help are too busy keeping the lights on and the servers running, or are buried in a never-ending series of projects so they rarely see the light of day, meet the customer, or engage in real learning with their colleagues? What if IT really never understands the business or if business people never really understand IT capabilities? How far can you go with that?

One of the root causes behind this all-too-common disconnect is cultural. But how do you change culture? That's an age-old question with what I believe is a surprisingly simple answer: culture is an outcome of behavior. According to John Shook, chairman of the Lean Enterprise Institute, "It's easier to act your way to a new way of thinking than it is to think your way to a new way of acting."[4] In other words, we change our habits and culture by doing and learning.

Another common root cause is structural; IT is often physically and organizationally separate from its business colleagues. I recently consulted with two Fortune 500 companies, each with architectural showcase campuses. Both wanted their IT to be more "aligned with the business," yet both housed IT staff off-campus, miles away, in cube-farm office parks. Perhaps this made sense from a practical facilities point of view, but nevertheless the message was clear: IT *is* separate, and it doesn't need to be co-located, or even nearby. As a result IT colleagues don't benefit from those casual conversations, spontaneous appearances at standup meetings, and the constant visual awareness that is so vital in a Lean environment.

To nurture a Lean culture, everyone must intentionally develop new patterns of behavior and interaction, which begins by creating new relationships among colleagues across disciplines and functions. And here is where we arrive at the essence of Lean thinking, which is much more than a collection of tools and practices. At its heart, Lean thinking encourages a collaborative learning enterprise. It's about respecting people and their ideas and providing an environment where they can thrive through experimentation. The primary lesson we have learned, over more than six decades of

Lean practice, is that cross-functional teams with a shared sense of purpose and supported by enlightened leadership can overcome incredible obstacles and achieve sustained success.

How Can We Overcome the Obstacles in Our Way?

In 2005, Southwest Airlines CEO Gary Kelley conceded, "In many ways, our technology is ahead, but technology at our airports has been behind." This stemmed, in part, from the fact that investing millions into a broad portfolio of complex (and sometimes fragile) technology seemed antithetical to Southwest's core philosophy to keep things simple. It also stemmed—in the words of Don Harris, Southwest's director of airport solutions—from the fact that the airline "has been technology phobic."[5]

But to support the requirements of the business traveler they were targeting for growth, the time had come for Southwest to bring IT fully into its strategic vision and daily work. Southwest turned a greater emphasis onto its IT capabilities—not by increasing the IT budget but by changing IT's focus to customer intimacy and service. Southwest accomplished this by engaging its IT team members in conversations and job shadowing with customer service agents. Team members visited airports, and by observing and talking with travelers they learned more about their experience. The result was the replacement of a collection of clumsy green-screen applications with an easy-to-use, internally developed airport management suite. From self-service kiosks to user-friendly interfaces for check-in agents, IT's contributions to the customer experience dramatically reduced wait times and accelerated check-in, ticket changes, and other traveler functions. This new system also reduced the time required to on-board a new customer service agent from nearly six months to several weeks.

In another of Southwest's programs to create greater customer awareness, IT team members were given opportunities to gain a firsthand experience of what it was like to be an *internal* customer of IT. For example, one senior systems architect flew to a small airport one evening to perform routine service on an outdoor skycap workstation. He came away with a richer understanding of the work and the issues—trying to operate a keypad while wearing gloves in frigid weather, the impact of humidity on screen visibility, how to better manage cords for access and safety, etc., while lugging heavy bags, answering questions, and offering helpful advice, all in the Southwest spirit of fast, friendly, and fun.

One of the most exceptional "know-your-customer" programs within Southwest is the opportunity for employees to fly standby—with a twist. Once airborne, traveling employees are invited to join the on-board service team, passing out beverages and peanuts, getting to know the customers in the unique, Southwest way.

With such an emphasis on customer intimacy and service, it's no wonder that Southwest is the only major North American airline never to have filed for bankruptcy. Even more impressive, it's the only major airline in the world to have posted a profit for the past thirty-nine consecutive years. At Southwest, it's not about IT, it's about customer experience, and everything about the culture and behavior reminds team members of that, every minute of every single day.

PACCAR's approach to cultural integration led them to create "the foundry," a dedicated workspace that facilitated cross-functional, enterprise-wide collaboration and innovation. This was a highly visual room, including a long stripe that ran the length of the room and symbolized the path to value. Although it's too early to measure the impact of TruckerLink on the bottom line, PACCAR has walked away with some impressive recognition, including being named as one of *Forbes'* "50 Most Innovative Companies" in 2011.

The result for both Southwest and PACCAR isn't just innovation that improves value to the customer. What both companies achieved is far greater. IT specialists have come out from behind the technology curtain, engaging as equal members of teams rather than as visitors, as transient (mercenary?) members of a temporary technology project. By creating a *product* with real, tangible, measurable, lasting customer value, business and technical team members come together as something larger—with a sense of shared purpose. They understand that they are creating a total experience for the end customer, a complete product. In this integrated environment, they feel a sense of belonging, of ownership, of *pride of workmanship* that W. Edwards Deming (father of the total quality movement) insisted is the heart of quality. Teamwork is the intangible, ineffable path to value, the *line-of-sight connection* between human beings, the products they envision and create, and those they serve.

Across all industries, IT is increasingly changing the way customers receive value, directly through IT-enabled products and services, and indirectly through more efficient product/service development, production and delivery, and customer support. Many innovations are hidden in the background, while others touch the end customer in new and unexpected ways. Vail Resorts, for instance, introduced a smartphone app to track guests' activity on the slopes so they can post (and boast) to their Facebook friends in real time. In the first year, 100,000 customers downloaded the app, resulting in 35 million social network impressions about the thrills of skiing Vail Resorts.[6]

And if one of those skiers has a mishap and spends his evening in a local emergency department, there's a chance he may be sent home with discharge instructions created with the time-saving technology developed by Callibra. Their Discharge 1-2-3 Composer application allows busy emergency care physicians to quickly and easily create detailed, customized information to help the patient understand and manage his care at home. And with one click, the discharge instructions can be translated into the patient's native language. This application saves about one hour per physician, per shift,[7] which equates to more patients seen faster with better patient outcomes.

Value isn't found only in commercial projects; it can also mean saving a life or rebuilding a community. In the past, families affected by natural disasters in less-developed regions of the world had to wait days, even weeks for communications and supplies to reach them. Now NetHope, a community of IT leaders from many of the worlds' largest NGOs and nonprofit organizations, has partnered with Cisco Systems to change that. When disaster strikes, NetHope teams quickly mobilize wi-fi hotspots, powered by car batteries, establishing instant communication, enabling relief organizations to reestablish supply lines and improve sanitation and living conditions for a six-year-old in need of a blanket, food, and clean water.[8]

We can all share inspirational stories about how vibrant companies across all industries add new and surprising value and improve our daily lives with creative use of information technologies. But that's not the purpose of this book. The key question is this: How can *your* enterprise deliver more IT-enabled innovation and value to *your* customers, better, faster, and cheaper than ever before?

Such breakthrough change isn't easy, but bringing the knowledge and capabilities of IT into every aspect of creating and delivering value to your customers can transform your enterprise. Just ask Amazon.com. In 1995, they entered the marketplace as an online book retailer with a bold vision. It's now difficult to distinguish exactly what Amazon.com is—far more than a bookseller, or even a retailer, it has become a highly sophisticated platform for global commerce. Nevertheless, when a box arrives on your doorstep, Amazon.com is acting in the traditional role of a retailer, in a new, disruptive, and delightful way. Most importantly, though, Amazon.com does not think of technology in the traditional sense at all—just listen to founder Jeff Bezos in his 2010 shareholder letter:

> All the effort we put into technology might not matter that much if we kept technology off to the side in some sort of R&D department, but we don't take that approach. Technology infuses all of our teams, all of our processes, our decision-making, and our approach to innovation in each of our businesses. It is deeply integrated into everything we do. Invention is in our DNA and technology is the fundamental tool we wield to evolve and improve every aspect of the experience we provide our customers. We still have a lot to learn, and I expect and hope we'll continue to have so much fun learning it.

The question is not about how you can imitate Amazon.com, Google, or other young upstarts. That is the wrong question for most of us to ask. The right question is *how do you start where you are, and using what you have*, make a real difference going forward, when virtually every product and service you design, develop, and deliver must have an integrated technology aspect that is meaningful to your customer? How do you do that quickly, and often?

This journey starts not with technology but with people.

What You Will Learn and How This Book Is Organized

Beginning in the fourteenth century, scientists, sculptors, philosophers, poets, financiers, painters, and architects converged in Florence, Italy. At the end of their day they congregated in the great halls of the city's patrons to dine and converse. These gatherings became known as *salons*, where the thought leaders of their time shared knowledge, integrating the principles and techniques among disciplines, sparking new ideas that led to significant advances in human insight and capability. These enlightened individuals viewed their differences in disciplines and culture not as barriers but as opportunities, and together they forged a new world—today we call this period of awakening and learning *The Renaissance*.

Is there a useful history lesson here? Has enterprise IT been struggling through its own Dark Ages of overspecialization, dis-integration, and misalignment? What can we learn from this earlier age of enlightenment in order to nurture our own?

This book opens with the reflections of Dan Jones, coauthor (with his longtime friend and associate Jim Womack) of many seminal works, including *The Machine That Changed the World, Lean Thinking, Lean Solutions,* and *Seeing the Whole Value Stream.* Dan's career has been a journey of grasping the essence of value within many of the largest value streams on the planet. He offers a unique perspective on the essential role that IT can play within the Lean enterprise now and in the future.

In Part I you'll gain an understanding of Lean principles and practices. You'll learn the importance of value streams and how IT capabilities enable them. You'll learn how to establish effective, collaborative, continuously learning cross-functional teams. You'll discover the Lean approach to leadership and management, creating frontline accountability, aligning change initiatives to strategy, creating enterprise-wide agility.

You'll also learn:

- Why IT plays an essential role in the ability of the enterprise to run, grow, and transform (Chapter 1)
- How to align resources to ensure that all individuals within the enterprise see and understand how their work creates customer value and how they are empowered to improve performance (Chapter 2)
- How to integrate IT capabilities with enterprise-wide activities to significantly improve the value customers receive (Chapter 3)
- How to leverage the knowledge and impact of IT specialists, manage scarce resources, and evaluate outsourcing options (Chapter 4)
- How to speed new ideas to market through the cooperation of IT development and operations (Chapter 5)
- How and what to measure in order to improve performance and increase value (Chapter 6)
- How Lean leadership and management systems differ from traditional methods and how they create a continuously improving, collaboratively learning enterprise (Chapter 7)
- Why fully engaged people are the most important element in a Lean learning enterprise (Chapter 8)

In Part II, you'll hear from thought leaders across several IT communities:

- Enterprise architecture
- Business process management
- Service management

- ERP and commercial off-the-shelf software (COTS)
- Lean-Agile software development
- Integration and data management
- Business intelligence

You'll hear their voices and their perspectives on how Lean thinking contributes to their practice and how you can apply these principles to add value to your enterprise performance.

It has been a glorious sixty years of experimentation with information technology, with a continuous stream of invention and innovation on all fronts. Moore's Law predicting exponential growth in computing power still prevails, breaking new limits with each passing year. And the extraordinary power and promise of the Internet, with universal access to vast stores of knowledge, and the ability to connect individuals, teams, organizations, and communities around the globe, is unparalleled in human experience.

In this new age of enlightenment, through the rapid developments in information access and mobility, customers are now better informed and more powerful than ever before. They want it all, they want it fast, and they want a satisfying experience. Bold, curious, innovative enterprises are learning how to deliver.

Think of this book as a twenty-first-century salon, where everyone, across disciplines and specialties, can come together to explore, learn, and harness this new potential. Welcome to the Lean IT Renaissance.

Notes

1. Richard Hunter and George Westerman, *The Real Business Of IT: How CIOs Create and Communicate Business Value* (Boston: Harvard Business Press, 2009), 2.
2. Gartner, "IT Spending and Staffing Report," January 27, 2009.
3. Susan Cramm, "Put IT Where It Belongs," *Wall Street Journal*, April 25, 2011.
4. John Shook, "How to Change a Culture: Lessons from NUMMI," *MIT Sloan Management Review* (Winter 2010).
5. Tony Kontzer, "Winds of Change," *InformationWeek*, March 28, 2005.
6. AdWeek, "Word of Mouth Awards," http://www.adweek.com/sa-article/best-word-mouth-136683.
7. Press release: "Callibra Named Winner of 2011 Chicago Innovation Award," November 11, 2011.
8. For inspiring NetHope stories visit http://hub.nethope.org/videos-2.

CREATING A FRAMEWORK FOR BUSINESS AND LEAN IT INTEGRATION

In Part I we'll explore the foundations of a collaborative learning culture focused on customer value. We begin by gaining an understanding of why information technology is essential to the enterprise-wide effort to improve operational performance (run), expand market presence and volume (grow), and innovate—creating exceptional value for existing and new customers in new ways (transform).

With that understanding, we'll establish a framework for alignment to ensure that every person within the enterprise sees and understands how their work creates customer value so that they are engaged and empowered to improve performance. In Lean terms, this framework is known as a *value stream*.

We'll then learn how to integrate resources from throughout the enterprise into value streams to enable collaboration (Chapter 3). We'll address resource constraints, discovering ways to leverage and expand knowledge and capability (Chapter 4). We'll explore ways to speed new ideas to market through the cooperation of Lean-Agile software development and IT service management (Chapter 5). And we'll learn how to measure performance in a way that enables us to continuously improve the value we deliver (Chapter 6).

Chapter 7 takes us to the heart of Lean leadership and Lean management systems, helping us to improve our effectiveness as leaders and managers to create a learning, growing, integrated, and agile enterprise.

Part I concludes with Chapter 8, an exploration of the force that lies within every great enterprise, a transformative energy capable of creating market-differentiating value, year after year, for customers and shareholders alike.

Chapter 1

In Pursuit of Growth and Innovation

Steve Bell

> Knowledge is an unending adventure at the edge of uncertainty.
>
> **Jacob Bronowski**
> Scientist and author of *The Ascent of Man*

WHAT YOU'LL LEARN IN THIS CHAPTER

- Why Lean IT plays an essential role in the ability of the enterprise to run, grow, and transform
- Why sustained success requires a dynamic balance of operational excellence and innovation
- Why a new approach to governance can help drive innovation and alleviate uncertainty across the IT portfolio
- Why it's more important to be a "learner" than a "knower"

The CIO is sitting in a large and well appointed but empty conference room, a cup of cold coffee beside him as he thumbs through his fifty-page project portfolio. Casually he says to me, "Ten percent of my annual $1 billion budget—over one hundred million dollars—is waste. It's not adding value to our business or our customers." Then he stops. He leans forward, lowering his voice: "You and I both know it's probably much more than that—I just can't say it openly."

Do the math. If even 10% of the IT annual spend is waste, what is the value of discovering and *permanently* eliminating that waste? And what about the waste in the rest of the enterprise caused by an ineffective relationship between IT and "the business"? Ten percent? Fifteen? If you could capture that, how would you reinvest the gains?

The game has changed—with cloud computing, social media, mobile computing, big data analysis, software as a service, and more—suddenly we all want IT to drive innovation and growth. And we want it now. But many enterprises are mired in IT waste, complexity, and cost—which saps our energy, our creativity, and our speed. We all know the waste is there, but we are often unable to identify it, let alone do anything about it. We devise elaborate mechanisms to track and control spending yet have difficulty answering seemingly simple questions about what a new IT product or service will cost. How can we make effective investment decisions without such a fundamental understanding?

According to a 2007 survey by the MIT Sloan Center for Information Systems Research, the average for-profit company spent 72% of its IT budget on run-the-business/keep-the-lights-on activities.[1] In 2009 PricewaterhouseCoopers reported this figure at 80%.[2] However run-the-business spend is calculated, and whatever the figure happens to be within your enterprise, every dollar spent keeping the lights on is one less dollar available to support growth and innovation, an important consideration for any IT organization that aspires to be a catalyst for change.

The Big Shift

How do we shift our thinking and redirect our investment to get more business and customer value from our IT capabilities? It's a two-step process (Figure 1.1). First, taking the Lean approach to *operational excellence*, we emphasize continuous improvement of speed, quality, cost, and customer satisfaction by aggressively reducing waste, unnecessary variation, and overburden. As operational performance improves, we can shift more effort, investment, and creative energy toward enabling and enhancing business strategy and innovation. This is where the second aspect of Lean comes into play: *product development.*[*]

---

[*] It's important to note that while Toyota Production System techniques usually attract the most attention, Toyota's *product development system* has made just as significant a contribution to their sustained success. —Jeffrey Liker[3]

Lean practices help business and IT stakeholders work together in rapid and continuous cycles of experimentation, improvement, and innovation to reach a balance of three complementary objectives:

1. *Run the business*: Providing consistent quality services and improving price-to-performance ratios while reducing cost and risk
2. *Grow the business*: Improving top-line revenue with existing business models through improvement and innovation of products and services, the processes that deliver them, and the IT services that enable them
3. *Transform the business*: Radical innovation of products and services, the processes that deliver them, the business models that drive them, and the new markets and customers they serve[4]

Run efficiencies free up resources for growth, and growth then funds transformation. But they are interdependent in another, less obvious way as well. You can develop a highly innovative product, but if you can't quickly and effectively produce, deliver, and service it, you have not created value for the customer. Worse yet, a fast follower may come along and take your idea and your customers with it. So growth and transformation require operational excellence for effective commercialization. Although this relationship is obvious in the long run, it is in the day-to-day interdependence of operational activities and product development that most enterprises struggle, and nowhere is that struggle more challenging than with IT.

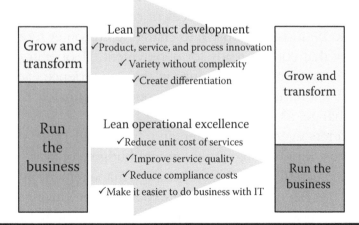

Figure 1.1   The big shift.

A Delicate Balancing Act

Run-the-business/operational activities are generally known—or are at least knowable. They are usually repeatable processes that can be standardized and continuously improved using Lean operational excellence techniques. In contrast, activities that enable enterprise growth and transformation often involve new and unknown situations, where variation and uncertainty produce the spark for innovation. These are the situations that we commonly associate with Lean product development, which includes software development.

However, software application development can also help to improve and automate many run-the-business activities, improving speed and service levels, reducing cost, and freeing capacity. In this way, Lean development and innovation can improve operational activities where occasional unknowns and disruptive events affect the existing standardized work.

Similarly, new products and services must also be designed with awareness for how they will be produced, delivered, and serviced in a standardized way as they are commercialized. Gaining an understanding of this requires input from those involved in run-the-business activities. So while they are subtly different, Lean operations and product/application/service development must cooperate if an enterprise is to grow and transform consistently (Figure 1.2).

Maintaining such a balance isn't easy because of the inherent nature of these two forces: operations and development. In the realm of IT, for example, operations strive for more standardized processes and less variation, while product development *requires* variation, and rapid change is the key to agility. Many software developers now believe in the Lean-Agile approach, which means that small pieces of code should be rapidly designed and deployed to be most responsive to changing customer requirements. But the moment that code is ready for deployment, IT operations often put up roadblocks to rapid change, because in their experience each individual change can cause a harmful service interruption. Fortunately this mindset is beginning to change, as we will explore in Chapter 5.

To make matters even more challenging, traditional IT governance practices tend to resist rapid change, with annual budget controls, and laborious, often bureaucratic portfolio and change management processes. Historically, IT has been both risky and expensive, producing highly inconsistent outcomes, so governance practices often attempt to *control* the uncertainty rather than work with it. Although the intent is to ensure that

	Lean operations	Lean product development
Run	Goal: Operational excellence Uncertainty: *low*	Goal: Develop new operational capabilities; product design for efficient production, delivery, and serviceability Uncertainty: *low to medium*
Grow	Goal: Improve flexibility and mass customization and efficiently scale in volume and geographic reach Uncertainty: *medium*	Goal: Incremental growth and innovation with products and services, processes, customers, and markets Uncertainty: *medium to high*
Transform	Goal: Fast and efficient commercialization of new ideas Uncertainty: *medium to high*	Goal: Radically new business models, products and services, processes, customers, and markets Uncertainty: *high*

Figure 1.2   Balancing Lean operations and development.

investments are made wisely and with appropriate oversight and controls, the result can be a loss of speed and agility accompanied by increased cost and, paradoxically, risk.*

If we are to realize a vision of transforming our companies and our industries with innovative use of IT capabilities, we need to achieve this balance between production and creation. We need a new relationship with risk. And to do that we need to better understand the very nature of uncertainty so that we can work with it rather than simply trying to control it.

Embracing Uncertainty

The CIO of a global energy company recently reflected on the similarities between research and development (R&D) and IT projects. In both, there are many technical complexities, variables, and unknowns, causing uncertain outcomes with each new project. The chief difference, as this particular CIO observed, is that with R&D there is a natural expectation that outcomes are uncertain and that the cost and time to deliver a successful result are unknown. This is the very nature of scientific research.

---

* "Requiring an 'accurate' estimate at the beginning of a project can dramatically increase project risk instead of decrease it as intended." – Scott Ambler and Per Kroll, IBM[5]

But with IT projects there is usually an expectation for known outcomes along with predetermined budgets and timelines. Through rigorous planning and control, stakeholders try to eliminate uncertainty and the risks associated with each project. But IT development is often an act of learning, not of production, and uncertainty is not only necessary but sought. Companies that successfully drive innovation quickly into the market have learned to embrace and exploit uncertainty as a source of competitive advantage.

Researcher David Snowden has developed a *sense-making framework* that helps us understand degrees of order and uncertainty so that we can take the proper approach to a particular situation. He postulates that there are four situational contexts: simple, complicated, complex, and chaotic.[6]

1. **Simple contexts** are ordered, known, and deterministic, where strict adherence to a formula produces the same result each time (e.g., baking a cake). Such situations should be approached with a standardized best practice. The proper approach is to "sense, *categorize*, and respond"—to strive to categorize the situation into a known solution to be implemented.

2. **Complicated contexts** are ordered, knowable, and deterministic; there are "known unknowns" (e.g., sending a rocket to the moon). Because there is one best solution to be found among the many variables and potential solutions, this is typically the domain of experts and expert knowledge, but experts have their blind spots too. A single "best practice" is inappropriate here, but there should be a set of "good practices" that may be drawn upon to configure the proper solution. The proper approach is to "sense, *analyze*, and respond"—to explore the situation in a scientific manner to understand the cause-and-effect relationships before prescribing a solution and then experimenting to ensure that the solution produces the desired effect.

3. **Complex contexts** are *un*ordered (not *dis*ordered, for there is an order of a higher degree) and dynamic (e.g., raising a child). Organic and human systems, including business organizations, are often complex; expertise is necessary but insufficient because systems are adaptive and respond to change in various ways, so rational assumptions do not always apply. With complex systems, patterns are emergent; we usually understand cause and effect only in retrospect, but using a past

example as a prescriptive model for responding to future change events is not appropriate because the system is not deterministic. Attempting to control a complex situation robs participants of the opportunity to learn new patterns. The proper approach is to *"probe,* sense, and respond"— to experiment, testing the behavior of the system to understand cause and effect and to determine the appropriate response. But the system is also dynamic, so what addresses the situation today may not work tomorrow; therefore, continuous monitoring is required to sustain performance.

4. ***Chaotic contexts*** are unknowable. No patterns exist—only turbulence. There are no right answers and many decisions to be made, often in situations of high stress (e.g., assisting at a multi-car accident scene). The proper approach here is to stabilize the situation, taking immediate controlling action to establish some sense of order: *"act,* sense, respond." There is a risk, however, that leadership may remain in the crisis command-and-control mode too long before shifting to complex domain behaviors of experimentation and learning.

What can we learn from this model of sense-making and response given our goal to simultaneously manage risk and achieve operational excellence while helping the business to grow and transform? Lean practitioners have learned that they must adapt their responses to the nature of each situation.

Simple and complicated situations are deterministic; as long as you follow the rules, the outcomes are predictable. This is the domain of many operational excellence efforts: taking a known or knowable process and standardizing it so that it is performed consistently and efficiently, with the understanding that the standardized work will continue to be improved.

But the most challenging endeavors, those that are transformational and often deliver the most value, also involve the most uncertainty and risk. These endeavors are, by this definition, complex, and they are often found to be in a chaotic state. First teams must stabilize them, so they can then be improved.

The skillful, innovative Lean enterprise learns to manage a portfolio of activities consisting of various degrees of uncertainty, always testing the boundaries for new discoveries, while continuously standardizing what is knowable. Thus, Lean thinking helps us to take on more unknowns and drive more discovery and innovation while producing better outcomes— faster and with less risk.

Improving the Value of What Is *Known*

When a team sets out to improve the operational efficiency and quality of repeatable activities, it often encounters a process that is not well understood, where every participant performs a task his/her own way, and there are no consistent measurements.

Because you cannot continuously improve random behavior, the first thing the team must do is *stabilize* the process. It does this by assessing the current state and determining the *one best way the team members can all agree on at the present time* to perform each step; in Lean terms this is called *standardized work*, which establishes a baseline of consistency to build upon. It's important to note that the manager is not telling the team what to do; the team figures out together how to best perform the work and then holds each other accountable for that behavior.

Once the process has been stabilized and standardized and the team establishes baseline measurements and visual management, it has a foundation upon which to continuously improve. The team then quickly finds and fixes problems, testing new ideas (hypotheses) one at a time by using the plan-do-check-act (PDCA) scientific problem-solving method. So the standardized work keeps improving over time, but at any point in time it represents the one best way the team can all agree on to do the work—ensuring consistency and a baseline for further improvement.

Thus, an IT organization can establish and sustain excellence in many operational activities, removing waste and freeing up capacity to be reinvested in growth and transformation. Note that even in a stable operations environment where so much is often already known and documented, each sudden variation is a new unknown, a reason to conduct another experiment to better understand the process. Occasionally there will be a disruptive event, like the adoption of cloud computing or another radically new technology, or an unexpected merger or acquisition in which multiple data centers must be consolidated on short notice. Such events initiate a need to experiment to discover the new, best approach.

The key ingredient for continuous improvement is a *team* with a sense of ownership and shared purpose and dedication to making things a little better each day. Lean thinking brings several paradoxes and counterintuitive notions to the table, and here is one of them: some on this team may initially fear that standardized work removes creativity and judgment, making the work mundane and uninteresting. This misunderstanding often causes resistance. Peter Senge once said, "People don't resist change. They resist being changed." When we help teams take ownership for the way they do the work, the way they measure the work, and for their outcomes, they respond with a sense of pride and a *desire to change* for the better. When a team eliminates the waste, the randomness, and the daily firefighting and frustration, this frees up time and energy and creates a space for creativity and innovation to flourish.

Improving the Path to Value in What Is *Not Known*

Growth and transformation investments are often new in every sense of the word: new products, markets, processes, and customers—even new business models. And with new initiatives come uncertainty, variation, and risk. Lean thinking helps in this domain too, but the approach is subtly different.

Consider one of the fundamental principles of Lean operations: *quality at the source*. Do it right the first time. Avoid errors, defects, and the rework, damage, and customer dissatisfaction they create. But in a development setting, paradoxically, we succeed when we fail faster and earlier; this emphasis on early failure in conditions of uncertainty significantly *reduces* risk, because we learn faster, in smaller increments, and thus avoid costly mistakes later. This approach is sometimes called "worst first," intentionally tackling the most challenging variables early in the learning process.

According to Don Reinertsen in *Managing the Design Factory*, "The fallacy in thinking that high first-pass success optimizes the design process lies in underestimating the important information generation that occurs with failure. … if we succeed at doing things right the first time we will have driven all information generation out of our design process."[7]

Innovation and transformation are an entrepreneurial journey, and there is much that even large, legacy enterprises can learn about how startups manage risk. "At its heart, a startup is a catalyst that transforms ideas into products," suggests Eric Ries in *The Lean Startup*. "As customers interact with those products, they generate feedback and data. That information is much more important than dollars, awards, or mentions in the press, because it can influence and reshape the next set of ideas."[8] So herein lies a great paradox of Lean development—we *reduce risk* by confronting uncertainty, early and often, through experimentation.

In this way, Lean thinking provides a safety net, helping teams to stretch, learn, and grow with less risk. Hypotheses and experiments are well thought out, discussed among peers, across disciplines, and with existing and potential customers. Lean thinking encourages testing the unknowns in small, bite-sized chunks. Smaller-scoped experimentation fuels continuous learning, which results in better products and better services, enabling the enterprise to respond more quickly to a dynamic marketplace.

What's Wrong with "Implementation Thinking"?

Some who encounter Lean thinking for the first time consider it to be a deterministic approach, mitigating risk through rigid practices. After all, it was first developed in a manufacturing environment and emphasizes standardized work, which to many suggests "Taylorism"*—with visions of men with stopwatches and clipboards treating human beings as machines. Yes, Lean helps an enterprise to identify good practices, but the standard created is temporary—until the next experiment where the team discovers a better way to accomplish the objective. For years, Mike Rother has studied the culture and behavior of organizations that thrive through continuous and collaborative learning by experimentation.† He cautions against the notion of certainty:

> Having an implementation orientation actually impedes our organization's progress and the development of people's capabilities. The way from where we are to where we want to be next is a gray zone full of unforeseeable obstacles, problems and issues that we can only discover along the way.
>
> The best we can do is to know the approach, the *means*, we can utilize for dealing with the unclear path to a new desired condition not what the content and steps of our actions—the solutions—will be. If someone claims certainty about the steps that will be implemented to reach the desired destination, that should be a red flag to us.[9]

Implementation is a word that is deeply ingrained in the culture and behavior of the IT organization, and in the way it manages projects. This is

---

* After Frederick Taylor (1856–1915), the industrial engineer who pioneered experiments in efficiency.
† Mike Rother and John Shook, authors of the popular *Learning to See* (Cambridge, MA: Lean Enterprise Institute, 2003), which introduced the practice of value stream mapping, both stress that a focus on the Lean tools and techniques themselves tends to distract people from the essential principles of collaborative problem solving and learning through PDCA experimentation.

often a natural blind spot for IT professionals because IT product development is often held to a false—or at least premature—certainty regarding scope, time, and cost of projects by the prevailing mental model of governance, project and program management, and financial control.

Consider the disappointing history of IT project failure. Early in every project there is a natural period of uncertainty, often called the *fuzzy front end* where strategic goals are transformed into tactical project objectives. While the natural progression of a project lifecycle leads to increasing certainty as the time of completion nears, it is during the fuzzy front end, when teams explore and experiment with uncertainty, that valuable insights and innovative ideas often appear. Yet there is a natural human tendency to try to push through this uncomfortable phase too quickly, arriving at a sense of premature confidence and certainty that too often leads to disappointment.

Peter Senge emphasizes this counterproductive leadership bias in *The Fifth Discipline*: "Deep within the mental models of managers in many organizations is the belief that managers must know what's going on. It is simply unacceptable for managers to act as though they do not know what is causing a problem. Those that reach senior positions are masters at appearing to know what is going on, and those intent on reaching such positions learn early on to develop an air of confident knowledge."[10]

Through years of guiding transformations, and during the development of a transformational leadership curriculum, the Lean Enterprise Institute has proven that authentic and lasting transformation requires leaders who *emphasize learning rather than knowing*. A Lean leader is comfortable saying, "I don't know, let's figure this out together."

By accepting uncertainty as an ally and chunking up projects into smaller and more rapid increments, the quality of decision making and outcomes improve, and the frequency and severity of project disappointments decrease. As a team moves *in the general direction of a vision*, they learn and adjust, step by step. At the conclusion of each small step there is a reflection on what has been learned, and the team then agrees on the next step toward the vision. By taking this step-by-step approach, the team ends up in a far better place than if it had rushed headlong according to a plan. However, the absence of a deterministic plan makes many people uncomfortable, especially when a significant investment is at stake.

Rother compares this incremental approach to finding your way through a dark room. You know generally where you are trying to go: the approximate location of a doorway across the room. But what obstacles lie in your path? The only safe way to proceed is one step at a time, learning from each step and planning the next. This is the essence of the scientific journey: when you suddenly bump into something solid, you pause, correct your course, and try again. But if you simply march confidently into uncertainty with a preordained and highly detailed plan, you're likely to suffer bruises (or worse) and end up frustrated. This, Rother points out, is the consequence of our infatuation with lists: project plans, action lists, checklists, and so on, which often lead us confidently astray. While giving us the sense of certainty and control, an overly prescriptive checklist (e.g., work breakdown structure, project budget) can make us unaccountable to actual results. By saying, "I did all the tasks assigned to me on schedule," it absolves each individual and team from watching the situation carefully, adapting to new discoveries at each step. This is how team members can report "all green lights" and "good progress" right until the moment the project fails.

Rother insists that the checklist approach is "an unscientific and ineffective method for process improvement. It is in actuality a scattershot approach: multiple action items are initiated in the hope of hitting something."[11] The checklist approach causes more variation and instability he concludes—not less. On top of that, it creates a false sense of certainty which means that expectations will hurt more when they are finally trampled upon. And perhaps most importantly, "implementation thinking" doesn't develop people's capacity for disciplined problem solving, which is the key to sustained competitive advantage.

It is clearly counterproductive to attempt to force certainty into a complex project because it works against the emergent forces of discovery, creativity, and innovation. By working with the uncertainty that naturally exists in the situation, teams may arrive at innovative products and solutions that create real value. This leads us in a direction that many would consider "inefficient" from the traditional project management perspective but results in faster and more effective discovery and commercialization of new ideas.

Consider *set-based development* (also called *forced innovation*)—designing multiple prototypes and simultaneously experimenting with different approaches and different levels of sophistication and difficulty with the results of each prototype informing the subsequent working design. If the advanced designs prove effective, they can lead to rapid innovation and radical new production introduction; if they do not mature in time for the current schedule, they accelerate the next cycle of development. But this approach involves greater investment and apparent duplication of effort and creates more failures (valuable learning experiences), which is discouraged by traditional efficiency thinking.

WHAT ARE THE VITAL FEW THINGS WE NEED TO KNOW?

At 3:24 PM on January 15, 2009, US Airways flight 1549 rolled down the runway at New York City's LaGuardia airport with 150 passengers on board. During the initial ascent, the jet struck a flock of Canadian Geese and instantly lost power in both engines. Three minutes later, the aircraft was floating in the Hudson River and all passengers were safely rescued. How did Captain "Sully" Sullenberger and his crew perform this remarkable feat? They had a checklist and the training and practice to know how to use it in a sudden and dire emergency. Clearly, checklists aren't inherently a problem; it's knowing how and when to use them properly that matters.

In *The Checklist Manifesto*, Harvard professor and surgeon Dr. Atul Gawande explores lessons learned from decades of airline safety procedures, hoping to learn how they may be applied in the field of Lean healthcare. He learned that in every cockpit is a folder of checklists that the crew uses for both routine and emergency situations. There is so much complexity in a modern aircraft that even the most seasoned pilot, especially in an emergency, can't be relied upon to remember every vital detail.

What struck Dr. Gawande was how short these checklists are. They don't contain every step the pilots need to perform a procedure. That would create an overly large list that would be counterproductive during an emergency. Anyway, he realized, you can't create a checklist that would handle every possible variable that arises in a real-life situation. These checklists, Dr. Gawande noted, only contain those vital few steps that are essential in avoiding catastrophic failure—lists of known issues that must be done right the first time. The rest is up to the skill and experience of the crew whose hands are on the controls, managing uncertainty second by second.

The checklist that Dr. Gawande teaches is what Lean practitioners call standardized work, which is how a team documents what is *known* so they can quickly spot exceptions and deal with unknowns—the sudden problems that inevitably occur in real life—such as a flock of geese. But when the process is entirely new, complex, or chaotic, there is no standardized work, no checklist—there is only past experience, fresh ideas, and hypotheses to experiment upon. In that case, what is known and what can be relied upon is the scientific experimentation process itself: PDCA.

The Fast-Follower Path of Innovation

Running the enterprise well—correction, not just well, but *very well*—can create its own path to market leadership by exploiting innovation. First does not always mean most successful, profitable, or sustainable. Sometimes *fast followers* become the market leaders. But fast followers need effective business processes to exploit someone else's idea.

Apple did not create the first MP3 player. The first two MP3 players, created by small technology companies in the late '90s, were minimally functional and lacked a legal way to download music. Compaq (later bought by Hewlett-Packard) followed quickly into this new market, significantly upgrading the technical capability, but they didn't invest in putting the whole value package together. Apple then took its bite of the market with the iPod. Elliot van Buskirk, technology editor for MP3.com, had this to say: "It wouldn't be too much of a stretch to assert that the entity now known as HP beat Apple in the race to make a high-capacity portable music player by three years—an eternity in the world of MP3 players—and still somehow lost."[12]

"At least half the cumulative operating profit for a new product will be generated in the first eighteen months after introduction," state the authors of *Fast Innovation*, "then commoditization will reduce margins during the remaining five to ten years of life and provide the other half of cumulative operating profits." Clearly, there is a reward for being first to market: introducing a disruptive innovation.* However, being able to take someone else's innovation and quickly introduce and differentiate your own offering can also pay dividends. "Sometimes a rapid follower can capture most of the profit, usually because the first mover *lacks strong operational execution or a lack of process innovation*"[13] [emphasis added].

To capture the top spot as a fast follower, you have to turn a better version of the innovation out *fast*—and deliver it better than anyone else. And the longer you lag, the greater the differentiating value must be. Research shows that *slow* followers will likely never recapture their investment in a new product; the bulk of the new profits are already taken in the first eighteen months. "In short, from an innovation standpoint," assert the authors,

---

* In *The Innovator's Dilemma* (Cambridge, MA: Harvard University Press, 1997), Clayton Christensen introduced the term *disruptive innovation*, something new that radically transforms the status quo, which may include the company's own current product offerings. This is contrasted with *sustaining innovation*, which is an incremental improvement on an existing product, service, business model, or market.

"better never than late!"[14] (Apple followed by three years with the iPod; more on that later.)

An innovation strategy requires funding an acceptable degree of risk with the introduction of new products, services, customers, and markets while maintaining operationally excellent processes to commercialize (produce, deliver, and service) them. If the governance model and decision-making framework isn't tuned to accepting this hybrid approach to uncertainty at the outset, if it insists on hard dollar/scope/time assertions at the beginning of every initiative, then you will most likely find a constant tension that tends to throw up roadblocks to growth through innovation.

From Innovation to Transformation

I recall a conversation with my travel agent at a cocktail party in 1996. She couldn't imagine people would someday not need her services or that she should begin planning for a new career. (By the way, I've since learned that discussing another's probable career obsolescence doesn't make for good cocktail party conversation!) But today we're not at all surprised when a new technology suddenly changes our lives. There are now legions of very bright and highly competitive people in every industry who are deliberately looking for ways to disrupt the status quo for fun and profit. They're smart; they're experienced; and, quite often, they're well funded. Many of them work in Web 2.0 companies with technology savvy baked into the company's genes. But many work in older companies—"intrapreneurs" who are eager to be disruptive and transformative in their own backyards.

Are any of these people working for you? To quote Will Rogers, "Even if you're on the right track, you'll get run over if you just sit there." Disruptive innovation results from taking a radical, unproven idea and monetizing it. This introduces the highest degree of uncertainty. In fact, that is the whole point! And that often means intentionally creating disruption within your own comfort zone, with your own products and customers. Get used to it. Make it happen. Remove the barriers that resist it. But don't rush blindly into risk; do it wisely. Fail early, fail fast, fail often.

If you don't deliberately invest in innovation, it's not going to happen. And if you do invest in pioneering new ventures, you can't treat these investments using the old model of IT change management and governance. It's just not going to work.

Nor is it going to work without fully integrated IT capabilities. We live in an age where skillful application of IT is an essential component of the value proposition for every enterprise because:

■ IT capabilities are integrated within virtually every product and service we deliver to our customers.
■ IT competency enables us to develop for, deliver to, and service our customers better, faster, and at a lower cost through continuously improving and adapting *business* processes.
■ IT savvy helps us listen more carefully to the voice and behavior of our customers through many diverse channels such as big data analysis and social media listening.

The Virtuous Cycle of Innovation

When an enterprise pursues growth and transformation, it is signing up for a continual dance with uncertainty, which requires repeated experimentation (and failure) in order to achieve sustained success. How does it fund the effort? By focusing on operational excellence to drive waste out of the routine run-the-business operations; this frees up capacity: people, money, and other resources for growth, which in turn drive additional profits to fund the transformation, which in turn requires operational excellence to commercialize and monetize—a virtuous cycle (Figure 1.3).

The challenge is that all three forces of change are interdependent; they play out simultaneously, yet differently, within each *value stream* (all the activities involved in delivering value to the customer; we'll explore value streams in depth in Chapter 2). Each value stream must therefore find the right dynamic balance of its portfolio of run, grow, and transform efforts according to the maturity of its product lifecycle and the needs of its customers. One-size-fits-all, top-down management and governance doesn't work here. Each team must have a clear purpose and a vision for the future. This calls for a new style of management and leadership.

Now back to Apple and the iPod. Why did they succeed when the initial developers, and even Compaq/Hewlett-Packard, did not? Apple was neither the first to market nor especially fast to follow. And when they did follow, their technology wasn't that much better than their competitors.

So why did they *wildly* succeed?

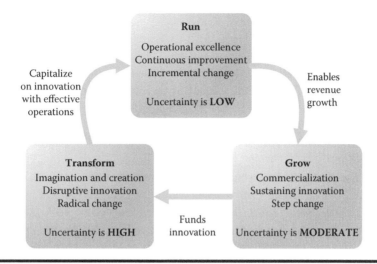

Figure 1.3 The self-sustaining cycle of uncertainty.

Apple delivered—and delivered in a *big* way—customer value. What good is a high-density portable music player *if there's no music to play?*

Apple swallowed the market. In this bold combination of innovation and commercialization, Apple delivered a *complete* product. They not only transformed the value of the personal music player and created a new business model, they also disrupted the music industry.

Once in a while a company such as Apple, Toyota, or Southwest Airlines comes along—one that seems to have an innate sense of shared purpose, teamwork, and a truly remarkable culture. We can't simply copy these companies. It's foolish to try. Each of us must find our own path, making a sincere and deliberate effort to invest in our own transformation—of our products, processes, business models, industries, IT capabilities, and our culture.

It all begins with teams of people with a clear sense of shared purpose—serving the customer and providing exceptional value. It begins when teams start asking the seemingly simple questions: *Who are our customers? What do they value? And how do we create that and deliver it to them?*

And with these questions, the Lean journey begins.

Notes

1. MIT Sloan CISR survey of 1,508 IT leaders conducted in 2007.
2. PricewaterhouseCoopers, *The Real Promise of Cloud Computing*, Technology Forecast, Summer (London: PricewaterhouseCoopers, 2009), 8.

3. Jeffrey Liker, interview, May 29, 2011.
4. R. Hunter et al., "A Simple Framework to Translate IT Benefits into Business Value Impact," Gartner Research, May 16, 2008.
5. Scott Ambler and Per Kroll, "Best Practices for Lean Development Governance, Part I: Principles and Organization," IBM developerWorks, June 15, 2007.
6. David J. Snowden and Mary E. Boone, "A Leader's Framework for Decision Making," *Harvard Business Review*, November 2007.
7 Don Reinertsen, *Managing the Design Factory* (New York: Simon & Schuster, 1997), 79.
8. Eric Ries, *The Lean Startup* (New York: Crown Business, 2011), 75.
9. Mike Rother, *Toyota Kata* (New York: McGraw-Hill, 2010), 7.
10. Peter Senge, *The Fifth Discipline* (New York: Doubleday, 1990), 234.
11. Mike Rother, *Toyota Kata* (New York: McGraw-Hill, 2010), 30.
12. Eliot Van Buskirk, "Introducing the World's First MP3 Player," *CNet Reviews*, January 21, 2005.
13. Michael L. George, James Works, and Kimberly Watson-Hemphill, *Fast Innovation* (New York: McGraw-Hill, 2005), 22.
14. Ibid., 18–22.

Chapter 2

Value Streams
Aligning Resources to Create Value

Steve Bell

Price is what you pay. Value is what you get.

Warren Buffett

WHAT YOU'LL LEARN IN THIS CHAPTER
- The Lean approach to aligning resources to the flow of value creation
- What a value stream is and how it enables people to see and understand how their work contributes to customer value
- How to continuously improve value stream activities
- The essential role of leadership in value stream improvement

Let's begin with the questions that are fundamental to Lean, questions everyone within the enterprise should *always* ask: *Who are our customers and what do they value?*

These questions lead directly to the *purpose*, the *true north* of every enterprise. Although simple, these questions can lead everyone within the enterprise on a journey of learning and discovery, jostling many basic assumptions and intruding on comfort zones. Such inquiries often produce unexpected insights about our customers and what they really want from us. These insights can guide transformative strategy.

Central to this question is how we conceive, create, deliver, service, and improve the product or service that our customers value. In Lean terms, this process is called a *value stream*. As the name implies, it relates to the flow of actions required to bring a product or service from concept to launch, from order to delivery, and from service request to customer satisfaction.

Who are our customers? Value can only be defined by the end customer.[1] But the flow to this end customer often includes many intermediate steps, each step represents an intermediary customer—either external or internal to the enterprise. These intermediate customers may consume a component product or service to create a finished product or service for the end customer. It's therefore essential to view a value stream as a series of interconnected activities, each serving the next downstream recipient of a process, with the goal of maximizing value to the end customer.

What do our customers value? The end customers are not homogeneous; often they are quite diverse. A single value stream may serve numerous end customers, and each customer may have a different perspective on value and a different way of measuring it.

Value is neither always tangible nor always easy for the customer to articulate. When asked to judge quality and customer service, many customers say they "know it when they receive it." Customers often know what they're used to being satisfied with, but when they are led on a deeper inquiry into their underlying needs,[*] they may discover a new definition of value. In some cases, it may be an extension of something already available—the better mousetrap. In other cases, however, customers may not even be consciously aware that they have a problem to be solved or that they want something new—this is the case when revolutionary new products appear.

The arrival of the Internet has, in many cases, entirely transformed the relationship between customers and their service providers and suppliers. In some industries it has radically redefined value and competitive advantage. How many enterprises are using the Internet in new and surprising ways to listen to their customers, to interact with them, and to observe their behaviors? In his article "Value Stream Management," Dan Jones comments on the disruptive voice of the Internet-enabled customer:

> [T]he web [is] opening up the possibility of turning customers from strangers to partners. The more customers know about what they could have and the way products and services are produced and delivered the more demanding they are becoming. They recognize they have an increasingly powerful voice! And they

---

[*] For a discussion of new techniques for understanding unspoken customer preferences, see the discussion of social media listening and big data analysis in Chapter 15.

expect providers to be able to deliver exactly what they want, when, where and how they want it and to significantly improve the experience of using these products and services while minimizing the impact on the environment. In return they may well be willing to share their plans and to respond to suggestions from providers.[2]

Lean thinking encourages everyone to better understand what their customers want—going to the source, known in Lean terms as the *gemba**, and observing customer *behavior* in order to create and deliver what they value. In return, the engaged customers may act with increased loyalty.

THREE SOURCES OF VALUE

The first of five principles introduced in *Lean Thinking* is this: "Value can only be defined by the ultimate customer."[3] From the customer's standpoint, the creation of value for the customer is "why producers exist."

However, according to Dan Jones, there are two more important dimensions of value to consider: the employee and the enterprise.

> Value to the customer is the least visible, but value of the employee is the most difficult to measure. Organizations often say "employees are our most valuable asset" [but they often behave otherwise]. Actually, that is the foundation for running an integrated, interdependent process, that you have skilled people running the process. Therefore the work has to be a learning environment. For effective learning and development it has to be hassle free at one end of the spectrum, and learning something new, being challenged, at the other end. And then finally there is survival for the organization, and profits for the shareholders. It has to be balanced among all three.[4]

---

* *Gemba* is a Japanese term meaning the place where the work is done and where the value is created. According to Jim Womack, the current situation along value streams is hard for anyone to grasp, but sustainable improvement is difficult unless everyone whose actions affect the value stream can see and agree upon the actual situation. Therefore, those touching the value stream need to take a walk in order to see and grasp the situation.

Visualizing the Value Stream

Once we have identified the customers and what they value, this awareness becomes the compass that guides our activities and measures our
performance. Anything that adds value to the customer is called *value
adding* (VA); unnecessary steps are known as *nonvalue adding* (NVA).
To improve a value stream we must carefully consider *all the steps* by
first asking does the step add value, and, if not, can we eliminate it? The
general rule of thumb is this: if we are performing a step and the customer knew about it, would he or she be willing to pay for it? Some steps
will be necessary due to regulation or other unavoidable circumstances,
but if given a choice, the end consumer would not pay for it. These are
known as necessary but nonvalue-adding activities (NNVAs) and should
be reduced when possible.*

In a value stream, a customer seeks a product or service, and a series of
steps (made up of processes and practices†) produces and delivers it to them.
This is different from the classic definition of a *process*, where inputs are
transformed into outputs (Figure 2.1).

What is missing in this depiction? The customer is missing; the customer's
definition of value is missing. A process may efficiently transform an input
into an output, but if the customer doesn't value the transformation then the
process should not be done. Many nonvalue-adding activities are this way—
we do things not because the customer wants them but because "we've
always done them this way."

A value stream is a closed loop where a customer requests and
receives value, as shown in Figure 2.2. The value stream encompasses all
the actions required to determine, create, deliver, and service what the
customer values.

There are three primary value streams that *every* enterprise must have.[5]
Lean applies to all three but in subtly different ways:

---

* Many NNVA compliance costs invest scarce resources in checking for defects, to make sure they
don't reach the customer. An enterprise should consider investing these resources, instead, in process improvement to prevent defects. Not only does the enterprise spend less checking for defects
(waste), but this investment pays many other dividends.

† Processes are a series of tasks that are generally repetitive, well-defined, routine, controllable, and
standardized. In contrast, practices are non-routine, highly variable, loosely defined, heuristic, and
require a degree of knowledge, judgment, and experience to carry out.

Figure 2.1   Classic depiction of a process.

1. The *development value stream* involves the design, development, testing, and commercialization of products and services that offer value to customers. This value stream starts with an idea, a problem to be solved, an opportunity to be met. It not only includes the development of a product or service to satisfy that need but potentially the creation of new processes and technologies to produce and deliver it, which may include the design and development of entirely new supply chains and business models. Development emphasizes learning and discovery and *seeks out variation* as a source of innovation, "failing" early and often, to develop robust and effective products.

2. The *operational value stream* includes the production and delivery of products and services. Operational excellence emphasizes waste reduction, improving the speed, quality, and cost of the processes while *seeking to remove variation.* Thus, Lean applied to development and operations is subtly different, an essential theme we'll explore throughout this book. In a design/build situation, the development and operations value streams often blend together as a hybrid.

3. The *service and support value stream* is interactive between the supplier and the customer, so the emphasis is upon creating a satisfactory

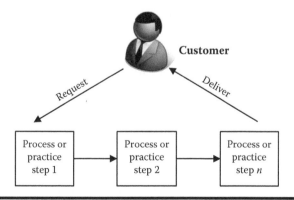

Figure 2.2   Simple depiction of a value stream.

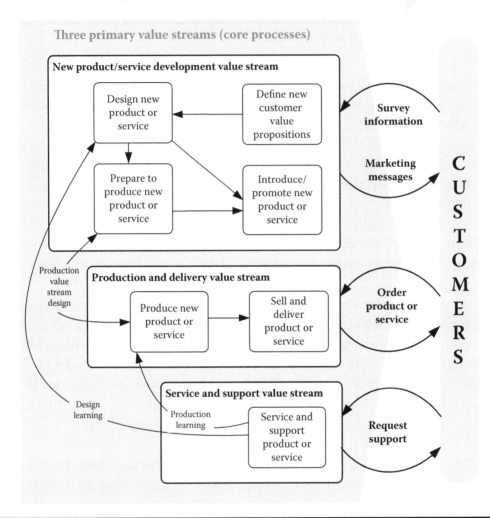

Figure 2.3   Three primary value streams.

customer experience. In a professional services industry, the operations and service and support value streams often blend together as a hybrid.

As you can see in Figure 2.3,[6] these three primary value streams are interwoven with multiple feedback loops [plan-do-check-act (PDCA) cycles], orchestrated by management systems and enabled through the flow of information. The end customer is the primary focus of these value streams. To study this diagram, I suggest you start with the customers' perspective on the right-hand side and work backward.

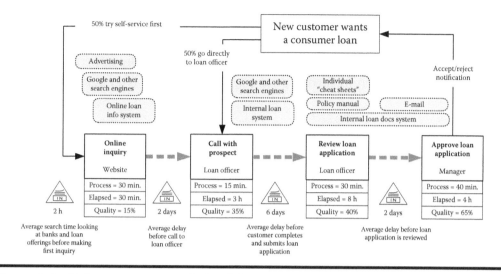

Figure 2.4 Value stream map of a bank loan application process.

Value streams are often depicted with a value stream map, as shown in Figure 2.4.* This example follows a customer through the process of applying for a consumer bank loan. This value stream begins when the customer searches the marketplace for loan information (or calls a loan officer directly) and finishes when the customer loan application is either accepted or rejected. From the customer's perspective (not the bank's), the ultimate outcome is how quickly and easily the funds are obtained.

This value stream map example is the composite of several real-life scenarios and generally reflects the proportion of work and wait time found in common business processes, leading Lean practitioners to suggest that typically over 95% of the time customers wait for value is unnecessary and should be eliminated. In this example, the total elapsed time from when a potential customer first makes an inquiry until the application is accepted or rejected is 97.5 hours (1 day = 8 hours). During this time, only 115 minutes of work is being done (2% of the total time, and it is likely that some of that work is also not necessary). What does this mean to the customer? It means they

---

* A thorough examination of the value stream mapping technique is beyond the scope of this book. To learn more, please see Mike Rother and John Shook, *Learning to See: Value Stream Mapping to Add Value and Eliminate MUDA* (Cambridge, MA: Lean Enterprise Institute, Inc., 2003); Dan Jones and Jim Womack, *Seeing the Whole Value Stream: Mapping the Extended Value Stream* (Cambridge, MA: Lean Enterprise Institute, Inc., 2002); and Beau Keyte and Drew Locher, *The Complete Lean Enterprise: Value Stream Mapping for Administrative and Office Processes* (New York: Productivity Press, 2004). See also the Lean Enterprise Institute's online value stream mapping workshop at http://www.lean.org.

must wait longer than necessary for what should be a simple and fast process. Rigorous value stream analysis can find and quantify waste, helping to prioritize improvement efforts, which often results in dramatically improved speed, quality, and cost, which in turn creates happy and loyal customers.

THE NEED FOR SPEED

A financial services client of mine engaged in a value stream mapping exercise of its commercial loan application and approval process. The client was shocked to learn just how long it took to process an application and how much waste of time, effort, and errors occurred along the way. They also engaged in voice-of-the-customer activities and learned that a faster response on a business loan application would, in many cases, offer a competitive advantage. If the bank could respond faster (and friendlier) than its competitors, the business customer might proceed with the loan, even if it was priced slightly higher than the competitors' offerings. This was, as the customers explained, because the bank's actions not only indicated an *intention* to focus on customer service (which is easy for *any* bank to say) but also demonstrated its ability to execute on this intention in a deliberate way. Moreover, speed from the bank translated to speed for the client. Learning if a loan would be approved would allow clients to make decisions and take action faster, and that, for many, represented value.

The value stream mapping technique originated in Toyota's manufacturing operations and has since been adapted successfully to virtually all activities in all industries. For example, value stream mapping of hospital emergency department flow has proven highly effective in many well-documented cases. Value stream maps measure time, quality, resources, and cost of the process. In many service operations such as the one depicted here, the customer remains actively engaged with the process throughout the life cycle. As you can see, the customer searches for loans, talks with loan officers, completes loan applications, answers questions when the application is being reviewed, and finally learns of acceptance or rejection. These all require ongoing engagement with the customer.

VALUE BEYOND NUMBERS

A global energy products enterprise that had been on a Lean supply chain journey for ten years decided to experiment with Lean within the IT organization. We chose a pilot improvement event (often called a *kaizen*) with the company's new employee on-boarding process because it was a frequent activity that engaged many people across several functions within IT and many other areas of the business. We brought together a team of eight people who had worked together (yet separately on their individual tasks) for years. We interviewed customers (in this case, hiring managers and, ultimately, new hires), gathered data, and value stream mapped the entire process: provisioning and setting up connectivity, a computer and devices, cell phone, security rights, application access, and so on. What this team learned surprised them: 7 hours of value-adding work required an average of 11.2 days to complete, accompanied by a ridiculous number of inquiries, phone messages, e-mails, frustrating delays and callbacks, errors and rework cycles, and so on. There was little standardization or coordination in how the work was done from one employee to the next.

The negative impacts of this broken process (not a process really, just a set of disconnected tasks) included lost new hire productivity, constant interruptions and rework for the technologists, wasted time for the hiring manager, and a poor new hire experience never to be forgotten by the employee. Through a relatively simple 2-day improvement event the team reduced the elapsed time from 11.2 to 4.5 days (a 60% reduction) with further improvements expected when they examined the hardware procurement process. Most notably, the team calculated a current state quality of less than 1%, meaning that the process was almost *never* done right and always created a problem that required later correction. The team set their initial future state quality target at 75%, believing that most failures were preventable by simple standardized work. At the end of the event, the human resources director requested her department be next on the list for a pilot *kaizen* event.

Although customer-centric, the traditional value stream mapping view measures the end-to-end process perspective but not the *customer experience*. For example, Figure 2.4 does not record how many phone calls typical customers made during the entire process, how long they waited on hold, how many times they left a message and waited for a callback, how many times their question was handed off to another individual (resulting in yet more waiting for callback), and so on. These individual customer interactions are often called *moments of truth*, and customers may care as much or more about the satisfaction they receive from each of these interactions (were they friendly, prompt, accurate?) than the total elapsed time. So it is often helpful to include additional customer perspectives such as customer process activity, quality, and satisfaction metrics to the traditional value stream map depiction. This can be done by using the *swimlane* mapping technique (Figure 2.5),[7] which represents the customer and provider flow of information and works as parallel pathways that interact with each other at various points along the value stream.

Another technique that is popular in a service and support setting is the measurement of *failure demand*, the amount of capacity used to do things (like returning phone calls and clarifying confusing information) that would have been prevented if done right the first time. This is a particularly useful measurement in a call center environment, where often 50% or more of the work is found to be unnecessary, and provides an economic argument to invest in service-level improvement.

Now look again at Figure 2.4. The start event of this value stream occurs when a new customer wants a loan; the end event occurs with the approval or rejection of the application. But what happens before that start event? What happens after approval or rejection? This value stream connects to other value streams within the enterprise, and collectively they may comprise an even larger enterprise-wide value stream.

To increase value to the customer, a team must consider all steps of the *highest-level* value stream together as a complete system. To look at anything less, for individuals or departments to suboptimize only a segment of the overall value stream, tends to shuffle waste around from one function/ department to another rather than eliminating it entirely. And even when waste *is* eliminated within a single step of the process, without a systemic view the localized benefits are often lost or absorbed in an ineffective process further downstream—resulting in the customer not realizing the value.[*]

The initial purpose of value stream mapping is to help the entire team grasp the situation by documenting the current state from a high level.

---

[*] An extreme example of this is Amazon.com. They did not seek to incrementally reduce waste within the traditional steps of the retail bookselling model. They completely eliminated most of the supply chain (value stream) and delivered value (fast, high quality, inexpensive, variety) directly to the customer. We'll explore this radically transformative IT-enabled value stream thinking throughout this book.

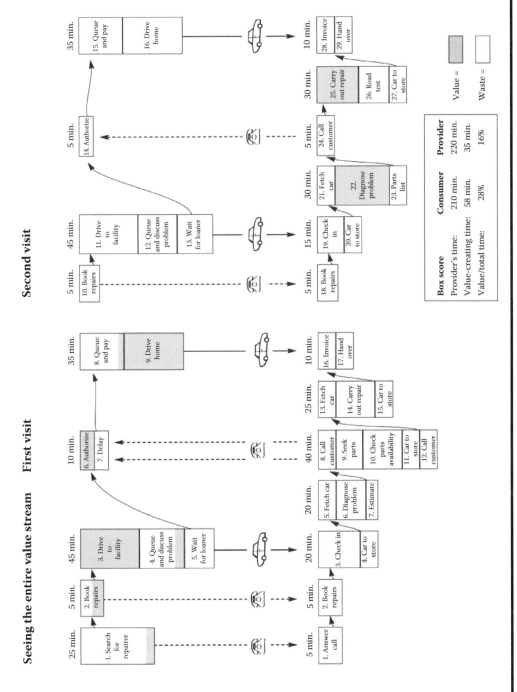

Figure 2.5 Customer-interactive value stream map.

This means that the team will identify, quantify, and prioritize the wastes, enabling them to move step by step toward the vision of an ideal state (the PDCA cycle) guided by facts and experimentation. So at the beginning, the value stream map is informative and directional. When continuous improvement cycles (*kaizen*) begin, deeper and more granular views focus in on specific segments of the value stream to make small, measurable improvements.

The collective, systemic view of the results of these individual experiments is shown on the value stream map. The results are compared to the associated improvement targets defined by the team. During the deeper dive (a *kaizen* that focuses on specific improvements at the process level) lower-level value stream maps may be used along with other types of maps and visualizations such as spaghetti diagrams, process maps, swimlane maps, fishbone diagrams, and other problem-solving tools and techniques.

LOW-HANGING FRUIT

By an anonymous Lean IT coach

One of the first problems that a newly formed team decided to tackle was historical inquiry on customer billing, which wasted time and effort as employees made daily trips across the parking lot to the poorly lit document storage room to locate archived paperwork. As the team began to examine the problem, the technologist team member shared a vital piece of information, explaining that the enterprise resource planning (ERP) system had been enhanced several years ago and now provided all the necessary information online to quickly respond to historical inquiries.

The solution became immediately obvious. Utilizing the ERP system capability and eliminating the hardcopy method would not only improve the speed of customer service and prevent daily treasure hunts to the document warehouse, it would also eliminate the long-term storage of those documents with an outside service provider, eliminating over $5,000 per month in fees. And on top of that, the team suddenly realized they no longer had to print and archive hardcopies, which meant it could save not only the space, storage cost, and labor to move countless boxes of paper around but that it could also stop printing over 100,000 unnecessary sheets of paper each year—an environmental win.

Excited and energized, the team invited the CIO to their *kaizen* report-out. When she asked why they had not acted on this problem before, members of the IT staff replied, "We didn't think we had permission" to invest time to work on the problem with their business colleagues.

Value Streams Are Fractal

The value stream map example of the loan application process shown in Figure 2.3 represents a single process within a larger enterprise-wide value stream. In this case, lending is one of several system-level value streams within the typical financial institution. So the full portfolio of enterprise-level value streams are broad and deep, comprised of a multitude of multithreaded supporting processes.* Core enterprise value streams are made up of a rich fabric of successively lower-level supporting value streams, most serving internal rather than external customers. In *Lean Thinking*, Jim Womack and Dan Jones describe these multidimensional value stream relationships as *fractals*, which are defined by mathematicians as "a rough or fragmented geometric shape that can be split into parts, each of which is (at least approximately) a reduced-size copy of the whole."[8] The basic principle of a fractal is that *a simple pattern*, a basic instruction set, repeated again and again, will create astonishingly complex, beautiful, and organic results. The veins within the leaves of a plant, the branching form of a lightning bolt, and the spidery flow of a river delta are naturally occurring fractal patterns. Womack and Jones illustrate the fractal patterns of Toyota management systems in *Lean Thinking*:

> A product line manager overseeing an entire product may work with a number of Value Stream managers at lower levels taking responsibility for different courses of the Value Stream. For example, a Chief Engineer (to use Toyota's term for a product line manager overseeing an entire automotive platform) works with a development leader in design, a Value Stream manager in the assembly plant, and Value Stream managers in each of the component plants working on major items assembled into the finished

---

* A Lean enterprise is a compound matrix structure, also known as a *network organization*, with many areas of overlapping responsibility and authority. This is why the discipline of business process management (BPM; see Chapter 10) may be especially useful to Lean practitioners and help them understand the flow of value streams within complex organizational structures.

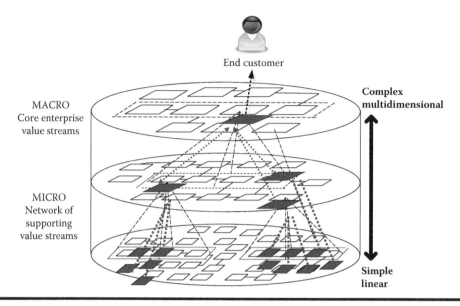

End customer

Complex
multidimensional

MACRO
Core enterprise
value streams

MICRO
Network of
supporting
value streams

Simple
linear

Figure 2.6   Value stream patterns as fractals.

product. Each manager is essentially doing the same job but with
varying scope—wide at the top and narrow at the bottom.[9]

This relationship is illustrated in Figure 2.6, which shows value streams at
multiple levels, effectively creating a network of supporting value streams that
in turn is supported by a management system to orchestrate their collective
efforts.* While such a comprehensive, fractal view of enterprise-wide value
streams may be difficult to unravel (see Chapter 10), it is helpful for all
individuals and teams to keep this perspective in mind, always seeking to
understand how their daily work contributes to the flow of value into the
hands of the end customer.

Value Stream Improvement

One of the most significant advantages with a value stream orientation is
the holistic awareness and visibility it creates. Everyone can see exactly how

---

* "The question that confronts every team that tries to model a process is how much to model.
  Supporting processes are just as important to the success of the enterprise as core processes. Often,
  however, there is no flow among the support processes. Indeed, even the various processes included
  in a given support group—like HR and IT—may have only [a] tangential relationship to each other.
  When starting out, we model the core processes, and then, when we are ready to focus on support
  processes we model them only as they touch any of the specific core processes." —Paul Harmon

each process fits into the larger picture of delivering value to the end customer, and more importantly, where it does not. This awareness creates the opportunity for continuous improvement and innovation that matters not just to the enterprise but also to the end customer.

Value stream improvement is a contact sport, a fully engaging experience for all. This means that all essential stakeholders must be engaged, because all perspectives—including the customer's—must be represented. Team engagement is essential for effective transformation of a value stream, and this changes the role of the frontline manager or supervisor from a director and controller to one responsible for developing the teams' problem-solving skills and encouraging them to experiment. This means that the manager must become more engaged with the daily work, "go and see" frequently, monitor progress to identify performance gaps, balance demand and capacity, create time and space for problem solving and improvement activity, bridge organizational silos, and remove obstacles* that get in the teams' way as they learn how to remove waste and improve outcomes.

Bringing a team together for the first time and preparing a map of the current state of a value stream can be a challenging experience for the team members who are asked to develop a clear and quantitative model of how the work is currently done. The initial discoveries are often sobering, challenging many unquestioned assumptions and habitual behaviors, and may highlight long-standing disagreements and misunderstandings. "For many employees, it may be the first time they've looked at their work as part of a process or value stream," says David Almond, former CIO and now a Lean transformation leader at the State of Oregon. "We had several employees tell us that they don't have customers and aren't part of a process, but rather perform a very specific function."[10]

When beginning the value stream transformation journey, many processes are unstable, chaotic, and poorly documented, guided by tribal knowledge and with limited baseline data available for a thorough analysis. Furthermore, if several individuals are performing the same task within the process, they often discover that they each perform those tasks slightly differently. What a team usually discovers, in a very visceral way, is that the value stream is bloated with wasteful, redundant, and even conflicting activities that were never seen from each individual stakeholder's limited perspective.[†]

---

* Often, existing management and measurement systems, and the assumptions underlying them, are the most significant obstacles to sustained improvement. We'll explore this further in Chapter 7.

† "Once you can see the processes by stripping away unnecessary detail, you can then look for the delays, overburden and root causes of common-cause variation that is having systemwide consequences." —Dan Jones

This realization can be both upsetting and motivating to the team. Members are often heard making statements like "Now I finally understand why this happens." But the excitement really kicks in when the team translates their new understanding into action, tackling the low-hanging-fruit issues that often yield breakthrough performance improvement in the very first PDCA cycle.* In virtually every *kaizen*, there is at least one forehead-slapping moment where the team members look at each other and exclaim, "Are we really doing *that?*" Such realizations are motivating (as long as there is no blame) and make a big difference not just in process performance but also in team morale. Early successes also motivate the team to seek out more improvements.

For rapid problem solving to work, all stakeholders must come together in close proximity, in a closed-loop discovery and decision-making cycle in which the results of one improvement cycle inform the next (PDCA). The team must have the authority to implement changes within clearly understood boundaries.† Once the team develops a shared understanding of the problems and opportunities, this naturally leads to a collective approach to improve the process so that it consistently achieves the desired outcomes. One of the first steps is for the team to meet the customers where they live (at the *gemba*) so the team can see and understand the situation firsthand. There are many ways to gain an appreciation for the voice of the customer, but actually going to the source is foundational. Through observing the customers' behaviors, combined with other methods of inquiry, the value stream team develops a clear and guiding vision of value through the eyes and voice of the customer.

Let's consider part of that last sentence again: *the value stream team develops a clear and guiding vision of value.* Visual management of the value stream is essential. It helps all participants to see, at a glance, where value is flowing and where it isn't. The essential purpose of visual management is as follows:

- *Self-regulating*: Conveying actual versus planned outcomes, enabling the team to spot the gaps in performance trends
- *Self-explaining*: Conveying quickly and easily the current situation and how the standardized work should be performed to prevent errors and variation

---

* This PDCA process is often guided by an A3 form, which describes the entire problem-solving journey on a single sheet of paper. The importance of an A3 is *not the form itself* but the disciplined problem-solving process and the simplicity and clarity that it encourages.

† "I find that many teams become demoralized because they are not properly constituted to attack the base problems. A frequent reaction I see is: 'You have the wrong people here—our managers *need* to understand this.'" —Mary Poppendieck

- *Self-ordering*: Instantly and intuitively showing when something is not right or is out of place

In an effective visual management environment, processes are stabilized and visualized so that abnormalities, quite literally, call attention to themselves *immediately* using a variety of simple and clever visual techniques. Physical line of sight is important, but in a geographically distributed enterprise the entire value stream often runs further than the eye can see, so access to computerized information systems that visualize the state of the process and notify stakeholders of abnormal conditions is often necessary.

Once a value stream is stabilized, visualized, standardized, and measured, the team is responsible for its ongoing performance. Leadership and management focus on oversight, coaching, and breaking down organizational barriers so that the team can succeed.

But something else happens when teams come together to identify how the work is done and how it fits together. Recall the comments David Almond heard among his staff—that they believed they weren't part of a process and didn't have customers; their job was just to perform a task. During the initial value stream mapping exercise, everyone learns to see how everything is connected, and how, ultimately, what everyone does affects others and the end customer. Everyone learns that with management support employees *can* conduct experiments and make changes that create real improvement, breaking down the waste and frustration they have until now learned to live with. That creates a sense of ownership and pride. *We do this. We make this happen!*

WHEN TECHNOLOGY BECOMES A LIABILITY

Technical debt is a term that has emerged from the Lean-Agile software community. Although there are many definitions for technical debt, my favorite is also the simplest: "a system that resists change." Unnecessary or obsolete code, architectural and design flaws, expedient workarounds, and the general tendency toward quick and dirty solutions are examples. The enterprise pays "interest" (lost time, inefficiency, additional change costs, business risk, frustration) until the debt is eventually "liquidated" by an investment to remedy it. If debt is left unmanaged, it can become crippling and eventually force a catastrophic intervention. Obsolete legacy systems are a form of technical debt, but a brand-new system can also create debt if it is designed in a way that violates architectural or design integrity, which makes it difficult to change later on.

The technical debt metaphor is useful for Lean thinkers in nontechnology areas as well. I like to think in terms of "process debt" where a faulty process is adapted with clumsy and expedient workarounds (including unwise investment in automation), building layer upon layer of process scar tissue that charges a daily cost, whereas the underlying process itself should be simplified, improved, or eliminated altogether.

Whether or not we can agree that technical or process debt should be added to the Lean taxonomy of waste, most of us *can* agree that such a burden of unnecessary complexity and resistance to change naturally exists within our enterprise. And it requires a deliberate effort to learn to see and remove this debt and to prevent it from appearing. Every time something new is added (a process change or new software logic), the team should consider ways to remove obsolete components— making debt removal part of your regular business case analysis, considering the *total cost* of ownership with each change.

There's More to Lean than Waste Reduction

Most popular Lean texts emphasize the elimination of waste (known as *Muda* in Japanese): those activities that consume resources but do not add value to the customer. The most common wastes include the following:[*]

- Inventory (physical and virtual)
- Overproduction (doing more or sooner than necessary)
- Delays
- The creation and correction of defects
- Overprocessing (doing more than the customer values)
- Motion
- Transportation
- Unused human potential

Waste saps the energy and enthusiasm of workers and diminishes the enterprise's capacity to create value for its customers.

---

[*] See Appendix C of *Lean IT* for many examples of IT waste to get you started on your own search; you can freely download a PDF at http://www.leanitstrategies.com/books.

But in addition to *Muda*, which receives the most attention, there are two more *systemic* impediments to value that must be addressed by management and senior leadership: *Mura* (unnecessary variation) and *Muri* (overburden). Together these three constitute the *three Ms*.

Mura is unevenness or variability—inconsistency in the content and flow of work that is caused by changes in volume (uneven demand), mix (work content), and quality. When excessive variation is present, there is insufficient standardization among products and processes, and each new customer request may create a one-off effort that requires special handling, which disturbs flow. Variability is often found in enterprises that routinely engage in the *diving catch*, a heroic but ultimately unsustainable effort that becomes an accepted part of the daily work and culture.

Customers naturally desire variety and flexibility, but these should be achieved while avoiding unnecessary complexity and chaotic behavior. It is the responsibility of management and senior leadership to minimize product and process variation whenever they can, encouraging standardized, modularized product design with component reuse and reconfiguration.

Management and senior leadership should also seek to reduce demand variation whenever possible, working with customers (internal and external) to smooth out demand patterns and eliminate counterproductive policies (e.g., month/quarter/end-of-year sales incentives that cause self-inflicted peaks and troughs in demand).

Muri is overburden—placing unrealistic workloads on people and equipment, which leads to stress, mistakes, rework, poor morale, and eventually burnout. Overburden also saps creativity and limits the ability to view a larger picture. It is the responsibility of management and senior leadership to remove systemic overburden through a focus on managing demand quality, quantity, and rate while encouraging standardized work, cross-training, and load balancing to create stable capacity conditions that support flow. Managers should pay careful attention to team status, priority, and load through *gemba* walks and daily review of visual management displays and by participating in regular team huddles.

Effective and self-sustaining continuous improvement requires employee engagement: it is everyone's responsibility to "learn to see" and remove waste within every value stream, using problems as catalysts for daily improvement. But in order to do that successfully and sustainably, there must be basic stability in the mix and rate of work, with a little *slack* (we'll explore this further in Chapter 4) factored into the daily cadence so everyone can stop to fix problems the moment they arise. When people are working at an unreasonable pace (overburden), they leave a trail of waste (poor-quality work, errors) behind them that creates systemic friction, which leads to even more waste.

Everyone, at every level of the organization, are responsible for two things: doing their daily work and improving how that work is done. At a time when most enterprises are asking more of everyone, the idea of "slowing down in order to speed up" seems counterintuitive. But consider the many seen and unseen costs associated with the three Ms—time, quality, cost, and customer satisfaction. Also consider the cost of employee dissatisfaction and turnover: onboarding costs and the loss of valuable knowledge, experience, and customer relationships.

In my experience, few people resign from their jobs; most resign from their management systems and leadership culture. Ultimately, it is the responsibility of management and senior leadership to create an environment that respects the individual and encourages individual contributions. This requires leadership to pay attention to the systemic conditions of unnecessary variation and overburden so everyone has time, energy, and focus to continuously improve each and every day, steadily moving the enterprise towards its true north purpose.

Notes

1. Jim Womack and Dan Jones, *Lean Thinking*, 2nd ed. (New York: Simon & Schuster, 2003), 6.
2. Dan Jones, "Value Stream Management," December 2, 2009, http://www.lean.org/common/display/?o=1284.
3. Jim Womack and Dan Jones, *Lean Thinking*, 16.
4. Dan Jones, interview, December 12, 2011.
5. Dan Jones, interview, July 19, 2011.
6. Paul Harmon, interview, December 14, 2011.
7. Dan Jones, "Lean Consumption Meets Lean Provision," Frontiers of Lean Summit, October 31, 2005, http://www.leanuk.org/downloads/LFL_2005/Day1_Plenary1_Jones.pdf.
8. Wikipedia definition of "fractal," http://en.wikipedia.org/wiki/fractal.
9. Jim Womack and Dan Jones, *Lean Thinking*, 322.
10. David Almond, interview, June 3, 2011.

Chapter 3

Integrating IT Capabilities into Value Streams

Steve Bell

Toto, I've a feeling we're not in Kansas anymore.

Dorothy
The Wizard of Oz

WHAT YOU'LL LEARN IN THIS CHAPTER
- How to identify your customer
- How to integrate IT capabilities with enterprise-wide value streams
- How and where IT capabilities integrate with business processes, products, and services
- How to nurture a team culture that emphasizes customer value

Now that we've examined the fundamentals of Lean value streams, let's explore how to integrate technologists and IT capabilities into them. Integration will naturally transcend the traditional separation of IT and the business. We are *all* the business, no matter what our individual specialty or function—marketing, logistics, finance, or IT—and we all serve a shared purpose of serving the end customer and sustaining the enterprise.

Who Is Our Customer?

A global services firm asked me to help them improve the performance of IT project delivery. We began by gathering key IT executives to explore and define *who the customer actually is*. They talked at length about business stakeholders, business customers designing the services, regulators, system designers, end customers, and the governance board—the body responsible for reviewing the business cases for the various IT projects—and selecting among them for the best fit with enterprise strategy. As they talked, I realized that they didn't have a true appreciation for what it was to be a customer—an end customer—of their enterprise. Theirs was an internal view. Ultimately, the group concluded that because the governance board decided which IT projects moved ahead, and which did not, the governance board was the customer.

It's remarkable how some teams can endlessly circle around this seemingly simple question. So let's establish one thing very clearly: the only customer that ultimately matters is the one that justifies our existence—the end customer that *consumes* our enterprise's products and services. The *purpose* of the enterprise is to serve these end customers, and it is their definition of value that must ultimately drive all actions and decisions. But the road to this simple conclusion is filled with twists and turns.

As we explored in Chapter 2, within the enterprise there are many interdependent value streams, and every downstream recipient of work-flow is considered a customer. Some business-IT value streams will touch the end customer directly when the customer places an order online, visits the website to gather information on a product or service, or purchases software or a software-enabled device. In these cases, from the perspective of a technologist, the answer to the question "Who is our customer?" is clear.

But there are many *supporting* value streams, such as when technologists act as internal service providers, enabling the business to serve the end customer. Is there a danger in calling such business intermediaries the "customer"? Could this thinking be the source of many long-standing business/IT alignment and integration problems? Hunter and Westerman in *The Real Business of IT* think so, suggesting that "calling the business a 'customer' simply conveys the idea that IT is not part of the business. If the IT team is talking about and helping to deliver on those outcomes, then 'alignment with the business' is a non-issue."[1] When thinking Lean we must consider the whole value stream so that we don't suboptimize, and if we perceive the business as the primary customer, we might do just that.

The pitfall occurs when those serving internal customers, as is often the case with technologists, lose sight of the fact that while they may be *directly* serving an internal customer, ultimately their work has value *only* if it enables their internal customers downstream to better serve the end customer. So while I may use the term "internal customer," the term represents one point within the overall value stream *leading* to the end customer.

Let's consider an example in which a team provides an IT service to an internal customer. From the end customers' point of view, that service is nonvalue adding (NVA); moreover, that service is not required for some external factor such as compliance, making it necessary but non-value adding (NNVA). Using those criteria, the activity should be eliminated as soon as possible.

But it may not be that simple. Consider this question: Does this IT service enable the internal customer to improve the value of the product or service he or she delivers to the end customer? For example, consider when an IT service facilitates fast and trouble-free internal communication and collaboration, allowing the business stakeholders to invest more time serving the customer and learning what they want. Would the customer pay for the company to improve its internal communication systems? No. But the customer *will* pay for improvements to the products and services they purchase, which may be enabled by the increased attention to their needs.

In many situations throughout the enterprise, but especially with IT services, this cause-and-effect relationship with end-customer value is often unclear; what seems necessary and value adding at first may not be upon closer examination. A classic example of this is found in *Reengineering the Corporation*, where the authors relate the story of a visit by Ford Motor Company executives to Mazda. In the accounts payable department, Ford executives were stunned to witness a staff of 5, where in the same role Ford employed a staff of 500.[2] Mazda devised a way to procure and pay suppliers for parts that eliminated many routine, time-consuming, error-prone administrative tasks. When assembly pulled a new part from the supplier, it automatically triggered a replenishment signal (called a *kanban*) to deliver another. And when a car rolled off the line, it triggered another *kanban* signal to pay the suppliers of all the components that were consumed in that unit—no intermediate inventory tracking, purchasing, or accounts payable invoicing processes (or information systems) were needed. That is why the Lean journey is iterative and continuous; each time a layer of waste is removed it exposes underlying assumptions that should be examined in a new way.

This is just one example of traditional business activities (purchasing, inventory control, and accounts payable) that add no value to the customer. Lean practitioners have learned that once a team penetrates the layers of assumptions and habits, going beyond "the way we've always done things," they can bring about a radical transformation, creating meaningful value and differentiation in the eyes of their customers.

THE MERGER

By an anonymous Lean IT coach

Our organization, a leading company in its market, was acquired in a merger several years ago when another very successful company in the same line of business purchased us. Given that both companies were in the same business, it was natural for the executives to seek out consistency across the two businesses, trying to reduce duplication. The two different application development groups were combined into a single development team. The IT operations teams were also consolidated into a single group. Once the groups were merged, the next focus was on standardizing some of the disparate processes.

Among the first targets for standardization were the release processes that the groups used. Prior to the merger, our company had daily releases, whereas the acquiring company had a fixed bimonthly release schedule. The Agile teams were asked to slow down releases to accommodate what was perceived as a more waterfall style, bimonthly release cadence. This caused quite a bit of consternation in both groups. On the one hand, we had teams that were indignant that they couldn't release as frequently as they wanted to. They had become accustomed to delivering to production fast and frequently. On the other hand, the operations groups were greatly concerned by the impact that such a rapid release schedule would have on their already tight postmerger resources.

A working group was formed with representatives from application development and IT operations to help see if together they could reconcile the problem. The first thing we did was to create value stream maps of the sales, product management, development, and operations functions for both businesses. It quickly became very apparent that the value streams for both businesses had been optimized for their distinct customer base. Our customers had come to expect rapid changes from us, while their customers were insistent upon a much slower pace of change. These differences were pervasive, even to the point of being written into contractual obligations with some customers. It became quite apparent that it would be very challenging to make changes to those value streams without hurting one customer base or the other.

We also discovered some rather alarming gaps in the value stream, especially around the sales and product management processes. It became apparent from the value stream mapping exercise that we had no idea how long it took requests to get from sales and marketing to development. By comparison, the release processes for each group were extremely well defined and customized to the needs of each customer base. With the value stream maps in hand we were able to persuade executives that the most compelling areas for potential process change were not in the operations area (which was already fairly rigidly constrained) but rather in the sales and product management domain. The focus was on better capturing customer ideas and organizing requests (formerly a black hole) with less emphasis on fixing the release cadence, which customers were already happy with.

What Are Integrated Business-IT Value Streams?

Rule number 1: It's not about IT. It's all about business outcomes and business performance.

Weill and Ross
IT Savvy: What Top Executives Must Know to Go from Pain to Gain

Actually, it's all about satisfied end customers.

Mary Poppendieck

It's both a floor wax *and* a dessert topping.

Chevy Chase
Saturday Night Live

Is it a business value stream? Is it an IT value steam? Is it an integrated business *and* IT value stream?

Bottom line: It's simply a value stream. It may be focused on product development, delivery, or service. Its team members—cross-functional and often co-located—may be mostly business stakeholders with a few technologists. In other cases, they may be mostly technologists with a lone member or two from "the business." Or they may be comprised of *only* technologists, as is often the case with enterprise-wide shared IT services or Web 2.0 companies. Depending on the nature of the capabilities being utilized within each value stream, the team composition and skillsets will naturally vary.

What the technologists within each team must do, however, is identify not with their function or skill set but with their team's *purpose*. This means shifting their thinking from "We are IT" or "We write great software" to "We create a better customer experience and value."

With this shift in thinking from function to purpose, the next question is how and where IT *capabilities* fit into the many fractal enterprise value streams. The purpose of IT products and services can be divided into three basic categories:

1. Enabling business processes to serve the end customer
2. Developing IT-enabled products and services that the end customer uses/consumes to realize value
3. Helping to identify what the customer really wants

All of these functions are involved in providing value to the end customer (see Figure 3.1).

Enterprise IT Services to Enable Improved Business Processes

After working with countless people in many enterprises, I've concluded that everyone using enterprise IT products and services (serving internal customers to enable and support business processes) really just wants four simple things: applications that work seamlessly and invisibly, help when they don't, sound professional advice when it's needed, and new technical "solutions" *only* when process simplification and improvement aren't enough.

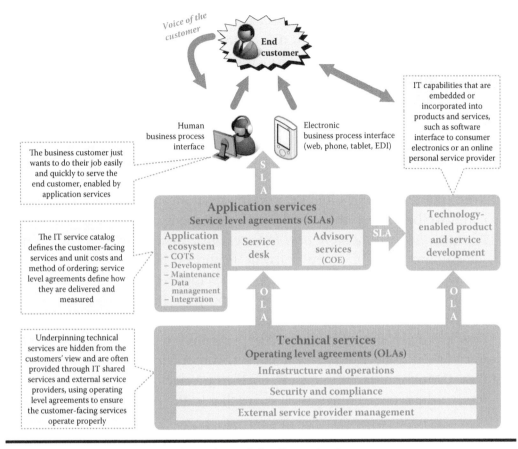

The business customer just wants to do their job easily and quickly to serve the end customer, enabled by application services

The IT service catalog defines the customer-facing services and unit costs and method of ordering; service level agreements define how they are delivered and measured

Underpinning technical services are hidden from the customers' view and are often provided through IT shared services and external service providers, using operating level agreements to ensure the customer-facing services operate properly

Voice of the customer

End customer

IT capabilities that are embedded or incorporated into products and services, such as software interface to consumer electronics or an online personal service provider

Human business process interface

Electronic business process interface (web, phone, tablet, EDI)

Application services
Service level agreements (SLAs)

Application ecosystem
– COTS
– Development
– Maintenance
– Data management
– Integration

Service desk

Advisory services (COE)

SLA

Technology-enabled product and service development

Technical services
Operating level agreements (OLAs)

Infrastructure and operations

Security and compliance

External service provider management

Figure 3.1   Enterprise IT services view of the flow of value.

1. *Systems that work and are easy to use*: When people settle into their work area, they turn on their computer, and then they start to work. This is the moment of truth, when people simply want quality information and reliable automation from their *application ecosystem* so that they can serve the customer better. It usually doesn't matter to the system user what lies *behind the curtain*—the supporting technical framework of data, integration, infrastructure, and other architectural components within which the application ecosystem functions.

2. *Fast, competent, and friendly customer service when something goes wrong*: When their busy day is interrupted by a system failure people want help, either self-service or a friendly voice to quickly restore their system to a functioning state with an immediate workaround if necessary, and with reasonable confidence that the problem will soon be fixed and won't happen again.

3. *Professional advice when it's needed:* When making a process or system change, the decision maker wants clear advice on matters including data access, application design and functionality, IT strategy, portfolio and project management, and help with technical standards such as architecture, integration, analytics, security, and compliance. IT can also add great value through insights into new business model designs and innovative product/service value propositions that leverage emerging technologies. Business people must ultimately take responsibility for understanding the technical and architectural implications of their decisions, but this requires a close working relationship with specialists who can help them grasp the subtle details and changing technical landscape.

4. *New product development and maintenance:* When a technology intervention (such as a new software feature) is needed to improve a business process, the person wants the change to be fast and of good quality, both in terms of fitness for the purpose intended and free of defects. But there must be safeguards to resist building something new if process simplification and improvement will do the job without introducing unnecessary new technical components, complexity, or cost. (Don't confuse this with IT-enabled products and services delivered to the *end* customer; we'll cover that in the next section.)

To ensure fast and cost-effective service, the first two (and perhaps the third) of these value-adding IT capabilities may be encompassed in the form of service offerings from which the internal customer may choose. These service offerings may be presented in some form of service catalog in which standard service offerings are clearly described and unit-priced and with guidance on how the internal customer may purchase and configure them to meet its special needs without excess customization or complexity. The internal customer receives a service level agreement (explicit or implicit) against which service delivery performance can be measured.

"If an organization doesn't have service offerings, then it is subject to whatever demands their customers care to invent," state the authors of *Defining IT Success through the Service Catalog.* "These uncontrolled demands will generate enormous variability and unpredictability in the skills and resources needed to deliver the service. Without service offerings it is impossible to drive standardization, which makes it impossible to drive costs down and reliability up."[3]

With IT services, internal customers should clearly know what they're asking for: what the services cost, how to request them, and how to know when they're working properly. Armed with this knowledge, customers can make well-informed consumption decisions and determine for themselves if they're receiving value commensurate with the cost.

The fourth value-adding capability of enterprise IT services involves developing, enhancing, and integrating the *application ecosystem,* such as extensions to an enterprise resource planning (ERP) system, to support and improve business processes. These changes are ideally to be continuously and seamlessly delivered into sustaining operations so that the internal customer may better serve the end customer.

For value streams tasked with developing and supporting the application ecosystem to enable business processes, the team will likely be composed primarily of technologists (developers, operations, architects, etc.), with customer representatives* actively serving on the team. It is important for all team members to participate in process improvement (*kaizen*) events, *gemba* visits to end customers, and other activities where the team gains firsthand experience with the business processes they support.

IT-Enabled Products and Services

In addition to product and service development that enables business processes, there is a separate domain of IT that develops technology capabilities that are incorporated into products and services delivered to end customers. These include software, platform, and infrastructure as a service delivered to customers online; software products delivered to customers in the traditional licensed form; and software embedded in products such as aircraft, automobiles, medical devices, consumer electronics, and other consumer goods.

The developers of these technical capabilities often don't report to the IT organization or identify with it. Rather they feel they are members of the multidisciplinary product development organization, which is comprised of a variety of specialties, including market research, product design, and engineering. But they certainly rely on internal IT services (application ecosystem, desktop, connectivity, and communication) to do their work and to deliver their technology-enabled products and services to their end customers.

---

* These may be internal customer representatives responsible for the design of business systems used internally to support end customers. These teams may also include end customers (or proxy representatives for them, such as customer surveys and focus groups) when designing self-service applications used directly by the end customer.

IT-Enabled Voice of Customer

Traditional methods of discovering what customers value include *gemba* walks, surveys, informal conversations, focus groups, and other "ask the customer" approaches, as well as formal methodologies such as Kano analysis and quality function deployment. But IT capabilities can help us to take this one step—one *giant* step—further. For example, emerging data analytics capabilities enable us to capture transactions, interactions, communications, and even the behavior (giving us insights into the unconscious intent) of our customers through various channels such as social media listening, online device monitoring, and big data analysis.

Such sources of transactional and behavioral data can help us better understand what our customers want, even when they may not know it themselves. Value stream teams tasked with developing and running IT-enabled customer behavior and sentiment monitoring and analysis applications will be primarily composed of technologists but will also include members of sales and customer service, market research, product development, and individuals with social science backgrounds such as sociology, anthropology, and ethnography. We'll explore this subject further in Chapter 15.

ING MOBILE CONSUMER BANKING THE LEAN-AGILE WAY

David Bogaerts and Jael Schuyer
Lean and Agile coaches

Amir Arooni
CIO Domestic Bank Channels
ING Netherlands

In 2010, ING chose to use Agile/Scrum techniques for developing a new mobile banking application. With plenty of ideas and the need to deliver the application as soon as possible, a new way of developing was necessary. Agile made it possible to launch a new application that matched perfectly with the customers' needs without a long time to market.

To develop a new and highly visible platform in a completely new way was a challenge, but there was full support from the senior responsible manager, and the idea originally came from first-line managers and employees. Developers worked closely with their business colleagues in the consumer banking value stream, developing and testing in two-week iterations. Daily stand-up meetings helped keep the team on track, and retrospective meetings after every iteration quickly improved process effectiveness, creating a very rapid learning curve.

Because we tackled the most difficult element first—security—we were able to provide a realistic go-live date as soon as this critical threshold was completed. This was the most difficult part of the transformation—our architects, risk-management, and application maintenance stakeholders pushed themselves with heroic efforts to help the Scrum teams continue sprinting at their rapid cadence. Now we are working on an enterprise-wide change of these formal structures and governance processes toward the creation of supporting expert groups who set frameworks for Scrum teams and answer ad hoc questions quickly.

With the first release of the new application, customer feedback was immediate and enthusiastic. An extensive analysis of application store customer feedback is now done on a daily basis and is used as input for new ideas and prioritization. The second (new feature) release brought a customer rating of 4.5 stars (out of 5), with customer comments such as "good to see that ING is doing something with our feedback" and "almost perfect." We were listening to our customers, and they appreciated it.

Value Stream View of IT Products and Services

Now let's look at these same IT products and services, not from an internal Enterprise IT services viewpoint as represented in Figure 3.1 but aligned with the three primary end customer-facing enterprise value streams (introduced in Figure 2.3). Figure 3.2* illustrates the distinction between the resources and services dedicated to individual value streams and those shared across several.

Although each of the three primary value streams serves the same end customer, they are different in nature and may require different types of enterprise IT products and services to support them. For example, product development may require special applications and technical capabilities such as product lifecycle management, 3D modeling, source code management, and automated testing. The production and delivery value stream engages

---

* Although this figure shows the technical, application, and business participants as separate, they collaborate within their value stream.

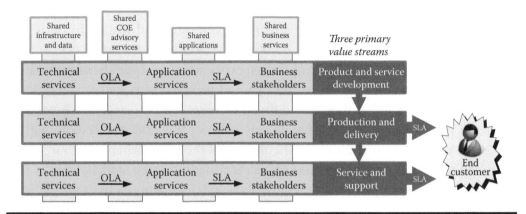

Figure 3.2 IT products and services in the three primary value streams. OLA, operating level agreement; SLA, service level agreement.

customers using transactional systems such as ERP for order management, delivery, support, and field service. The service and support value stream manages customer relationships and interactions through customer relationship management, social media, and analytical applications. At the same time, all three primary value streams are likely to share many enterprise application and infrastructure services, data, center of excellence advisory services (discussed in Chapter 4), and business services among them, hence the fractal nature of enterprise value streams.

CAPABILITY MAPPING

Capability mapping is a modeling approach that helps to associate enterprise strategy with value stream design across the enterprise. Every enterprise has many *capabilities* that, to distinguish them from value streams or processes, are *expressed as nouns and not verbs*.[4] In other words, capabilities are what the business does—not how it does them. At first this seems abstract, but it's an important distinction.

Capabilities common to most businesses include customer management, procurement management, product/service management, human resource management, financial management, asset management, and so on. By mapping enterprise-wide capabilities to individual business units, their value streams, and the detailed business processes and information systems that support them, leaders can define how the basic capabilities are distributed and enabled across the entire enterprise.

Consider procurement management as a general capability, for example. This includes underlying capabilities such as vendor management and product acquisition management. Let's say that leadership determines that procurement management is a significant strategic enterprise-wide weakness and/or opportunity it wishes to address. Where do they start? What value streams or processes do they begin with? This can be a daunting question. Without a coherent vision, their efforts are likely to be scattershot, lacking in a holistic approach that may yield only localized improvements—falling short of enterprise-wide transformation.

A capability map helps connect the dots across an enterprise, identifying all of the value streams, supporting processes, and information systems that contribute to this particular capability in some way. The figure below shows a simplified view where capabilities are distributed across various centralized and decentralized operating models of a single global enterprise.

Once this capability mapping schema is defined, it's possible to select and prioritize among them, communicating strategic targets down to each value stream manager and team that has an important role in performing that particular capability; this may be useful for strategy deployment, a Lean management technique we'll explore in Chapter 7. Viewed from the bottom up, the capability map may also help individual value stream managers and teams see how their activities relate to others so that they can coordinate improvement efforts toward targeted capabilities.

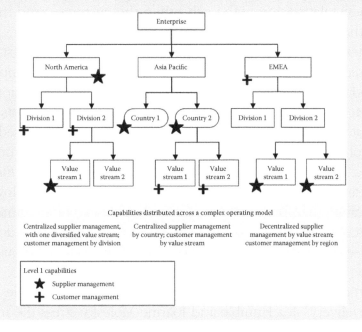

Capabilities distributed across a complex operating model

| Centralized supplier management, with one diversified value stream; customer management by division | Centralized supplier management by country; customer management by value stream | Decentralized supplier management by value stream; customer management by region |

Level 1 capabilities
★ Supplier management
+ Customer management

Maintaining Continuity with Product-Focused Teams

One of the most common terms in IT is *project*. A project has a beginning and an end, and the team's relationship with the customer is transient; teams are assembled, and upon completion of the project they are disbanded. Experts are often shared across several projects at once, causing unpredictable interruptions and bottlenecks, and often they are shifted to the next project even before the current one is fully completed—which can cause problems during release and customer adoption if someone must be called back in to address a problem.

In moving to value stream thinking, it's important that teams (and their managers) begin to see their work not as projects but as *products*. In this product-centric view, *projects are enhancements to products.*[5] This is the case whether the product is to be delivered to the end customer or whether the product is used to support the internal business processes, such as an order management or product development system.

In contrast to projects, which have a beginning and an end, a product has continuity over time: a lifecycle. As one product lifecycle begins its decline, another enhanced product or product family is in line to replace it in a deliberate evolution, creating continuity with products and in understanding customer desires and market behaviors. Another important distinction is that project teams are often temporary, whereas product teams may remain intact through many product lifecycles; the teams, their knowledge, and their relationship with each other, the customer, and the marketplace strengthens and develops.

In an orchestra, individual players aren't motivated to play loudest or fastest; their shared purpose is the creation of a perfectly balanced symphony. Similarly, product teams right-size and align resources (people, equipment, contractors, etc.) to continuously deliver small-product enhancements and services at a steady, sustainable rhythm. The cost is predictable based on the composition of the team, and the value it delivers is based on the run rate (i.e., pace, cadence, drumbeat, takt time), which determines how much *throughput* the value stream can produce over time. As a result, value stream flow based on products rather than projects creates a predictable rate of investment and improved outcome quality—easier to plan, budget, and measure—delivered in rapid release cycles that can respond quickly to changes in the business environment.

In their article "Why Enterprises Must Adopt DevOps to Enable Continuous Delivery," Jez Humble and Joanne Molesky stress the importance of a product orientation across the entire value stream and the necessity for shifting roles and responsibilities among team members:

> Treat each strategic service like a product, managed end to end by a small team that has firsthand access to all of the information required to run and change the service. Use the discipline of product management, rather than project management, to evolve your services. Product teams are completely cross-functional, including all personnel required to build and run the service. Each team should be able to calculate the cost of building and running the service and the value it delivers to the organization (preferably directly in terms of revenue).
>
> In a product development approach, the central application management function goes away, subsumed into product teams. Non-routine, application-specific requests to the service desk also go to the product teams. The technical management function remains but becomes focused on providing IaaS [Infrastructure as a Service] to product teams. The teams responsible for this work should also work as product teams.[6]

This second paragraph highlights the interdependent relationships among product teams and the shared services that support them, which are themselves distinct product teams. This illustrates the fractal nature of primary and supporting value streams.

You may have noticed that use of the words *product* and *service* tend to blur together from the customers' perspective. As products are developed and released, they are incorporated into the existing service delivery and management framework so that there is the potential for rapid and continuous transition from product (development) to service delivery (operations). Thus, an integrated value stream team must include representatives from development *and* operations (which may include external service providers from both disciplines) working closely and continuously to create end-to-end flow. This is the basis of the DevOps movement, integrating the culture and practice of Lean-Agile development and IT service management toward the goal of continuous flow from design to delivery. We'll explore this further in Chapter 5.

Products require lifecycle continuity not just with teams but also with leadership and strategy. For this reason, the role of the value stream manager is to help ensure that all aspects of the product have clear alignment and accountability. The value stream manager often has profit and loss and budget responsibility and is ultimately accountable for business and customer outcomes. He or she confers this responsibility to the team, ensuring that the flow of value to the customer is made explicit and visual.

The value stream manager may also maintain a strategic roadmap for the product, describing a multiyear vision for the future. This roadmap may be used to correlate long-term goals with short-term release plans and to guide budget and investment decisions. The roadmap also acts as a compass heading to guide continuous improvement and innovation efforts. There is often an executive sponsor to oversee the value stream performance and to advocate for it in strategic discussions. (We'll discuss the role of the value stream manager and the Lean management system framework in Chapter 7.)

LESSONS WE HAVE LEARNED FROM VALUE STREAM REORGANIZATION

Brian Wellinghoff

Director of the Lean Journey
Barry-Webmiller Companies

We are a diverse, decentralized manufacturing company committed to a people-centric Lean culture with nine operating divisions and thirty facilities in North America. We are currently in the process of converting our enterprise from traditional silos to value streams. Approximately 50% of the organization has made the change.

A particular source of creativity and uneasiness has consistently come from our engineering departments. Traditionally, our engineering teams were divided from the organization in second-floor offices. Through the transition to value streams, the engineering department has been reconstituted as teams co-located within their value streams, closer to the production area.

While the hesitancy to move and lose the status of a personal office was meaningful to all engineering associates, after several months, the vast majority of engineers recognized the value of enhanced communication with sales, planning, and assembly. After the first year or two we saw a sharp increase in the number and marketability of product innovations, and we are now launching more new products than at any other period in our history.

However, the effect of value stream transition on engineering leaders has been more acute. Many spent their entire careers progressing in a technical specialty (mechanical, electrical, hydraulics, etc.), a parallel I could envision for many IT professionals as well. In our organization, those engineering leaders with broad communication and coaching skills became our value stream leaders and love the larger scope of impact they have on the organization. Those who prefer a technical focus often lead new product development—and although the number of team members is smaller, it allows them to do more of what they truly love. There are still a few, however, who feel Lean is an endless series of people who ask, "Why do you do it this way?"

I can see obvious parallels to our experience when applying value stream thinking to IT. It could mean breaking up the IT teams from their current technical fiefdoms and co-locating IT professionals within value streams, closer to where the value is delivered. I could see some IT leaders being similarly resistant to this new approach. Encourage them to embrace the change—it'll be worth it.

Investing in an IT Value Stream Transformation

There is an initial price to pay for value stream orientation, as Lean manufacturers learned decades ago when they started rearranging their factories from functional silos to value streams. According to Gartner, "When resources are removed from functional silos that optimize skill utilization and head count, and placed in multidisciplinary teams that optimize process outcomes, then head count may actually go up. The reason is that as resources are spread across many permanent teams, it becomes impossible to use a fraction of a resource."[7]

As we learned in Chapter 2, the long-term benefits of value stream flow often outweigh the incremental cost increases of value stream resource reorganization; this is the counterintuitive Lean principle of economies of *flow* over economies of *scale*. Even when total costs initially increase, if the velocity, quality, and capacity improve, then the business and its customers will realize more value. The cost accountants' reductionist view is overruled by just-in-time value delivery to the customer.

Perhaps just as important as the productivity benefits of flow is the reduction in complexity and the overhead required to manage it. When an organization has too much work in progress and too many projects in flight at one time—with several projects assigned to each team and with teams regularly sharing scarce and specialized resources—considerable effort is required just to plan, schedule, and manage people and the work they are doing. Significant productivity is lost as specialists jump from one incomplete project to another, and moving bottlenecks create complexity and chaos on a daily basis. Lean manufacturers learned that implementing sophisticated planning, scheduling, and control systems (material requirements planning and advanced planning and scheduling systems) only made matters worse. One small deviation in reality caused extensive recalculations of all the interdependencies—making schedules "jittery" or "nervous," causing the people working on the shop floor to become equally jittery and nervous.

In the end, Lean manufacturing practitioners learned that when value streams are aligned and made to flow at a steady pace, the need for sophisticated planning, scheduling, and management systems, the overhead to care and feed them, and the cycles of instability they create are greatly reduced. Lean factory floors evolve to simple visual management, with pull signals regulating a smooth flow of work. When integrated business-IT value streams are adopted, these same benefits may be realized; for a small-scale example, observe a Lean-Agile software development system in action. (We'll examine Lean-Agile flow further in Chapter 5.)

Let's be clear that value stream alignment, other than in the exceptional cases of highly standardized, repetitive production, is never quite perfect—whether in a factory or an IT setting. There are many issues in a dynamic environment that are constantly destabilizing flow: new products, new technologies, sudden demand changes and interruptions that cannot be buffered, staff illness and turnover, equipment failure and unplanned system outages, and so on. And larger projects, those that require several teams to orchestrate their work, necessarily require more planning, scheduling, communication, and control—in some cases this may require automation. But there are many examples of development and operations teams who coordinate megaprojects and programs using mostly iterative communications and visual management techniques (such as *kanban* and Scrum).[*]

---

[*] See *Scaling Lean and Agile Development* by Craig Larman and Bas Vodde (Boston: Pearson Education, 2009).

In general, when an organization strives to align its resources along value streams, and when teams can visualize flow with clear line of sight to customer delivery, then the team can sense and respond to disturbances instantly, and the overall environment naturally stabilizes. It becomes easier to plan, manage, and control with minimal effort. The nonvalue effort that was once put into scheduling and managing complex and often chaotic flow can instead be redirected toward continuous improvement; every time a new factor suddenly disrupts flow, the team immediately senses and swarms, identifying and addressing the root causes of instability. This is why a naturally adaptive value stream team can be so effective.

The Magic of Team Dynamics

Value stream reorganization often causes radical changes not only in the type of work that individuals perform, but also in the physical arrangement of people and equipment, and the virtual rearrangement of the information flows that support the flow of work. In many subtle and not-so-subtle ways, this changes how individuals relate to each other and to their workspace. Many times I've heard someone exclaim, "Why do I have to give up my private cubicle to sit in an open space with the rest of the team?" Although I feel some sympathy for the individual, Lean development and delivery is a continuous and collaborative learning process, and the benefits of team co-location in a highly visual and interactive community space are too great to ignore.

When physical co-location isn't practical, teams should come together frequently in a highly visual setting (or a virtual collaborative workspace for distributed teams) for huddles, planning sessions, and retrospectives. As an intact, integrated value stream team, business and technical colleagues work together, sharing skills, developing relationships with their customers, and exchanging different perspectives, all of which help the team continuously fine-tune its value stream. As the team forms, storms, norms, and eventually learns to perform as an integrated team, new patterns of work and interaction evolve.

As application development teams move to rapid release cycles with more emphasis on prototyping and testing through each cycle, the balance of work among team members will shift, encouraging more collaboration among specialists who used to work separately. Some programmers choose to work in pairs; two people with a single keyboard may seem inefficient to many, but this collaborative practice produces high-quality code, and "some seasoned programmers describe working in pairs as more than twice as fast."[8] Testing specialists become engaged earlier in the release cycle to help customers define their own testing parameters and scripts as part of the requirements definition process. And architectural specialists continue their involvement beyond the initial architecture review, as release transitioning to operations engages many aspects of infrastructure and architecture.

As technical specialists shift their focus to helping the team perform better, the most knowledgeable experts find themselves spending more time teaching and mentoring and less time performing the actual work. While in the short run this might slow down progress a bit, in the long run it develops more capability, flexibility, and flow across the enterprise. According to Johanna Rothman, an ardent supporter of team development, there are common myths that need to be dispelled, such as the following:

> Myth #1: *If we plug just the right resources into the projects at just the right times, we can make the projects work.* Money is a resource. Desks are resources. Software might be a resource. But people? They are not resources. They are living, breathing, wonderful humans. When you take a person out of one team and attempt to "plug" that person into another team, you might get lucky. But don't count on it. Flow work through teams. Keep the teams together.
>
> Myth #2: *Only an expert can do this work.* There is some work that only experts can do. The real question is: how much? Never let experts work alone. I ask experts to pair with non-experts when they work on their areas of expertise. And when you remove the experts from the team, a funny thing occurs. The team pulls together and works as a team, not as a disjointed group of individuals. You want a team to work fast? Remove the experts. The team will work together and fast to discover what they don't know. They will share what they do know.[9]

According to Tom Poppendieck, "The cycle of forming, storming, norming, and performing takes months, which makes keeping teams intact for long times very important. Even adding, removing, or changing one member of a team causes significant disruption. It is not just domain knowledge but familiarity and trust in each other that makes a huge difference."[10]

In the bestselling book *Drive: The Surprising Truth About What Motivates Us*, Daniel Pink shows us that people and teams perform best when they are allowed to organize themselves and their work (autonomy), invest in doing the work well (mastery), and strive for something larger than themselves (purpose). These same principles are behind a successful Lean transformation: teams own their processes (autonomy) and are responsible for their continuous improvement (mastery), with a focus on value for the customer (purpose).[11]

In my experience, software development teams (and IT organizations in general) often feel they have a chronic *capacity* problem—not enough people or time to keep up with the business needs. Teams are burdened with huge backlogs, and when they deliver something to their customer they're often told it doesn't meet their needs. Once teams gain experience with just-in-time delivery of small features in short cycles, in close contact with their customers at all times, they learn that their problem isn't capacity but *quality*—their valuable time has been wasted writing software their customers don't need and won't use. This is when Lean thinking really sets in, and the team develops a sense of autonomy and mastery, focusing clearly on what the customer really values—the purpose.

We are talking about more than just teams here; we are talking about relationships, which is why the first line of the "Agile Manifesto" emphasizes "individuals and interactions over processes and tools."[12] For example, technologists may feel challenged by the lack of technical expertise of their nontechnical (business) team members as they ask questions and offer suggestions without full comprehension of the technical issues. Although this too may initially slow the team down, these seemingly naïve questions can stimulate outside-the-box thinking, leading to innovative approaches that may otherwise not have been considered. This mutual trust and curiosity also helps the team to grow and learn together; business partners develop technical competence while IT partners deepen their understanding of business processes. The key watchwords are *respect*, *patience*, and *interaction*.

When a team is kept intact for a long time, many beneficial things can happen. The team can establish a relationship with its customers, intuitively and collectively understanding what they really want. The team can develop a relationship with its product and a sense for its evolution over time. The team members develop a working relationship with each other, and they become familiar with the environment they operate within, learning to see and eliminate obstacles from their path. When people become a *team* in the true sense of the word, they develop a shared purpose. This is the bottom-line principle of a value stream: teams that learn how to learn, solving problems and adapting to sudden change, are a source of competitive advantage that cannot be imitated by a competitor.

Notes

1. Richard Hunter and George Westerman, *The Real Business of IT* (Boston: Harvard Business Press, 2009), 36.
2. Michael Hammer and James Champy, *Reengineering the Corporation*, rev. ed. (New York: HarperBusiness, 2001), 42–47.
3. Rodrigo Flores, Bill Fine, and Troy DuMoulin, *Defining IT Success through the Service Catalog (Pink Elephant Guides)* (Zaltbommel, the Netherlands: Van Haren Publishing, 2007), 40.
4. William Ulrich and Michael Rosen, *The Business Capability Map: The "Rosetta Stone" of Business/IT Alignment* (Arlington, MA: Cutter Consortium, 2011).
5. Alan Shalloway, James R. Trott, and Guy Beaver, *Lean-Agile Software Development* (Indianapolis: Addison Wesley Professional, 2010), xxxix.
6. Jez Humble and Joanne Molesky, "Why Enterprises Must Adopt Develops to Enable Continuous Delivery," *Cutter IT Journal*, August 2011.
7. Colleen M. Young, *Six Steps to Process-Based IT Organizational Design* (Stamford, CT: Gartner, 2006).
8. Alistair Cockburn and Laurie Williams, "The Costs and Benefits of Pair Programming," jacques.dsc.ufcg.edu.br/cursos/map/recursos/XPSardinia.pdf, 2000.
9. Johanna Rothman, "Three Myths and Three Tips," http://www.jrothman.com, December 1, 2011.
10. Tom Poppendieck, interview, December 14, 2011.
11. Daniel H. Pink, *Drive: The Surprising Truth about What Motivates Us* (New York: Riverhead Books, 2009).
12. Mike Beedle, Arie van Bennekum, Alistair Cockburn, et al., "The Agile Manifesto," http://www.agilemanifesto.org, February 2001.

Chapter 4

Leveraging Value Stream Resources

Steve Bell

> The ruin of any work is a divided interest.
> Concentrate—concentrate. One thing at a time.

Mark Twain

WHAT YOU'LL LEARN IN THIS CHAPTER

- How to leverage scarce talent and effectively manage skillset gaps
- Why slack capacity is essential for optimal performance and innovation
- How to use low-tech visual techniques such as *kanban* to promote flow and manage constraints
- The role centers of excellence (COEs) play in ensuring overall IT performance and furthering innovation
- How to assess outsourcing from a Lean perspective
- The significance of the new social enterprise

By now you're probably wondering just how you're going to spread your technologists and technology assets across your enterprise's value streams. Once you've mapped out the primary value streams and the supporting value streams underlying them (Chapter 2) and formed a general idea of the IT knowledge and skillsets required to optimize value creation within each (Chapter 3), the next task is to create intact teams. Unless you're a technology-focused or Web 2.0 company, chances are you'll have more value streams that require IT participation than you have technologists.

This is not a unique challenge, but it is a difficult one—whether you have an IT staff of 3,000 or 3. For example, a client of mine, a young, progressive financial services firm that emphasizes personalized service to regional customers, relies heavily on technology to streamline processes, enabling them to compete with global enterprises many times their size. Their IT organization is quite small, and their participation in all value stream teams is essential, yet stretching these technologists too far is clearly counterproductive and unsustainable.

Senior leadership understood the need to increase the working knowledge of everyone throughout the enterprise on the technology-related capabilities and potential obstacles of every value stream. Mentoring spread quickly, and soon nontechnologists were able to apply their unique knowledge and skills with a new appreciation of the systems upon which they relied. The firm made careful choices about outsourcing, keeping valuable customer touch points in-house and using commercial off-the-shelf (COTS) software wherever possible. In the end, it was encouraging how all parties stepped up and took ownership for the technology they needed, keeping it simple and customer-focused. All enterprises will need to think and act like this, no matter how large and sophisticated, if they are to exploit technology advancements without becoming overwhelmed by them.

Aligning and Visually Managing Flow

Many IT managers have difficulty quantifying their capacity and are therefore unable to make reliable commitments. This is a very uncomfortable situation to be in. It's usually not a failure of management skill but a fundamental problem with organizing work as projects rather than as products (as we explored in Chapter 3).

When preparing for value stream reorientation, several products or services that once passed through the traditional project "job shop" may now be divided into separate value streams because of different workflow paths or velocities. For an example that most of us have direct experience with, consider the flow of an automobile service shop when Lean thinking is adopted:

> Pre-diagnosis involves a careful telephone or e-mail discussion with the customer about the nature of the problem using a checklist administered by a staff member with sound technical knowledge.

A second customer contact just prior to the service confirms there are no new problems (and also increases the likelihood the vehicle will be brought in on time). And an inspection of the vehicle the moment it arrives at the dealer confirms the diagnosis and provides the customer with the precise cost of the repairs.

A few types of jobs account for a large fraction of total car repairs. For example, mileage- or time-based tune-ups on vehicles that are otherwise running fine. By creating different value streams—one for high-volume jobs which can be done quickly, another for more complex jobs that can be accurately pre-diagnosed, and a third for jobs where the problem is not known prior to detailed investigation in the service bay—it is possible to smooth and speed the flow of work for most jobs with tremendous benefits for customer response time and process productivity.[1]

With a traditional approach, the car waited for an empty service bay, and that's all there was to it. But in the Lean approach, some value streams are optimized for speed and efficiency while others are more adaptive, handling uncertainty and variation better. The same thinking about flow can be applied to many IT activities and the value streams they support.

Gartner's *Six Steps to Process-Based IT Organizational Design* explains:

Virtually every IT organization must face a process transformation [which will] inevitably drive radical changes in organizational structure. Traditional IT service delivery and organizational models achieved efficiency at the expense of effectiveness. [When computing power was expensive and scarce] it made sense to maximize the utilization and life cycle costs of assets.... This approach to resource orchestration inevitably resulted in functional silos. The optimized process-based organization is horizontally focused on outcomes, not vertically oriented around skills.[2]

This is the same shift in focus from asset utilization to process flow that Lean manufacturing has been advocating for decades. In any situation where work is designed to flow, the people doing the work must be able to manage their flow. They must be able to visualize the line of sight from start to finish so that they can instantly and intuitively know if work is flowing and respond quickly when there is an interruption. When creating a value

	What is displayed	How the team benefits
Demand	How much work is in the queue, of what type and duration; differentiation between planned and unplanned work; patterns of demand stability, predictability, and load.	The team can use this information to influence and improve future demand patterns.
Work in process	How much work is in process, the mix of work types, size of jobs, sequence of work; velocity/flow of work; blockages; pull signal when more work is needed.	This helps the team to prevent too much new work from being started to avoid congestion and overburden; team members communicate on daily work and signal for help when someone is suddenly overburdened or has a problem.
Problems	Where interrupts, delays, and errors are occurring; visually trigger problem analysis and corrective action.	The team can monitor patterns to prevent future problems; use as input data for *kaizen* activity.
Status	When work is scheduled, when it is underway, the pace of work, when it is expected to be complete, when it is completed.	The team can visually communicate with customers and other stakeholders, preventing interruptions for status inquiries; the display helps to visualize velocity and bottlenecks so informed demand/capacity-balancing decisions can be made.

Figure 4.1 How *kanban* can enable workflow.

stream, the team should establish a visual management system, and one popular technique is *kanban*,[*] which is both a form of visual management and workflow control (Figure 4.1).

Kanban is deceptively simple and surprisingly powerful, often using nothing more than sticky notes posted on a wall, where each note represents a unit of work. *Kanban* can be a very low-tech, high-touch way for teams to self-organize and manage their workflow. One of the key objectives of *kanban* is to limit work in process. Introducing too much work is a sure way to create congestion, confusion, quality problems, and interruptions—all enemies of flow. In addition to helping the team optimize flow, *kanban* is also helpful for managers, stakeholders, and customers to visualize the status and pace of work, helping them make informed decisions while minimizing team interruptions for status inquiries. And when a problem arises, *kanban* makes it immediately apparent, a visual beacon signaling for the team to swarm and solve the problem.

---

[*] *See Kanban* by David Anderson (Sequim: Blue Hole Press, 2010). Note here we are not just talking about *kanban* as used by Lean-Agile software development; the technique can be used to visually manage any type of workflow.

SPEEDING UP

By an anonymous Lean IT coach

We are a leading online payments company, and our business is all about creating new payment "gateways." We are typically able to create a new payment gateway in roughly two to three months. However, there are some teams who can create them much faster—somewhere on the order of two weeks. Executives asked us to find out what it would take to reduce our development time down to that two-week number across all teams. We did a value stream mapping of the entire gateway development process, and what we discovered is that the actual development time for each gateway is fairly trivial. Instead, the largest amount of time was spent up front in deciding which gateways to commit to development and justifying that commitment.

There were also considerable differences in performance between teams that had fixed roles (product management, business analysts, developers, quality assurance, etc.) that seemed rather process-bound and teams that tended to ignore or deemphasize their roles. These less role-oriented teams tended to just get on the phone and call the customer directly rather than waiting for product management or other roles to do it for them.

So it was a combination of understanding where the process tended to get stuck—which the value stream mapping made visible—and a corresponding emphasis on less role-specific behavior that helped us understand what the differences were between the high-performing teams and the laggards. There seemed to be an interaction between the process and the role orientation of people working the process. We didn't really appreciate this until we looked at all of the steps to get through the system and then asked ourselves why some teams were faster than others in the same situation.

Shared Talent

Shared resources are a serious threat to value streams because they are difficult to manage and can interrupt flow. You should strive to eliminate shared resources when you can and deal with them proactively when you cannot.

As an enterprise rearranges its people (and other resources such as equipment, facilities, etc.), scarce technologists must share their skills with others across multiple value streams. This means that individual specialists must take time from their current responsibilities to train others, which can be problematic in several ways. First, it's likely that the specialist is already working at capacity (or beyond); second, the special knowledge and skill may require a significant investment to train others; and third, there's prestige in being the specialist, and the individual may be resistant to sharing that prestige.

And who do they train? It will likely be other technologists whose own skills must also be spread across several value streams. So in effect, the process becomes cross-functional training—creating a population of technologists, each with one or more core specialties but also multiskilled in a broad range of other capabilities.* What results are multiskilled people who are more flexible and adaptable and capable of performing many more tasks— albeit more slowly—than a specialized resource. The technologists must also impart some basic knowledge to the nontechnical team members as well to raise the technical awareness and self-sufficiency of the team in general. The team members will then be better able to learn from each other, to quickly swarm and solve a problem, and to balance workload when a team member suddenly becomes overloaded. An added benefit is that individuals with broader knowledge complementing their specialty knowledge will often be more innovative since they bring ideas together from a variety of perspectives and experiences.†

Another approach to address the occasional shortage of talent, especially when dealing with shifting skill requirements and volatile demand, is to create a core intact team, supplementing it with contract workers as needed. When the majority of the team is intact and familiar with each other, the interruptions caused by the introduction of a new member can be minimized. Here is an area where standardized work may be helpful, developing standard processes and tools that help to quickly onboard contractors with less downtime and disruption to the rest of the team.

---

* A helpful technique here is the *skills matrix*, a grid that displays on one axis the team members and on the other the various skills, both business and technical, required by the value stream. At each grid intersection there is an indicator of the degree of competence of each team member for that skill. When displayed in a common area, the skills matrix serves to visually communicate what individual skills require development, and it also helps business and IT stakeholders to understand and appreciate the breadth of skills required to keep the value stream flowing.

† A popular theme in innovation is to comprise teams of "T-shaped people." The vertical bar on the T represents depth in a single field, and the horizontal bar is the ability to collaborate across disciplines; the goal is to gather and apply knowledge across multiple areas of expertise. For more on this topic of multidisciplinary innovation, see *The Medici Effect* by Frans Johansson (Boston: HBS Press, 2006).

A QUESTION OF SCALE

One of my passions is to bring Lean thinking to organizations that are working to improve the lives of the three billion people who live on less than US$2 per day.* While many enterprises experience shortages of technologists, this is especially true among nonprofits and nongovernmental organizations (NGOs) who often face the same systemic complexities as for-profit entities but with proportionally fewer staff. A Dartmouth study found that large nonprofits/NGOs spend one-fifth of what for-profit entities do on IT. And smaller nonprofits spend only about one-twentieth.[3] For most, it's simply impossible to form an intact team for each value stream, and resources to hire temporary support may not exist, so resource sharing and multitasking are necessary.

For example, consider the archetypal small nonprofit with three (or less) individuals supporting basic IT functions:

- *System administrator*: Responsible for managing networks, e-mail, communications, databases, licenses, security, backups, and other administrative tasks
- *Desktop support*: Responsible for maintaining equipment and software, configurations, devices such as printers and scanners, upgrades, etc.
- *Developer*: Responsible for a variety of development tasks, this person is often also responsible for website and social network applications and (formally or informally) involved in managing the content; this person may also be responsible for supporting business applications, integration, and business intelligence

Each of these individuals may experience excessive and erratic demand from multiple sources because there may be few formal governance mechanisms in place. Some work requests are small, whereas others are large in scope and duration. Some are planned while others appear suddenly. Some requests may be poorly specified, and most are marked URGENT. Some work can be performed individually, whereas other tasks must be coordinated as projects among the three individuals/roles.

---

* For more information, visit http://www.Lean4NGO.org.

In such a situation it may be helpful to first create a very simple *kanban* wall where each individual is represented as a horizontal lane, and there are just five columns: requested, queue, in process, problem, and complete. Each unit of work is represented as a sticky note; colors and markings may be used to indicate size or type of project—whether it is planned or unplanned, performed individually or collectively, and so on. Each collective project may also have a visual project timeline and a task list posted nearby. In addition, periodic tasks and planned maintenance events can be posted on a public schedule for everyone to see and plan around.

The initial result is that by making the demand, the amount of work in process, and the flow of work visible to all, the team can have quick and effective daily standup meetings, minimize interruptions, and keep track of priorities. Over time, the team may improve its work patterns, leading to a greater proportion of planned versus unplanned work. Visualization of workload and flow to others in the organization encourages better planning and thus a (potentially) more stable and higher-quality demand pattern, creating a rudimentary form of visually enabled governance and portfolio management.

The Importance of Slack

To continuously improve a value stream it's necessary to create a small amount of *slack* capacity so that teams have the time and space to respond to normal variation and to address problems as they occur. However, it's human nature to try to keep scarce and expensive resources busy and running at 100% capacity while continuing to think that this will lead to improved productivity and efficiency. There's just one problem: it's wrong. Mathematical queuing theory proves, and it's well documented in both Lean manufacturing and Lean-Agile software development practices, that when a resource is overburdened (beyond a *planned* utilization threshold of approximately 80%) productivity plummets. Interruptions escalate, task switching (thrashing) accelerates, flow ceases, delays and errors increase, and physical and mental stress builds up, all of which causes a loss of concentration, more errors, burnout, and eventually turnover.

Counterintuitive as it may be, it's proven that building slack into a plan generally causes productivity and quality to increase. It's important to understand that slack is *not* excess capacity or lost time; when the normal variation of daily work does not consume this slack time, then it can be used for continuous improvement or innovation activities.

So here's the problem: the importance of slack is well documented and mathematically provable.* One of the more notable examples of an enterprise employing slack for improvement and innovation is Google, which is famous for maintaining a 20% slack factor.[4] Yet when I speak to most IT professionals about this subject, they roll their eyes with a *"Yes, but..."* look. I've concluded that this is a chronic problem within the traditional culture of many IT organizations and business in general. I used to insist that it was unsustainable, yet I see enterprises continue to push the overburden/utilization envelope year after year, and there seems no end in sight. Of course, they continue to miss deadlines, and their best people continue leaving, but the practice of chronic, systemic overburden (*muri*) continues unabated.

Lean thinking opens the door for enterprise stakeholders and decision makers to engage in realistic, data-supported discussions about slack and how it improves speed, quality, cost, customer satisfaction, and quality of life. Measure the costs, measure the long-term outcomes, and decide for yourself.

TALES FROM THE DUNGEON

To help meet the expanding need for technologists, a client of mine, a global enterprise with an IT staff of over 1,000 individuals, created a deliberate career path. The entry level of this path was an IT helpdesk position. The company felt this role provided important experience with the full range of skills and relationships across the enterprise. Many who began at the helpdesk and rose through the ranks considered this a rite of passage. Although the company hired great people with great potential, the turnover rate for the helpdesk was more than 60%, and customer satisfaction (those calling for help) was suffering. Something was clearly not working.

One of our first *kaizen* events at this company was to help the helpdesk. Although technically they were called the "service desk," throughout the enterprise many just called it "the dungeon." There, in a windowless basement, fresh college graduates sped from crisis to crisis,

---

* For an entertaining exploration on the subject, see *Slack: Getting Past Burnout, Busywork, and the Myth of Total Efficiency* by Tom DeMarco (New York: Broadway Books, 2001).

triaging on the run, creating sporadic and often incomplete documentation after each incident. When they did attempt proactive problem prevention, they were constantly interrupted.

The first thing we did was to create slack; management invested in temporary resources to create some breathing room. Then we formed teams and began tackling issues, one by one, as a series of *kaizen* events. First was the inadequacy of the knowledge base, which contained obsolete and incorrect information caused by a combination of overburden (not enough time to properly document during the call), the lack of documentation standards, and insufficient time for periodic maintenance of the database. Once the knowledge base quality improved (which improved first-call resolution and thus reduced failure demand from repeated callbacks), we then emphasized more customer self-service capabilities (because the database quality was improved), which further reduced the call volume. Finally, we started a mentoring program, where the more experienced staff helped with onboarding the newcomers, improving support quality and capturing vital knowledge before they moved on. This in turn caused additional improvement in the quality of the knowledge base. In less than six months, turnover started dropping, and customer satisfaction improved. But if management hadn't invested in slack time, none of these efforts would have gotten off the ground.

Technologists: To Matrix or Embed?

A line-of-business manager, an early Lean adopter within his large enterprise, promoted *kaizen* to reduce operations waste within his division. His unit quickly realized significant productivity benefits, which allowed him to release excess staff to other business units. With his budget freed up, he hired his own software development staff (although he was required to call them "technical specialists" because he wasn't allowed to hire "software developers"). This created an *embedded* cross-functional team of business and technical specialists, reporting to this line-of-business manager, who quickly began delivering small, focused applications that drove additional revenue for the unit.

At the same time, however, the CIO branded this group of renegades as the "shadow IT" team, which was meant to be derogatory. The team, however, accepted this as a badge of honor, adorning their work area and engaging in lighthearted antics consistent with their name. Over time, this investment proved a success and the manager was rewarded. But it was not without consequences, because this technical team—disconnected from the formal IT group—deviated from enterprise standards, creating technical debt for the enterprise. For this reason, it's important that technologists coordinate with their peers in IT, even when they are embedded into a value stream.

Technologists can be matrixed into a business value stream team while reporting directly to the IT function, or they can be embedded and report directly to the business. Generally, the more directly the value stream affects the end customer, the greater the inclination for technical specialists to be embedded so they report to the business and identify directly with its purpose. It's also important to consider recognition and compensation tied to these organization and reporting structures; if misaligned incentives are left in place, they will create strong, often silent, resistance.

A LETTER TO MY *SENSEI*

Linda Ray

Director of Business Systems
W. W. Grainger

Dear Tom,

In our last coaching session you congratulated me on the work that we had done so far and left me with a final thought: Can I better use visual management tools? For many months, I did not get it. Then it hit me— neither my team nor I could see the flow of our SAP development and maintenance work or the problems. The team and I decided to use A3* thinking to improve our visual management system and, Tom, the best thing is we built it. Today, we have a new visual management board that is aligned to our value stream. We no longer view it as a board that's only used to satisfy management. Even more importantly, it has helped us better engage our business partners because now they can easily see the status of their work requests. Talk about a new level of transparency.

---

* A3 is a one-page summary that guides a team through the disciplined PDCA problem-solving approach.

Today, my team and I are talking about barriers and obstacles as work moves through the value stream; every day we are becoming more comfortable making problems visible. We were able to reduce our backlog and make time for the team to focus on creating standardized work and improve their documentation. The best yet—with our newfound capacity we were able to devote one of my team members to another key project. This not only satisfied a key business need but also fulfilled a skill/career development desire of one of my team members. All improvement opportunities that I could never get to in years past!

I realized that as a leader I can easily escape a spreadsheet or status update—I just hit delete. But with visual management, I can't escape it. Although there are days when I go home and wonder if it is all worth it, I find myself continually inspired by team members who try to improve their work every day so that we can keep up with the business's needs.

Centers of Excellence

Centers of excellence (COEs), also called *communities of practice* or *competency centers*, are shared groups or affiliations of subject matter experts that represent a discipline where the enterprise values *standardization* and *innovation*. As we mentioned in Chapter 1, these two values are complementary because standardized work reduces waste and unnecessary variation (Lean operations thinking), freeing up time and mental energy to pursue experiments to unlock creativity and innovation (Lean development thinking).

IT-related COEs may include enterprise architecture, security, compliance, integration, data management and governance, business process management, business intelligence, service management, software development, and external service provider management. General enterprise COEs may include Lean, safety, compliance, and strategic planning.

In a large enterprise, one or several technical specialists may be dedicated to a COE, or they may individually be dedicated to value streams and establish the COE as a formal coalition of experts (i.e., they report to the value stream and have some time allotted to the COE). In a smaller enterprise, a specialist who may be assigned within one or several value streams may also float around representing one or several COE disciplines. In many cases, COEs are formed as a mixture of these various approaches.

There is a potential contradiction at work here; in Chapter 3 we emphasized that by removing "experts" from the team, teams will develop the necessary skills themselves. But now we're talking about a central group of experts with influence on enterprise-wide standards that guide decisions of the individual teams. There are various approaches to integrating such expert knowledge and standards into value streams; the most important point is not to create experts that are disassociated from teams that are doing the daily work. "I've seen cases where a centralized 'architecture group' subtracts value," notes Jez Humble. "I always emphasize the importance of architects involved in the coding, so they get to see the real consequences of their prescriptions."[5]

Because COEs promote enterprise standards, they can become naturally resistant to change and innovation because change often disrupts standards. But when approached with the proper mindset, a COE can act as an incubator, a stimulant, and a cross-pollinator for new ideas. The inclination of the COE toward innovation may depend upon the general enterprise disposition toward standardization. "A way to prevent this is to ensure that COE representatives must 'go see,' communicating via personal interaction instead of documentation with the rest of the organization," suggest David Bogaerts and Jael Schuyer, Lean and Agile coaches at ING Netherlands. "We see that if COEs are far from the shop floor (either they choose to be or are pushed back) and do not get the chance to interact with the people who are doing the work, they lose touch with the real place (*gemba*) and have trouble adding value."[6]

When a value stream team wants to push the envelope of a standard, it should lead to an exploration, and perhaps an experiment, but not an argument. The COE should communicate the purpose and assumptions behind the standard: the enterprise-wide benefits for its adoption and the potential long-term costs for its violation.* Then an informed tradeoff decision is possible, with a clear escalation to leadership if necessary. The CIO is usually the final word on IT standards. "However it is important that the CIO avoid becoming the *"C-I-No"*— an obstruction to business experimentation supported by technology."[7]

COEs can play a *leadership* role in innovation, both opportunistically and by design. For example, an IT innovation might pop up unexpectedly when a value stream team conducts an experiment that produces positive results, and the COE members promote it widely. An enterprise may also deliberately encourage a COE to become an applied research and development center, enabling individual value streams to experiment in bringing

---

* "Note that industry methods for estimating Total Cost of Ownership in this way remain immature." —Charles Betz

new changes to market quickly. When properly integrated within the value stream culture, COEs can become useful frameworks for the propagation of new knowledge across the enterprise while acting as strategic balancing agents between standardization and innovation.

Shared Infrastructure and Operations

There is a significant trend these days toward consolidating, virtualizing, and outsourcing many shared IT functions, often into the cloud, in order to reduce cost and administrative burden while hopefully improving service levels, flexibility, and scalability. Let's take a Lean view of this trend.

According to Gartner, "One of the biggest mistakes companies make with Lean is focusing too heavily on driving cost out of the business. Building a huge data center may give you great economies of scale, for example, but it may also reduce agility and flexibility."[8] As a steady flow of releases from numerous development teams converge onto a consolidated production platform, congestion, delays, and quality problems may result, and flow ceases.

Although there are clearly economies of scale that argue for massive consolidation of utility computing capabilities, we must carefully consider the unseen costs and unintended consequences from a Lean *economy of flow* perspective. Is a constraint introduced by a shared infrastructure component going to cause delays in the continuous delivery of new IT products and services through the individual value streams served by this massively scaled and shared resource? By seeking high utilization of scarce resources are we inhibiting the flow and realization of value we are seeking?

The conclusion? With each decision we should consider the total cost of ownership from a Lean perspective. While the enterprise should seek to take advantage of low-cost, highly scalable shared services, they should balance this objective by encouraging each value stream manager to perform a rigorous value stream analysis, looking at all the strategic factors that contribute to speed, flow, and agility—not just operating cost.

To Outsource or Not to Outsource

"One day soon, you may not own or manage a single piece of hardware or software. Companies and people in far-flung places will be storing, managing and maintaining your data and applications," suggests the *CIO Magazine* article "The CIO as Supply Chain Manager." "With a services-based infrastructure, the CIO and teams are increasingly moving from building and integrating technology to managing a vast supply chain of technology partners."[9]

IT management and governance must now oversee a growing array of sophisticated and interdependent services from a variety of suppliers that often do not have experience working with each other. Although each may offer significant skills and advantages, they may not collectively offer the ability to prevent systemic failure, or the capability to quickly diagnose and respond if it should happen. That responsibility lies squarely on the enterprise that hires their services. The cost and performance benefit assumptions of such a widely distributed IT supply chain are worth considering carefully, compared with the additional quality, security, and complexity risks that it introduces.

Fortunately we have a model to study and learn from: MIT's Lean Aerospace Initiative, in which teams have spent years researching some of the most complex, extended supply chains on the planet. Just imagine all of the parts and supply chain relationships that must come together to design, build, and maintain a satellite, spaceship, or large aircraft. In *Lean Enterprise Value: Insights from MIT's Lean Aerospace Initiative*, the researchers emphasize the nuances of coordinating the activities of multiple enterprises, *and the central role that value stream organization plays*:

> Practitioners and scholars have long struggled with the conflicts, disconnects, and misunderstandings that often develop among supposedly collaborating organizations. Commonly, they attribute these to direct economic conflicts or to differences in culture. But the root cause probably lies elsewhere. It may have more to do with the way *value* does or does not flow through such an enterprise. More specifically, it may relate to the challenges of coordinating the multiple interacting flows of value in an [extended] enterprise.
>
> Each value stream has its own set of imperatives that cannot be ignored while constructing mutually agreeable value propositions across multiple value streams. Hence, value streams are the key building blocks for the multiprogram enterprise and key levers for organizational transformation.[10]

The point is that a clear value stream alignment across all stakeholders, including external service providers, is necessary to mitigate the potentially competing motivations of all players. Consider the experience of the manufacturing industry. During the past two decades, many U.S. manufacturers outsourced to China and other low-cost producers only to learn that there were many important considerations beyond just unit cost: lead time, shipping and expediting costs, communication delays, quality problems, cultural differences, intellectual property risk, and ultimately the loss of the knowledge and relationships of the employees who are displaced. In fact, the growing trend in many U.S. manufacturing enterprises is *insourcing*, rebuilding skills and knowledge that, years ago, were sent away. Perhaps we will see the same reversal in IT services someday as the pendulum continues to slowly swing back and forth—as it always has.*

There are valid reasons to outsource IT services, but you should examine your own situation critically, with a long-term view to value creation and total cost of ownership, not a short-term view of cost reduction. To successfully outsource, you should first clearly understand the services you're currently receiving. If the process you're outsourcing is fundamentally flawed or poorly understood, shipping it out won't necessarily reduce cost or improve quality and satisfaction. You may pay the price for outsiders to figure it out for you and then force-fit their own best practices onto your operations with little regard for the business or human cost of such disruptive change. Now it may be that's what you want to do, but this should be a deliberate and informed choice, not an accidental one. But there is a better way, and that is to take ownership of your processes, understand them, improve them, and then decide how best to run them.

In order to make a well-informed decision and ensure a successful transition if outsourcing is chosen, you should first do your homework, unraveling the entanglement of interdependent IT products, services, and people that currently exist. The authors of *Defining IT Success through the Service Catalog* state the matter as follows:

> With such a flexible taxonomy of nested IT services, the difficult design question is determining where to draw the line. In other words, how much detail is too much detail? Based on our experience, an IT service should be defined and made a visible component of the service offering if a competitor or external service provider includes it as an optional service in their offering [or if] calling it out will help explain differentiation from a competitor.[11]

---

* "We are already seeing this in our organization." —Anonymous Lean IT coach from a multinational financial services enterprise

This viewpoint suggests that some aspects of outsourced services may appear to be cheaper only because the enterprise has not recognized or factored in all the formal and informal services and benefits they are accustomed to receiving from their internal service provider.

One approach to this challenge is to first apply Lean thinking to the IT services you are considering for export. Stabilizing and standardizing your processes* first will allow you to more clearly define the services—those presently consumed as well as anticipated needs. It will also provide you with a more accurate basis of cost to run these services. According to Kurt Milne, executive director of the IT Process Institute and coauthor of *Visible Ops Private Cloud*:

> We interviewed thirty IT executives about their private cloud lessons learned. A focus on process was consistently mentioned as a key competency needed to ensure success. With high degrees of automation and standardization of system configurations, identifying and eliminating the causes of process exceptions is absolutely critical to delivering IT as a service. Exceptions kill automation and require manual intervention usually by highly skilled IT professionals that are already a limited resource. Eliminating variance is the "secret sauce" for those looking to optimize service levels and reduce costs simultaneously.[12]

Some enterprises discover that once they have improved these processes, outsourcing doesn't add up. And if it does, Lean thinking can help make for a smooth transition.

A Lean Approach to Outsourcing

Most enterprises pursue outsourcing to operate more efficiently (run) and scale to meet new opportunities (grow). But done wrong, outsourcing can

---

* In addition to standardizing your processes you may also need to simplify the underlying architecture. Many IT systems are expensive and painful to maintain because they have become so complex—this precludes successfully outsourcing or virtualizing them. A big prerequisite of success is standardization of your platforms and technologies so the automation piece (build, test, provision, deploy) doesn't become prohibitively complex and expensive. If you're going to move in this direction with Brownfield systems, you'll almost certainly have to rearchitect many of your systems up front in order to continue meeting your SLAs when you move to the cloud. That cost will be amortized over time, and of course migration can (and should) be done incrementally, but it's essential to recognize and evaluate the up-front cost when considering these options.
—Jez Humble

be deadly for innovation[13] (transform). To make the right strategic decisions on outsourcing, we must therefore consider the long-term strategic context.

When executed properly and for the right reasons, the transition to an external service provider can relieve pressure on internal resources. These resource gains, of both financial and human capital, may then be reinvested with a focus on services that will grow and transform the enterprise. But outsourcing run-the-business services does not mean that you can abdicate responsibility for them. As the number of external moving parts increases, so do the handoffs and potential failure points, so the skills for relationship management, contract management, and supervision must become stronger within your enterprise.

If an outsourcing relationship proves successful, there is a good chance that, over time, the scope and depth of capabilities they provide the enterprise will expand. Thus, the importance of coordination, communication, and continuous improvement of the external services providers' activities increases as well. But these external sources are separated from your enterprise by distance, time zones, culture, and organizational boundaries of management and communication. These relationships are often complicated by complex contractual agreements, with metrics that may not align with activities that drive your business outcomes and process improvement efforts. In addition, you are most likely not the only customer that the external providers are serving with the same pool of resources, so you are often subject to the whims of shifting priorities and resource conflicts.

Another important factor to consider when weighing the outsource equation is what customer touch points will be delegated. Customer interactions, precious *moments of truth*, often create value that can't be measured in a strictly financial analysis. An example of a customer touch point that is frequently outsourced is the customer helpdesk. In this service, it is the vendor, not the enterprise, who engages with the end customer when a problem occurs. Recall the question that drives every value stream: *Who is the customer, and what do they want?* What most customers want when they call a helpdesk is more than a friendly voice and a solution to their problem. What they *really* want is to not have encountered the problem in the first place.

Hearing where your customers are encountering problems is the first step required in preventing them from recurring. But if you have outsourced this point of contact, how and when will you hear about the problem? When outsourcing such direct customer connections to external service providers who are motivated by cost and efficiency (and perhaps even by financial gain for repeatedly solving the same problem each time one of your customers calls) and who have no relationship with those who can address the root causes of the problems, many opportunities for improvement and innovation may be lost. Worse yet, you'll never know it.

The enterprise should carefully weigh the value of customer touch points and consider retaining some in-house, continuously improve those processes, and create a direct channel of communication from the voice of the customer to those who design your products, services, and processes. To create a successful outsource relationship, the enterprise should view the relationship not as a vendor resource but as a partnership, and set the expectation within the contract language that the partner will participate with you in continuous improvement. In addition, when possible, hold the service provider accountable for outcomes—not just activities. This accountability will likely add cost to the contract, but without it—without a contractual requirement that your partner will evolve and improve with you—you will have effectively reverted to the situation you are seeking to eliminate: a siloed, underperforming IT function that does not align and integrate with the enterprise value streams to deliver customer value. And if you do attempt to retroactively build continuous improvement into the relationship, you may be met with unreasonable fees or even active resistance because service providers may actually profit from your poor processes.

The more enterprise run-the-business performance relies on the expertise of outside organizations, the more it must develop a framework for engaging these partners, individually and collectively, in active continuous improvement. Lean is about continuous, collaborative learning, so whatever capabilities you intend to outsource should be accompanied by a framework to promote and internalize that learning. As this occurs, the Lean management system (the subject of Chapter 7) extends beyond the boundaries of the enterprise into the extended value streams. In the end, all participants in value streams, whether internal employees or external service providers, must identify with the shared purpose of their value stream if Lean behavior is to flourish throughout the extended enterprise.

The Emerging Social Enterprise: From Transactions to Interactions

Ours is a world of rapid innovation and continuous global interaction and collaboration. The lines of separation among customers, teams, internal and external service providers, partners, and influencers are blurring.

Information, ideas, and interactions are constantly flowing through myriad channels. This new, collaborative world is exciting, but it can also be a recipe for complexity and chaos if we don't handle it skillfully. How do we guide this new energy with a light hand without trying to control it? How do we strike a *balance* among speed, efficiency, and innovation? How can we offer our customers a better experience while at the same time being cost-effective?

According to technology futurist Geoffrey Moore, radically new pathways of communication and commerce are being created, and "the planet is wiring itself a new nervous system."[14] The traditional *systems of record*, large-scale transactional systems (such as enterprise resource planning) have provided the infrastructure for the rapid growth of global commerce over the past two decades, just as the railroads and highways enabled industrial growth in the century before. But new pathways are now evolving rapidly, and Moore calls these *systems of engagement*—taking instantaneous business-to-business and business-to-consumer communication, content, interaction, and collaboration to a new level.

Traditional systems of record are built upon relational databases, massive stores of *structured* data, with rules that protect the integrity of the data and the processes they support. But with the explosive growth of *unstructured information*—documents, audio, video, photographs, images, conversations, web conferencing, chat sessions, wikis, and more—comes the challenge of how to integrate highly dynamic multichannel content into the daily processes of the business in a useful and manageable way.

Let's take just one early example of this trend. Many companies have incorporated online chat into their traditional customer service offerings, serving customers faster, better, *and* more cost-effectively rather than making them wait for a live voice. With the booming market in social and mobile applications, we will encounter many more opportunities to interact with our customers in real time while they are using our product or service or about to purchase it. Along with these new opportunities comes the potential to create waste on a very large scale if we're not able to integrate these capabilities with the processes they are supposed to support.

Let's not lose sight of the simple fact that processes remain the lifeblood of every enterprise. What W. Edwards Deming said decades ago remains true today: "If you can't describe what you are doing as a process, you don't know what you're doing." Overlaid onto these processes and the transactional systems that support them is a rich fabric of relationships and experiences.

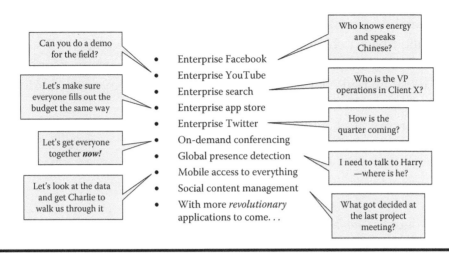

Figure 4.2 Systems of engagement for B2B: A new view for enterprise IT.

Each of these interactions is a moment of truth for someone, somewhere. "Social business systems need to be implemented within a context, and that context is the processes that drive the business," insists Moore. In order to do that, the social (human interaction) fabric of these new social media systems must be overlaid onto the transactional systems of record we use to automate those processes (see Figure 4.2).[15] "If you're stuck with only systems of record, trying to play a game in a collaborative value chain, you are well and truly stuck." The correct architecture is to build systems of engagement on top of systems of record (and the processes they support) in a way where they act together. While that's easy to say, "it's a decade's worth of work for a corporation to do,"[16] suggests Moore. And quite frankly, even the largest and most sophisticated enterprises are just beginning to realize the true nature of what social technologies can do to enhance value to their customers, while many clever and nimble startups circle, nipping at their heels.

How does a traditional enterprise, with decades of enterprise legacy systems, navigate these treacherous waters without creating more fragmentation and technical debt? How do business leaders know which of these emerging technologies are hype—time-wasting distractions—and which really add value and differentiation? None of us has a crystal ball, but we do have a set of *guiding principles*: continuous improvement, respect for people and their ideas, and a focus on our core value streams that serve our customers. After all, that's why an enterprise exists in the first place. Each emerging new technology should be viewed in this context, as an *experiment* in value creation—plan-do-check-act.

The speed of growth and change may be accelerating, but the nature of value creation hasn't changed. Ask yourself: How can we align all stakeholders in a way that they have a line of sight to their customer, enhanced through these myriad channels of communication and interaction? How can everyone measure the waste and the value?

With value stream alignment, teams can experiment their way through the tumult.

Notes

1. Jim Womack, *Gemba Walks* (Cambridge, MA: Lean Enterprise Institute, 2011), 189–190.
2. Colleen M. Young, *Six Steps to Process-Based IT Organizational Design* (Stamford, CT: Gartner, 2006).
3. Hadley Fuller, Brad Lang, Aaron Mihaly, et al., "Nonprofit Technology Needs Assessment and Guide, for Upper Valley Nonprofits," May 21, 2008; for Prof. John Vogel's social entrepreneurship class at the Tuck School of Business at Dartmouth, Hanover, NH.
4. Mark Striebeck, "Creating a Testing Culture," Lean IT Summit presentation, Paris, October 14, 2011.
5. Jez Humble, interview, June 2, 2012.
6. David Bogaerts and Jael Schuyer, interview, March 17, 2012.
7. Richard Hunter and George Westerman, *The Real Business of IT: How CIOs Create and Communicate Business Value* (Boston: Harvard Business Press, 2009), 33.
8. Leon Erlanger, "Smart Enterprise Insights: Going Lean," http://www.smartenterprisemag.com/showArticle.jhtml?articleID=217701405&pgno=3.
9. Zohar Gilad, "The CIO as a Supply Chain Manager," *CIO Magazine*, December 7, 2011.
10. Earll M. Murman, Thomas Allen, Kirkor Bozdogan, et al., *Lean Enterprise Value, Insights from MIT's Lean Aerospace Initiative* (Palgrave, 2002), 217.
11. Rodrigo Flores, Bill Fine, and Troy DuMoulin, *Defining IT Success through the Service Catalog (Pink Elephant Guides)* (Zaltbommel, the Netherlands: Van Haren Publishing, 2007), 42.
12. Kurt Milne, interview, May 31, 2011.
13. Chris Murphy, "Innovation Atrophy," *InformationWeek*, May 30, 2011.
14. Geoffrey Moore, "A Sea Change in Enterprise IT," AIIM, 2011.
15. Geoffrey Moore, "The Future of Enterprise IT," http://www.youtube.com/watch?v=P5zWZagA4ps.
16. Ibid.

Chapter 5

Speeding Ideas to Market

Steve Bell

> Water is fluid, soft, and yielding. But water will wear away rock,
> which is rigid and cannot yield.
> As a rule, whatever is fluid, soft, and yielding will overcome
> whatever is rigid and hard.
> This is another paradox: What is soft is strong.
>
> **Lao-Tzu**
> Chinese philosopher (6th century BCE), *Tao Te Ching*

WHAT YOU'LL LEARN IN THIS CHAPTER

- How to create a continuous flow from problems and ideas to experiments and solutions
- How Lean is applied differently within development and IT operations and how they may harmonize with each other to create flow
- How Lean thinking can benefit Agile software development practice and how Agile lessons can strengthen Lean
- How technologists within value streams can reduce unnecessary complexity and technical debt
- How to create fast and effective Lean IT governance

In Chapter 1 we explored the interplay of complementary forces at work: a creative force and a productive force, development and operations. One of the central themes of this book is that we must learn to balance and integrate these forces, creating rapid learning cycles that propel us toward our strategic goals in a continuous run-grow-transform cycle. Now, with a foundation of how integrated business-IT value streams function established in Chapters 3 and 4, let's take a closer look at how this dynamic balance can work.

It's easy to recognize and appreciate the creative force at work in development. But the creative force is also essential in operations. Consider the quote from Lao-Tzu about how the flow of soft water can carve through the hardest obstacles. The Taoist philosophers insist that everything has its own nature, and it flows best when we understand and work with this nature. The nature of operations is efficiency: determining what is known, standardizing it, and making it flow continuously and efficiently. Variation is the opposing force, the rock in the flow, and it is to be avoided when possible. However, in this way variation is also the catalyst for change, a disruptive force for the continuous improvement of operational performance. Thus, the creative force of improvement and innovation is found within the nature of operations.

On the other hand, the nature of development is creation. It *seeks* variation and uncertainty, to experiment with the unknown, to encounter obstacles, to learn, to create something new. If we attempt to drive out variation, to turn the creative process into a rigid one measured by ordinary standards of productivity, Lao-Tzu would say that we destroy its nature. If we assert Lean *operational* thinking within development, we risk becoming *Taylorists*, trying to force a rigorous pace and numeric controls onto a dynamic and unpredictable process of adaptive learning. Yet there is some nature of operations within the development process as well, and product development professionals have learned that applying process discipline can lead to improved speed of innovation.[*]

For the wisdom of a more contemporary philosopher on this issue, we turn to Rodney Dangerfield, who would probably lament that the operational teams chugging away to keep the lights on and the servers running "get no respect." This is despite having to be quite creative in the face of increasing demands, continuous budget cuts and threats of outsourcing, and disruptive architectural shifts such as virtualization, cloud, and mobile computing. All the while their colleagues, the developers, are considered by many to be cutting edge and sexy. This perception is misguided; development and operations must be on the same team (DevOps), acting with the same purpose, innovating together so they can quickly and continuously introduce new ideas, products, and services to their customers.

---

[*] See Allen C. Ward, *Lean Product and Process Development* (Cambridge, MA: Lean Enterprise Institute, 2007); Don Reinertsen, *The Principles of Product Development Flow: Second Generation Lean Product Development* (Redondo Beach: Celeritas Publishing, 2009).

Keep in mind that Lean represents a set of principles and practices rather than a methodology, and these practices adapt as they are applied in each new environment. Lean thinking began in manufacturing, and this is where many of the original practices emerged that we use today. But if taken too literally, focusing on tools and techniques within a *production* context, Lean thinking can lose its relevance to a service or development organization. Lean has crossed functional boundaries, out of manufacturing into development, services, and sales; it has also crossed industry boundaries, into healthcare, financial services, and the public sector. Each time it crosses a boundary, Lean practice adapts to the new landscape, to the nature of these new situations. And with it the thinking and the language must subtly change, but the basic principles remain the same. That is what is happening now within the emerging practice of Lean IT. And it is with this spirit of continuing evolution that in this chapter we explore how Lean thinking can harmonize this dynamic balance of development and operations across all IT disciplines and communities and across the extended enterprise.

According to Jeffrey Liker, author of the popular series of books on Toyota:

> The Toyota Production system (TPS) and Toyota's Lean Product Development System (LPDS) are based on the same set of underlying principles, but they look different in how the tools are applied and how the process is made to flow. In any kind of process that is purely based on knowledge work and involves complex project management, such as the design and development of a system (e.g., hardware or software design) or even the construction of a complex unique system like a new data center, LPDS will provide a more familiar model that can be easier to apply than TPS.[1]

Nevertheless, there is a natural tendency for Lean practitioners to use manufacturing metaphors when describing the Lean development lifecycle. This can be a nails-on-chalkboard moment for development professionals because it is against their nature. However, according to Liker, there really isn't such a disconnect with Lean manufacturing as one might think:

> I think the biggest problem with the manufacturing metaphor is that people take it literally and think they are making software

design look like a factory process. But in Toyota *a factory process is not a factory process*—it is a continuous improvement, learning process. It involves the same kind of design iterations. The problem comes in when you view the system mechanistically instead of organically—as a human-technical system—that you try to simply copy solutions in the mechanistic world. Whether the metaphor is design or manufacturing the imitation of tools and structures approach has limited chances of success.

I think it is much more fruitful to start with product design as a metaphor. Ideas like common architectures, design reuse, parts commonization, towering technical competence, driving the voice of the customer through every stage of the design, set-based design, etc. are all very powerful and you would miss those typically with a manufacturing metaphor. I think we have barely scratched the surface of what is possible with the continuous design, development, delivery and operations of complete systems using Lean principles.[1]

THE RELATIONSHIP OF LEAN AND AGILE

The Agile software development community is the most mature example of Lean thinking within the domain of IT. Three decades before the publication of the "Agile Manifesto" in 2001, many were already experimenting with iterative development. For example, see the 1970 article by Dr. Winston W. Royce, "Managing the Development of Large Software Systems,"[2] which calls attention to the risks of the waterfall method and suggests an iterative approach.

The Lean and Agile communities are now communicating, sharing, and learning from and with each other. In fact, Agile software development and Lean product development share the same foundations; many of the founders of the "Agile Manifesto" were influenced by many of the same people (Taiichi Ohno, Shigeo Shingo, W. Edwards Deming, Peter Senge, and Hirotaka Takeuchi) and followed the same examples as those in the Lean community decades ago. Many popular techniques, such as *kanban* and Scrum, which are complementary and not competing methods when skillfully applied, share common Lean roots. But I have discovered that while most in the Agile community are familiar with the history of Lean,* many in the Lean community (especially in the manufacturing world) have a limited awareness of the depths of Agile practice.

There is much Lean practitioners can learn from Agile in terms of listening to and interacting with the customer, automated testing to discover defects early and remove them quickly, continuous integration and delivery, pair programming and problem solving, creative uses of *kanban* and other visual management techniques, iterative project management (Scrum), virtual team communications, the value of team dynamics, and more. And beyond the tools and mechanics, the combination of art and science that Agile has applied to rapid learning and creation is inspiring.

Similarly, there is much the Agile community can learn from Lean practitioners, particularly about the fundamental *principles* of Lean, which explain not just how, but *why*, Agile practices can be so effective when adopted properly. The Lean emphasis on overall value streams can be helpful to enhance the value of Agile practice to the enterprise and its end customers (as we'll explore in this chapter).

For example, I have seen situations where Agile teams develop an antagonistic relationship with management because they perceive them as a source of interference and disruption to the teams' performance. According to the authors of *Lean-Agile Software Development*, "Although Scrum may help teams isolate themselves from dysfunction in the organization (which can lead to limited improvement), it is better for them to help the organization become more functional."[3] And the emphasis of transformational leadership and the importance of an integrated Lean management system (discussed in Chapter 7) can help focus and coordinate Agile and Lean efforts across an extended enterprise to deliver fast, flexible flow of value to end customers.

---

* There are several popular Agile-related books that do a good job relating the underlying Lean principles, e.g., *Leading Lean Software Development* by Mary and Tom Poppendieck (Addison Wesley, 2009); *Lean-Agile Software Development* by Shalloway, Trott, and Beaver (Addison Wesley, 2010); and *Scaling Lean and Agile Development* by Larman and Vodde (Addison Wesley, 2009).

From a Problem to a Solution

When we consider the idea-to-adoption value stream, it's natural to think that the goal is to write and deploy code faster. But the objective is *not* software development velocity; it is to solve a problem or deliver a new idea quickly. Often this means improving a business process or enhancing a product while writing *less* code, perhaps even *removing* some wasteful elements (process and technical debt) that no longer add value.

Too often, however, teams gravitate to technology as a quick fix to a problem when a simpler, nontechnology solution may prove equally effective—or better. Whenever technology is identified as a possible countermeasure, the team should first ask: What are we hoping to accomplish? Is there another way to arrive at the goal without creating unnecessary technical complexity and cost? Such restraint and reflection will pay dividends in the long run, preventing accumulation of technical and process debt, accelerating the ability to change, and simplifying and streamlining products and processes.

So let's start by examining the relationship between a core *business* value stream and the underlying application development and deployment (DevOps) value stream that supports it, with the intention of improving performance while avoiding unnecessary complexity and technical debt. The core value stream team analyzes and experiments with a problem or idea using the plan-do-check-act (PDCA) approach, resulting in a process improvement that may (or may not) require a change to the software used to enable that process (e.g., a custom-developed application or enhancement or a change to the configuration of a commercial off-the-shelf system).

The core team is comprised mostly of business stakeholders within the value stream, but at least one technologist is essential for contributing understanding of the underlying systems and the technology strategy in general so that the team can make informed decisions. And since the technologist actively participates in the day-to-day process improvement efforts, he or she is more capable of determining the role (if any) of technology and guiding the development and deployment when it is needed. This relationship is illustrated in Figure 5.1.

If and when the team identifies a legitimate need for a technology intervention, this creates demand in the queue for the DevOps team, a supporting value stream comprised mostly of technologists along with a few business representatives. Many enterprises have a role that plays an intermediary between the business and IT, acting as a translator (e.g. business

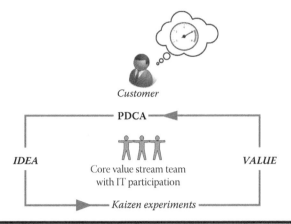

Figure 5.1   The idea to adoption value stream.

analyst). One client called this role an "ambassador between warring factions." In my experience, having an intermediary reinforces the separation between the two organizations and prevents direct interaction, shared learning, and the development of an enduring relationship. Ideally (when the business can justify it), this should be an intact team comprised of business and technical colleagues dedicated to the value stream, producing a steady cadence of application enhancements.

How to Capture Problems and Ideas

How do we prime the pump to get the continuous flow of problems, ideas, and value moving? In my experience, in every value stream there is an abundance of waste to be eliminated, problems to be solved, and ideas to be explored. Quite often, however, people already know where the waste is and have terrific new ideas, yet for a variety of reasons they aren't able to act on them. So the first step is often simply to bring all the right people together across the entire value stream (including representation from technologists) so that everyone sees the big picture.

When a value stream team is formed and *kaizen* efforts start to deliver positive results, teams develop *eyes for waste*, often causing a deluge of pent-up issues to rise to the surface. I always encourage this team to start making a list of known problems and ideas and then post them on a visual management display to facilitate problem identification and solving. Problems, issues, and ideas come from many sources—we all have a few we'd like to do something about. Each *kaizen* and value stream mapping session turns up a few new discoveries that are added to the list. The service desk ticketing system can usually produce some useful data as well. And once the team posts this list in a public area, inviting input by hanging a pen nearby, others may begin sharing their ideas.

The team may call this list a *parking lot*, an *issues list*, an *improvement board*, a *kaizen opportunity list*, or something similar. Whatever it's called, this list is an honest and visible acknowledgement of the obstacles and opportunities that lie ahead. In the spirit of Lean thinking, "problems are treasures" that open the door to continuous improvement. But this list is not a backlog; it is not a commitment that any one of these issues is going to be solved. In fact, many issues that seem to be problems are only symptoms of deeper problems. This list contains valuable input for problem identification and root cause analysis.

The public display of known problems and opportunities can be therapeutic for the team and act as a catalyst for stimulating questions that illuminate even more problems and ideas. This catalytic effect is especially important when other teams pay a visit during a *gemba* walk (also known as a "waste walk") to learn from each others' problems and to reflect on shared concerns. But be aware that for some, a visual display of their problems can feel threatening. Leadership must set the tone that problems are caused by poor processes, not bad people; only in a blame-free and trusting environment will all stakeholders freely expose their problems.

The goal of the issues list isn't to gather the most problems; in fact, if it is allowed to grow too large, it can become burdensome and counterproductive. The issues list is valuable raw material for problem solving. Often a list of hundreds of problems can be reduced to a handful of underlying relationships and root causes, using visual tools such as fishbone (*Ishikawa*) diagramming, mind mapping, and value stream mapping. Visual categorization of problems, and their myriad symptoms that may appear as problems, may help the team unravel complex situations into individual root causes and countermeasures that can be quickly tested and validated through PDCA experimentation cycles.

Visualizing the issues list is helpful beyond the borders of the team as well. Some of the same or similar problems may occur in several value streams and spread throughout the enterprise. One of the responsibilities of Lean managers and leaders is to "go see" and look for commonality across different value streams. Viewing multiple issues lists also helps DevOps value stream teams see opportunities for common solutions and component reuse.

Once the team has a list, how do they use it as a catalyst for a series of rapid experiments that yield the best results? Teams must prioritize their problems and symptoms in a way that supports strategy so that the most urgent rise quickly to the top for rapid experimentation. But when we create this list of issues for experimentation, if we're not careful we'll start thinking of it as a *checklist*:* first we'll solve *this* problem and then we'll solve *that* problem, in a tidy, preordained sequence. The issues list simply represents the problems that the team believes are most important to solve, but it should only work on them *one at a time* (see Figure 5.2). At the end of each experiment, the team reflects on what has been learned and then decides what the next problem is to be solved. It may be the next one on the list. Or it may not.†

Continuous improvement is a hands-on team sport. It's often messy, as problems suddenly appear out of nowhere. If you take this issues list idea too literally, it may seem very procedural, inflexible, and slow. If

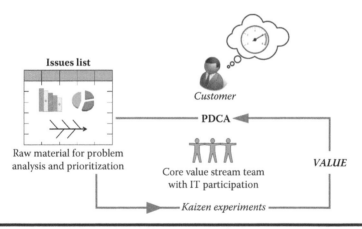

Figure 5.2   How an issues list feeds the core value stream PDCA cycle.

---

* Recall in Chapter 1 that we discussed Mike Rother's caution against using checklists or an implementation mindset. Eric Ries in *The Lean Startup* (New York: Crown Publishing, 2011) says much the same thing when he emphasizes validated learning, one experiment at a time. This one-step-at-a-time approach may feel slow at first, but it's the scientific method and the only way to be sure you are continuously learning and not jumping to unprovable assumptions and misguided "solutions." And if you're truly addressing root causes, you will find that one countermeasure may eliminate many related symptoms and problems at once, so the accumulative effect of incremental improvement (when problems are well chosen) can be fast and significant.

† "This buffer is best thought of as a short 'what are the most important things to learn next list.' The output of the 'flow' validates whether the hypothesis is correct or not. The team is building and validating its understanding of the customer problem and potential solutions by trying things and keeping (process and code changes) the things that work." —Tom Poppendieck

that's what you're thinking, think again. All problems aren't alike—some are large and complicated, requiring preparation, whereas others are tiny, urgent problems that shouldn't wait to be literally "put on the list." In fact, if you make someone wait to act on such a spontaneous problem-solving moment, the moment may pass and be lost forever in the rush of daily work. And there is no waste more tragic than the loss of a really good idea.

A quick and easy *kaizen* can take just a few minutes yet result in huge incremental gains, especially if you realize the benefits day after day. But such rapid responses need to be disciplined PDCA events. This is where a manager becomes a coach, helping the team to practice the art of problem solving every time a problem arises.

THE PINK STICKY MAN

By an anonymous Lean IT coach

One customer setup process of ours was very inconsistent. The high error rate impeded not only client servicing but ultimately the revenue stream as well, because some customers became frustrated and left. A *kaizen* was launched, including stakeholders from the corporate offices and sales representatives from the field who reluctantly participated merely "to be polite."

In the first exercise we value stream mapped the current state of the process and put bright pink sticky notes on any area that was a pain point that contributed to errors. The map was covered with pink. As the *kaizen* progressed through problem analysis, the team defined a new target state where it expected to reduce the errors by at least 90%.

At the report-out of the *kaizen* to the executive sponsors, one of the sales representatives began presenting his segment, and while talking, he began putting pink sticky notes all over himself. He concluded by saying, "When we came to this *kaizen* we [sales] did not see the point. We thought the computer system was just a nuisance. We had no idea that because we were not following the process we were causing so many errors, rework, cost, and frustration for our customers. Bringing us all together to understand the whole process has opened my eyes and made me realize that I don't want to be a pink sticky!"

When Problems Need Technology Solutions

As the value stream team experiments with problems and ideas, every now and then a countermeasure requires technology assistance. This creates demand in the supporting DevOps value stream.

Because a technologist is on the team that identified and experimented with the originating problem or idea, the countermeasure is likely to be legitimate and is stated in terms that the technologists can work with: a "story" of what the business needs to accomplish, which can be translated into technical requirements. This story is entered into a development buffer—along with all the other demands—to be prioritized and sequenced into development by using whatever project and workflow management methodology the team has adopted (*kanban*, Scrum, etc). This relationship between the business value stream problem-solving cycle and the supporting DevOps value stream is depicted in Figure 5.3.*

Although these stories seem well defined, they shouldn't be considered as "work orders" for efficient production as in a factory, but as experiments to be conducted in order to better understand what will solve the customer need. In order to exploit the uncertainty and create viable solutions, the team wants to "fail early and fast." Unlike a production environment, the team does not pursue "quality at the source" and try to do things right the first time—it expects variation and in fact seeks it out because it's through testing the boundaries of uncertainty that the team validates new ideas. Teams may use forms of simulation, working with customers to determine "if we built this, would it solve your problem?" Simulations may involve storyboarding, user-interface mockups, or other low-tech techniques to validate the approach before the first line of code is written. So even now that we've entered the realm of development, teams should do whatever they can to write less code and "defer commitment" until they can validate the need for

---

* This illustration makes a distinction between the core business value stream, which includes a few technologist members, and the supporting DevOps value stream, which includes a few business members. This may seem to be an "IT and the business" dichotomy, but it's not. In many (most?) Web 2.0 companies, it's just one value stream team because the business process and product *are* the technology. But in nontech-focused companies (e.g., healthcare, education, manufacturing, public sector, etc.), most people in the core value stream aren't technologists; their technical counterparts are on the core team to help them. But when the value stream has an intact DevOps team serving its needs, it "belongs" to the business. When the supporting DevOps (or other IT service) value stream is shared among several core value streams, a sense of separateness naturally results, but this can be overcome by frequent *gemba* visits to each business value stream "customer" in order to encourage interactions and promote collaborative learning.

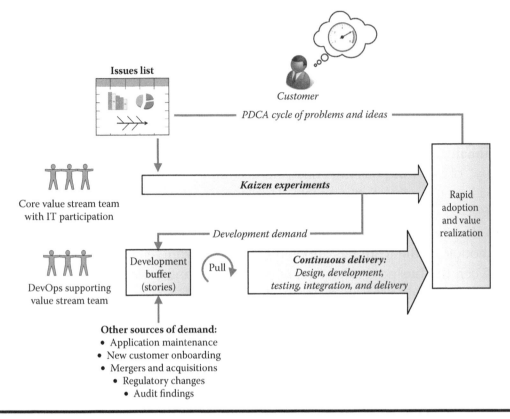

Figure 5.3 Core business and supporting DevOps value streams.

the code, at which point they can then create the "minimum viable product" necessary to deliver value to the customer in each cycle.

In *The Lean Startup,* Eric Ries describes this approach as "hypothesis pull." When engaged in breakthrough innovation and in situations of extreme uncertainty, customers often don't know what they want. And we may not even know who the customers are. We may not even be able to frame a good problem statement. We may have the germ of an idea, but we must prove the *value hypothesis* to determine whether an idea has merit before we spend too much money or time on it. "Our goal in building products is to be able to run experiments that will help us learn how to build a sustainable business. We figure out what we need to learn and then we work backwards to see what product will work as an experiment to get that learning."[4]

When the team compresses problem-solving time from months to weeks, or even just days, this enhances its ability to adapt to change and ultimately to *drive* it. Many technology-driven enterprises now deploy new capabilities daily, even hourly, and the trend toward rapid delivery is accelerating.* "With a small, cross-functional team, it should be possible to push the germ of an idea out to production and get feedback in hours," says Jez Humble. "Obviously, this needs careful thought and analysis to work out what the germ should be, but it is totally possible."[5]

If it's possible to execute an emergency change in a few hours, might it be possible to establish a cadence of minor changes every week? To find out, invite someone along to observe and gather data the next time you execute an emergency change, and later have the team value stream map the process to identify the first round of obstacles to be removed.

Now ask yourself this question: What obstacles are preventing you from solving problems and delivering new capabilities (process improvements and/or system changes) monthly, or even weekly? What do these obstacles tell you about your workflow? Are these obstacles technical in nature? Are they related to your management systems? What if you could analyze, quantify, and systematically eliminate those obstacles to accelerate innovation?

Creating Flow from Idea to Value

Let's say that you are already practicing, or at least experimenting, with various Agile techniques. What if you discover, after a value stream analysis, that the element slowing you down is *not* the velocity of the development team? What if there are other constraints that get in the way between the idea and its realization? That is, in my experience, often the case. Why is that, and what can we do about it?

Figure 5.4 illustrates a common and wasteful pattern where new ideas pass through various disconnected stages before they finally enter the development buffer: capturing ideas, turning them into a business case, applying traditional budget and governance mechanisms, and finally jockeying for position and priority as the time for development approaches. Then there's the handoff to operations and finally to the end user. These are all stages that commonly introduce delays and further challenges. As you can see, there can be many impediments to flow that are outside the development team's sphere of control and influence.†

Under these conditions an Agile development team may become suboptimized, relegated to becoming just another siloed function within a value

---

* See Kent Beck, "Software G-Forces," http://www.youtube.com/watch?v=KIkUWG5ACFY.
† "Improving development makes no difference here. With the widespread adoption of Agile approaches, we see this situation much more often." —Tom Poppendieck

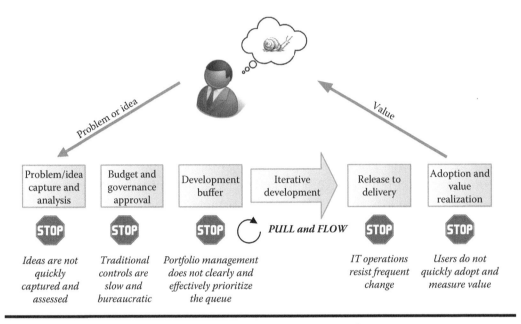

Figure 5.4   Stop and go: when development value doesn't flow.

stream that does not flow. When the team *sees the whole* value stream flow, it can prevent this from happening. Tom Poppendieck suggests that "this can only happen if the team is not just an Agile software team but is a truly cross-functional value stream team from idea assessment and approval through delivery and operations support. This real team will be a good bit larger than 7+/–2 people that Agile talks about."[6]

What exactly is this larger team that Poppendieck is referring to? It might be the core business value stream of which the DevOps team is a part (or an extension). And the obstacles to flow might be related to the management systems imposed by the value stream itself or even the governance systems in place throughout the larger enterprise. What can the DevOps team do about that? According to Tom Perry, Agile coach and senior program manager at CyberSource Corporation (a subsidiary of VISA, Inc.), "I've seen plenty of teams that were well aware of the larger value stream but were unable to make a case to change the upstream or downstream processes. It's one thing to change the development team's process; it's quite another to change the business process."[7]

The responsibility for removing systemic impediments is often in the hands of enterprise leadership (influenced by the value stream manager) because it transcends the authority of any single functional manager, hence the distinction that is often made between "system" and "process" *kaizen*.

Lean Governance to Promote Innovation

Governance serves an important purpose: guiding the decision-making processes of a complex enterprise. However, it is often heavy-handed and disconnected, which can stifle innovation and agility. Governance "gone wrong" can do the following:

- Force change and decision making into slow periodic cycles, often tied to the annual budget.
- Attempt to manage risk by trying to predict, and even control, the future. By disregarding the natural forces of change, variation, and uncertainty that exist in creative activities, it can make deviation from the plan someone's "fault," which stifles innovation.
- Encourage more projects to be launched (work in process) than can be efficiently performed.
- Promote large projects that attract the most attention during the funding process.
- Encourage project thinking, measuring success as achieving project cost, schedule, and scope (adherence to plan) rather than product thinking, which considers the value created over the entire lifecycle.
- Create the conditions for a game to be played to advance special interests rather than a mechanism for optimizing enterprise-wide outcomes.
- Reduce portfolio managers into making tactical tradeoff decisions and short-term interventions (what W. Edwards Deming calls "tampering") that increase instability and variation in the long run.

The traditional practice of IT governance is primarily guided by two frameworks: Control Objectives for Information and Related Technology (COBIT) and the Project Management Institute's Organizational Project Management Maturity Model. These frameworks are sophisticated and mature, but they are also highly structured, prescriptive, and encourage command-and-control behavior *when they are applied inappropriately.*[*] As we explored in Chapter 1, this can lead to more, rather than less, risk, as well as lost opportunities for innovation.

---

[*] In 2011, the Project Management Institute announced a formal Agile Certified Practitioner program, recognizing Agile practice as a formal project management methodology. In 2012 COBIT 5 was released. This new version places a greater emphasis on enterprise value.

While there is plenty of rhetoric around the need for innovation, the truth of corporate behavior is often quite the opposite, insists Gary Hamel, popular business strategist and author of *What Matters Now: How to Win in a World of Relentless Change, Ferocious Competition and Unstoppable Innovation*. Top-down control is "toxic to innovation," he says. "We need organizations that are passion-filled, creative and malleable. To put it simply, bureaucracy must die."[8]

In their series of articles on Lean governance best practices, Scott Ambler and Per Kroll of the IBM Global Agile development group describe two common antipatterns related to ineffective governance:

- *Governance for governance sake*: Also known as "bureaucrats run amok," this is a governance body whose focus is on ensuring that the appropriate documentation is created by development teams at the appropriate times.
- *Control through governance*: This is a governance body whose focus is controlling and directing development teams instead of enabling them. You know that this is occurring when the governance body spends most of its time crafting edicts, procedures, and/or policies for teams to follow.[9]

In addition to the challenges introduced by traditional IT governance, there is a problem with budgets, which many consider a necessary evil of corporate financial governance. Not only does an annual budget consume significant effort each year to create, it is typically followed by eleven months of nonvalue management activity, explaining why results no longer match it—an example of the waste that "checklist thinking" can cause.* There is a growing recognition that traditional budgeting perpetuates management command-and-control thinking and may actually be counterproductive, reducing planning effectiveness while introducing more risk, especially in volatile business conditions.

Once a large project is approved and funded, those requesting the project may have to wait months before resources are available and the work begins. By the time the project is finally delivered, requirements may have changed (or they perhaps weren't accurate in the first place because they

---

* Visit Beyond Budgeting Round Table at http://www.bbrt.org to learn more about a Lean approach that goes beyond budgeting, using rolling forecasts, flexible budgets, and event-driven planning to encourage agility and frontline accountability. Also see "Let It Roll" by Russ Banham, *CFO Magazine*, May 2011 (http://www.cfo.com/article.cfm/14570220).

were forecast too far in advance), and the customer ends up waiting too long and eventually becomes disappointed. This entire process is virtually guaranteed to produce unsatisfactory outcomes, and no amount of additional "control" can prevent it.

Despite all of the negative associations with traditional IT governance, however, there is no question that the basic intent is valid: ensuring that decisions are made by the right people, for the right reasons, in a responsible and accountable manner. As IT capabilities become more interwoven throughout the enterprise, and as systems become more complex, integrated, and dynamic, the potential risks and the need for good governance increase. And the more an enterprise relies on external service providers, the more leadership must develop a framework for engaging these partners, individually and collectively, in effective decision making.

In a Lean world, all of this must be achieved without sacrificing value for the customer. An enterprise is actually made up of many value streams, each serving a particular customer base. Each value stream should be treated individually; some are in the maintenance phase of their current lifecycle, emphasizing operational excellence, whereas others are in startup or growth mode and dealing with far greater uncertainty. Some are in a market-leading position, whereas others are trying catch up. Some are serving geographic regions or markets that are growing, whereas others are in decline. Each value stream team must therefore have the ability to manage its own portfolio of activities and investments to support its particular strategy and the specific needs of its customers through the right balance of run, grow, and transform initiatives.

To illustrate this important point, I asked David Bogaerts and Jael Schuyer of ING Netherlands to explain what Lean governance means to them:

> In our experience, a key element of establishing flow is that a business value stream determines a clear product vision—let's say looking ahead two years. Based on this vision, ideas are formed, including what is required in terms of software development. These ideas are translated into themes, something we can realize in six months or so. These themes are transferred into smaller items, concrete and clear enough to put onto a development team's backlog and *kanban* board. These stories are crafted by business and technical colleagues working together, and are of such a size that a single development team can realize several of them in a single iteration of two to four weeks.

Since a value stream has a vision which is continuously translated into themes and into small stories, a continuous flow of work for development teams is created. Since a team works in iterations of several weeks, new priorities can suddenly be selected by business representatives and inserted quickly into the flow, without having to struggle through approval delays. The implications for budgeting and governance are significant: since we (the value stream team) have a vision and a constant flow of work, we can build stable teams with a *stable funding flow*. Organizations that work on a traditional governance method can only dream of stable funding, continuous resource availability, and rapid throughput of fresh, high quality ideas.[10]

This story illustrates the Lean principles of *customer pull, flow*, and *level scheduling* (also known as *heijunka* scheduling). Managing a backlog in this way allows for changes to be made to the sequence until the moment a story is pulled into development. If a new story is suddenly elevated to the top position, the one that was "bumped" down the priority list must only wait one release cycle before its turn comes around again, so little harm is done. And when the business (and its customers) prioritize and pull stories in near real time, their precision is excellent—there is an immediate need for a solution; they can define it clearly, it gets built quickly and is tested by those who need it, and it is *adopted immediately*.

So how can we create a Lean governance and budgeting framework that supports such individuality of each value stream and encourages the rapid flow of new ideas into experimentation and investment? By establishing a management system where individual teams have the authority to manage their own decisions on business process improvement and application development, within clearly established funding limits, and with a fast escalation path whenever there is a question. Because the development budget is a stable monthly run rate, there is no need to micromanage funding decisions. And risk? As development is performed in small iterations, a team constantly focuses on testing and integration. With each iteration, the team's ability to work together improves and leads to a culture focused on interaction, individual accountability, and quality outcomes.

As Jim Womack says, "The Lean manager realizes that no manager at a higher level can or should solve a problem at a lower level; problems can only be solved where they live, by those living with them."[11] Lean governance should not seek to control people; it should encourage them to make informed decisions within their sphere of responsibility and accountability, promoting rapid experimentation and validated learning. In a Lean management system (which we'll explore further in Chapter 7), decision rights should be assigned as close to the work and customer as possible, ideally into the hands of each value stream team that is accountable for its own strategic roadmap. Doing so will speed decision making, innovation and value delivery to the end customer.

WHAT IS CONTINUOUS DELIVERY?

Jez Humble
Coauthor of Continuous Delivery

Continuous delivery promotes the seamless transition of release into production. While the practices suggested by continuous delivery (continuous integration, testing, and release) may support any software development methodology, it is particularly well suited to a Lean-Agile approach. In enterprises, continuous delivery requires close collaboration between development, testing, and operations staff—a *cultural transformation* advocated by the DevOps movement.[*]

One of the key elements of DevOps philosophy is known as "infrastructure-as-code"; it suggests that it should be possible to provision and evolve infrastructure in a fully automated way based on templates stored in version control. If you're doing it right, you should be able to go from bare metal to a production-ready stack using a fully automated process, which might include spinning up virtual machines, configuring operating systems, middleware (including databases), networking and firewall configurations, and, of course, deploying and configuring your software. One important side effect of this goal is that you should be able to restore service in the event of a catastrophic failure in a deterministic time (assuming your configuration and data is backed up).

You only really get the full benefit of this approach if software development teams can self-service their own environments, both for testing purposes and for deployment to production. In this model, the

---

[*] See "Hitting the Wall: What to Do When High Performing Scrum Teams Overwhelm Operations and Infrastructure" by Jeff Sutherland and Robert Frohman for an example of how Lean thinking helped to break critical operational bottlenecks that appeared once development velocity increased. This article is available at http://jeffsutherland.com/HittingTheWallHICSS2011final.pdf.

operations team manages the infrastructure but provides access via application programming interfaces with their own service level agreements (SLAs) for services such as utility computing, storage, and so forth (e.g., Amazon Web Services). However, with power comes responsibility. If the development team is managing the lifecycle of the infrastructure, it must also own the SLAs for the services it runs on the infrastructure. This forces developers to take responsibility for the cross-functional characteristics of the application (capacity, availability, security, etc.).

Of course most systems rely on multiple services or components working together, so development teams must also be responsible for making sure that when they release a new version of their service they don't break any of the downstream services that consume it. This can be enforced through continuous integration at the system level—making sure that the new version of your service passes acceptance tests in a fully integrated environment. One way to reduce coupling in the service-oriented architecture model is to deploy new versions of a service side by side with the old one, so that services that depend on it can choose when to "upgrade" by consuming the new version of the service.

Creating a Continuous Flow of Ideas and Innovation

This comprehensive idea to adoption value stream example (shown in Figure 5.4) illustrates a fundamental point of Lean thinking: you must consider the whole system if you are going to achieve authentic transformation. This holistic view is not something that comes naturally to most because it's in our human nature to be tribal creatures that stay within our comfort zones and organizational silos.* Taking a *product* lifecycle view to a value stream, rather than a project or task view, requires imagination and vision.

After each cycle of improvement, the entire team should reflect upon what it has learned (what Scrum practitioners call a "retrospective").† This actually

---

* "The problem is that our tribes are too small. They are centered around skill set rather than around purpose. If all members of the team had first-hand knowledge of the people who will use their solution and the problem and context they work in, the tribe would include these people, and this knowledge would provide purpose and define quality. Separation of solution analysis, design, and implementation is one of the root causes of the pain we all live with." —Tom Poppendieck
† Reflections held on a scheduled basis and those that occur at milestone events (such as a *kaizen* report-out) are important. However, it's also important for everyone to *continuously* reflect, with eyes wide open to spot waste whenever it appears.

involves two different aspects: what the team has learned about the problem it's trying to solve and what it has learned about the process of solving it. The first question leads the team into the next cycle of solving the customer problem. The second question leads the team to reflect on how to make the team work more effectively (and possibly faster) with each subsequent learning cycle. The first is about doing the work; the second is about improving how the work is done. They are both necessary and mutually reinforcing if a team is going to sustain improvement and innovation over time.

Years ago the focus was on continuous development, which gave rise to various iterative methodologies that are generally included under the term Agile. Now we have brought operations onto the team with continuous delivery (DevOps). According to Tom Poppendieck, this trajectory suggests the future journey for many enterprises:

> Now many organizations are emphasizing *continuous design*, where there is just enough up-front design to get started, then the design happens an iteration or two ahead of the coding. The technical folks are not just involved, they are essential contributors to the design because they need a deep understanding of the customer problem to be able to make the best technical choices. If you follow this to its logical conclusion, we are approaching an ideal state: the *continuous flow* of ideas to solutions, where the notion of a release becomes irrelevant, it is a batch concept that is the antithesis of Lean flow.[12]

Now this is certainly not practical in *all* cases; there will always be systems of such size and complexity that a multiple release approach is necessary.* Some large projects may always require several interdependent teams working in concert. But even in megaprojects and programs, with multiteam interactions, the size of each change should be reduced whenever possible in order to increase the speed, reduce the complexity and risk of each learning cycle, and improve agility.

There is a lesson here that we can learn from Lean history. In a factory, the Lean principle of *pursuit of perfection*† often meant setting an *ideal state*

---

* In the article "Agile Scaling Factors," IBM's Scott Ambler lists geographical distribution, team size, compliance requirement, domain complexity, organizational distribution, technical complexity, organizational complexity, and enterprise discipline as considerations when selecting a particular Agile process, team structure, and tools (http://www.ibm.com/developerworks/mydeveloperworks/blogs/ambler/entry/agile_scaling_factors?lang=en).

† The fifth Lean principle introduced by Jim Womack and Dan Jones in *Lean Thinking* (New York: Free Press, 2003).

target of one piece flow. Some production situations allow this to happen (such as automobiles, which are individually configured on the line), but many others are simply impractical to produce in quantities of one (such as boxes of cereal or batches of chemicals). But you'd be surprised at how clever teams often radically reduced their batch size, thus increasing speed and agility. In the same way, the ideal state to pursue in DevOps may be daily or hourly changes; clearly some companies have been able to reach and sustain this velocity, and many more are striving for it.

But a particular team or system may never reach that rate—and for valid reasons. What the team can and should do is ask how to cut the current batch size or cycle time in half. This question becomes a hypothesis for experimentation—for testing the boundaries. With each cycle, as old obstacles are overcome, new ones appear. Some cycles result in improvements, whereas others do not. But if the team is truly practicing PDCA, something useful is learned with every cycle.

The "pursuit of perfection" is often misunderstood. There is no such thing as perfection because there is always room for improvement. Teams should never be satisfied with the status quo; they should always work to anticipate and determine the next problem to be solved. This endless curiosity is the key to enterprise agility.

Notes

1. Jeffrey Liker, interview, May 2, 2011.
2. Winston W. Royce, "Managing the Development of Large Software Systems," *Proceedings of IEEE WESCON*, 26, 1–9, 1970.
3. Alan Shalloway, Guy Beaver, and James R. Trott, *Lean-Agile Software Development* (Boston: Addison-Wesley, 2010), 89.
4. Eric Ries, *The Lean Startup* (New York: Crown Business, 2011), 201.
5. Jez Humble, interview, December 15, 2011.
6. Tom Poppendieck, interview, December 14, 2011.
7. Tom Perry, interview, December 12, 2011.
8. *Industry Week*, interview with Gary Hamel, "For Innovation to Flourish in Your Organization 'Bureacracy Must Die,'" May 25, 2012.
9. Scott Ambler and Per Kroll, "Best Practices for Lean Development Governance, Part I: Principles and Organization," June 15, 2007.
10. David Bogaerts and Jael Schuyer, interview, March 17, 2012.
11. Jim Womack, "The Mind of the Lean Manager," in *Lean Enterprise Institute Electronic Newsletter*, July 30, 2009.
12. Tom Poppendieck, interview, December 14, 2011.

Chapter 6

Measuring Value

Steve Bell

Nowadays people know the price of everything and the value of nothing.

Oscar Wilde

WHAT YOU'LL LEARN IN THIS CHAPTER
- Why a focus on cost reduction does not ensure value creation
- The basics of Lean accounting and how it can help you identify problems, guide improvement, and increase value delivery
- How to choose the right measures to guide continuous improvement of IT products and services
- How measurement for measurement's sake can get in the way of people doing the right things to create value

We all want to create value, to feel a sense of pride from a problem solved, to see a good idea brought to life, to know that a job has been well done. And we all want satisfied—better yet—*delighted* customers.

What is it about the enterprises that we admire the most? What do we appreciate about them? Stop and think for a moment. Who is it you really *look forward* to interacting with—and why? It is likely that you admire their passion and commitment to the complete product and to the customer. You look forward to appreciating the experience, knowing that they care enough to pay attention to the things that matter to *you*.

Such pride and commitment to customer value is real. But how do you measure it? And more importantly, how do you measure the behaviors that cause it to happen? Although culture, the outcome of these behaviors, could be an enterprise's most vital asset, it is not something that appears on a balance sheet.

Herein lies one of the paradoxes of Lean thinking. We've all heard the phrase "what gets measured gets done." That's true. But it's often not carried out in a purposeful sense but rather as a controlling, dominating force. W. Edwards Deming insisted, as so many practitioners have learned for themselves, that running a business "by the numbers" does not create sustaining value. The "modern management system," as Jim Womack describes it, often transforms the creative potential of people into a dull routine to produce short-term financial outcomes.

The purpose of measurement in a Lean setting is not to *control* behavior. It is to help guide decisions and actions through an understanding of cause and effect to realize desired outcomes. The best measurements are created by the people doing the work once they have a shared understanding of what they're doing and *why*—how their work relates to the larger effort to create value for the customer.

Cost through the Lean Lens

Giving blood is an instant and guaranteed way to lose weight. But it's not an effective or healthy long-term strategy. In the same way, Lean practitioners have learned that a primary focus on cost reduction does not create lasting value, and may, in fact, cause harm.

Cost cutting has been a focus in IT for years now, and many CIOs feel beaten down, leading to *innovation atrophy*, "a condition where risk taking and daring become so neglected amid belt tightening, quick ROI [return on investment], outsourcing, and plain old fear."[1] Many enterprises intensely focus on IT cost reduction because cost is the only element they feel they can understand, measure, and control. When the only reliable means you have is a brake pedal, then that's what you'll use. But an emphasis on cost cutting can cause an enterprise to continue doing the wrong things. Worse yet, indiscriminate cost cutting may inflict irreparable injury to the long-term health of the enterprise, shedding valuable knowledge, skills, people, and relationships.

The key is to understand the difference between cost cutting and waste reduction. "My focus has been the elimination of waste to create capacity," says Mark Katz, CIO of Esselte, a global office products manufacturer with popular brands such as Oxford and Pendaflex. "A lot of CIOs [use] typical cost-cutting strategies: you squeeze your suppliers for bigger discounts, eliminate projects, cut staff, and cut services. But all four of those strategies will put you in a terrible position to respond when business gets better and you're asked to do more."[2]

So what does waste really look like, and how does it differ from head-on cost reduction? Waste is the cause; cost is the effect. Consider failure demand, which we discussed in Chapter 2. This is the amount of capacity consumed by rework that should have been done right the first time. If you can find the reasons for failure (cause), you can eliminate the wasted capacity (effect) and realize more value from your existing people and other resources. In many situations (a service desk is a good example), failure demand can often consume 50% of the team's capacity. By performing rapid, frequent problem analysis and prevention [using Lean techniques to enable the continual improvement of IT services, a foundation of IT infrastructure library practice (ITIL)], you can drive failure demand down, which increases capacity and improves customer service at the same time.

There are many other forms of waste to look for, and they're usually not hard to find: delays, redundancies, handoffs, searches for information, unnecessary variation, task switching, poor communication, inconclusive meetings, ineffective measurements, and so on. Who knows where this waste is? The people dealing with it every day. It doesn't take much effort to help frontline workers learn to see waste in their daily work, but it's usually more difficult for executives and senior managers because they're further away from the daily flow. That's why leadership and management often don't understand just how important it is to form the teams, map the flow, quantify the waste, find the root causes, and eliminate it patiently and methodically. Waste reduction is primarily a bottom-up activity, and leadership's role is to create the conditions in which this can happen (recall the Chapter 2 discussion of the three Ms).

According to David Almond, Lean transformation leader and former CIO for the State of Oregon:

> Many people look at Lean events as cost-benefit exercises. Our team was constantly asked to develop rigorous selection criteria for Lean projects so that only those with the biggest benefits were worked. The idea of tackling small efforts to build experience and develop Lean thinking was not understood. The line staff seemed to appreciate the experience and value of Lean more than management, because they could see the tremendous accumulative effect

that small, rapid waste reduction efforts would have, not just on productivity but also morale.[3]

Let's return to the basic premise of this book: focusing on what adds value to the customer helps everyone identify and eliminate waste from the routine run-the-business operations. Operational excellence frees up capacity: people, money, and other resources for growth, which in turn drives additional profits to fund innovation and transformation, which requires operational excellence to commercialize and monetize. Run-grow-transform is a self-sustaining cycle. And the cycle begins by eliminating the waste within the daily work that saps our energy, creativity, and enthusiasm.

Measuring Value the Lean Way

Lean practitioners have learned through decades of experience that traditional management accounting* practices, which intend to help guide business operations, can actually be harmful. Toyota's Taiichi Ohno once said, "It was not enough to chase out the cost accountants from the plants. The problem was to chase cost accounting from my people's minds." What did he mean?

Management accounting deals in financial abstractions while attempting to *control* daily operations, and it often confuses the important issues.[†] For example, charging enterprise-wide IT shared services and overhead costs to business operations continues to be one of the most frustrating challenges for IT professionals. Shared costs are pooled together, and arcane overhead allocation and chargeback calculations shift these costs from one profit and loss column to another, often leading to endless, and usually pointless, debates. It is usually impossible to tie these abstract cost allocations and the resulting variances back to the originating activities and the value they may or may not produce; thus, they can't help you improve. But they can waste your time and distract you from the activities that produce the desired outcomes. This is the irony of measurement-induced waste.

---

* We are not talking here about financial accounting, which addresses legal, tax, and regulatory requirements.
† I began my career as an accountant and have an appreciation for both the theory and practice of management accounting and the application of cost accounting in a production environment. So my criticism of management accounting is from an experienced, very pragmatic viewpoint.

Furthermore, when misguided measurement systems are a strong influence on behavior, workers and managers attempt to align outcomes with the numbers imposed, gaming the system to achieve short-term performance objectives and rewards rather than creating sustaining value for the customer.

In contrast, the discipline of Lean accounting is more operationally minded, focusing primarily on *individual value stream performance*— tracking relevant cash-basis financial and operational metrics and nonvalue activity that should be eliminated.*

An important element of Lean accounting is the "box score," which is described in Figure 6.1. The box score represents the value stream team's *current hypotheses* about cause and effect: what activities cause successful outcomes and how those activities can be measured and visually displayed to help the team reach their targets. Measures of these activities may become effective leading indicators for performance improvement, and so the box score is displayed on a wall in the work area,† becoming the centerpiece of the visual management system for each value stream.

IS ANYBODY WATCHING?

By an anonymous Lean IT coach

During a *kaizen* we reviewed our client auditing process. For this one particular client service automation product, it is critical that the reporting in the field offices reconcile with corporate operations. The standard process for all field offices, over fifty of them, included an extensive package preparation process: running reports, auditing the reports, sorting them, labeling them, and bundling them into a package that was then shipped overnight to corporate operations. The process was very thorough and time consuming; great care and caution were applied.

---

* To learn more, see *The Lean Business Management System: Lean Accounting Principles & Practices Toolkit* by Brian Maskell et al. (Cherry Hill, NJ: BMA Press, 2007).

† For example, the box score for an IT service desk (helpdesk) may include the following measures displayed in the work area: number of calls per day/shift, number of repeat calls, average call wait time, frequency and trend of most popular incidents, number of new problems identified, number of errors discovered in the knowledge base, customer satisfaction survey responses, etc. These are just suggestions; the team should select measures based on the problems they are experiencing and the areas in which they need to improve.

Both the preparers and the recipients attended the *kaizen* and worked together to map the full process. The preparation process was documented, but when corporate operations were asked what they did with the package they received, their answer was simple: *they threw it away.* They didn't use it at all.

It turned out that over the years the need for this package had been replaced by system access, file transfers, and other data management processes. Once the immediate frustration and incredulity subsided, the field offices were thrilled to no longer have to compile this package, saving them significant labor, material, and shipping costs. Steve Bell shared with us that this is a common discovery made by *kaizen* teams about unnecessary accounting activities, reporting, and audit controls.

	Lean	*Traditional*
Focus	Value stream performance against strategic targets.	Organization performance; departmental reports to compare annual budget to actual results.
Costing	"Real numbers"—direct costs summarized by value streams.	Allocated indirect and standard costs that absorb overhead.
Variance analysis	Comparing actual versus target activity to understand where the performance gaps are so they can be addressed.	Standard cost variance analysis that tries (unsuccessfully) to associate abstract allocations with actual activity to drive corrective action.
Profit drivers	Profit comes from optimizing flow and value to the customer; excess capacity provides flexibility.	Profit comes from full utilization of resources; excess capacity is waste (mass production thinking).
Transactions	Unnecessary transactions are wasteful.	Detailed transactions are often captured simply to drive cost allocation calculations.
Control	Processes are simple and visual so they are self-regulating.	External financial, operational, audit, and governance mechanisms attempt to "control" operations.
Accountability	Frontline workers establish cause/effect relationships and create measures that guide performance improvements toward targets.	Managers set numeric objectives and attempt to control performance through abstract financial and operating reports.
Performance reporting	Box score: single-page value stream summary showing relevant cash-basis financial and operational metrics, capacity utilization, and nonvalue activity to aid decision making.	Commonly financially oriented, based on cost accounting assumptons; these are difficult for nonaccountants to understand and of limited use in daily problem solving and prevention.

Figure 6.1 Comparing Lean and traditional accounting.

Measuring Value: The Customer's Point of View

The Lean-Agile software development community has moved from lengthy waterfall projects toward rapid iterations with an emphasis on speed and visibility, which encourage learning and improvement. Agile measures often focus on the mechanics of the development process. Common examples include reducing release cycle time, batch (story/release) size, the amount of work in process, the amount of integration and testing, the number of defects discovered, and the degree of engagement of all value stream stakeholders throughout the lifecycle. These are good *process* measures, but they do not ensure the desired outcome: value to the end customer.

The only way to ensure this outcome is to measure the end-customer benefits realized through each iteration; this is the CA of the PDCA cycle. Did it do what customers wanted it to do? Did it help them realize the value they anticipated? Did it help the team learn something new?

This is an essential point that Eric Ries stresses in *The Lean Startup*, explaining that measuring progress by the number of stories "delivered" can be misleading. Ries suggests measuring *validated learning*: "knowing whether the story was a good idea to have been done in the first place."[4] And how do you measure that? The development team is responsible for validating each story, measuring the outcome and confirming the benefit with the customer, *before moving on to the next story.** The backlog thus becomes a series of individual experiments—not a predetermined checklist. This is the scientific method applied in conditions of great uncertainty, where every next step is into the unknown.

In addition to measuring the outcomes of application development, it's also important to measure the performance of the operational systems the applications rely upon. In the past, measures of IT operations performance have usually been stated in technical and operational terms: response time, availability, applications supported, service outages, administrative headcount, and so on. While useful for managing daily IT operations, such measures are meaningless to business partners and end customers. In fact, their

---

* Ries suggests measuring each story, yet in a Scrum environment what is often measured is the outcome of each release, which is made up of several stories. However, this complicates measurement because there are several stories involved and thus multiple variables to consider. Scientists are careful to isolate their variables when they design experiments so they don't receive ambiguous results; with plan-do-check-act we should try to do the same. This is why continuous testing and integration of each individual work unit is important.

inappropriate emphasis may reinforce the suspicion that technologists don't understand what the business—and the end customer—really want: outcomes. These outcomes may include customer satisfaction, increased sales, improved customer retention, increased market share, increased percentage of sales represented by new products and services, reduced operating costs, and so on.

To define useful and meaningful measures, value stream business and technical colleagues must *together* learn how the various IT systems and services—and the applications upon which they run—contribute to desired business and end customer outcomes. However, associating IT-related activities with such end-of-pipe business outcomes is easier said than done. In fact, in May 2011, *CIO Magazine* declared the following:

> IT value is dead. Business outcomes are the real and only measure of IT worth. Yet shifting the focus from technology outcomes to business performance isn't easy. Calculating technology value using business terms is an evolving art. CIOs who attempt it readily admit that it involves some guesswork. So where to begin? Anywhere. Just get started.[5]

This prescription to "begin anywhere" isn't very specific, but it's certainly a call to action and experimentation. So where shall we start—and how? Let's follow the causal chain of activities and outcomes along the three primary value streams (introduced in Chapter 2) from the end customer all the way back to the underpinning technical services, as shown in Figure 6.2. In this illustration we'll suggest a variety of measures a team may consider, but it's essential for the team to select their own measures depending on the problems they are experiencing and the areas they need to focus improvement efforts upon.

Each of the three primary value streams delivers value to the end customer, helping to produce the ultimate business outcomes. Are they easy to define? Simple to measure? Clearly not. This is why it is essential for each value stream team to figure these measures out for themselves. This is the value stream journey, and it starts by understanding the flow of value from the customer's perspective.

Let's consider how the internal application support services (application ecosystem development, integration, maintenance, service desk, and professional advisory services; see Figure 3.1) serve the business customer. We're

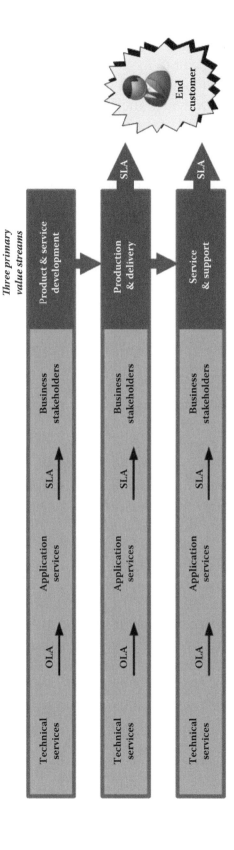

Three primary value streams

Box score examples *(for discussion purposes)*

Technical services

- OLA attainment
- End/business user downtime events caused by technical failure
- Frequency of problem-solving events
- Technical education and cross-training
- Release testing automation
- Asset utilization in production
- Technology product obsolescence
- Early COE involvement in new projects
- Ratio of planned/unplanned work
- Staff retention/churn in critical areas
- Security threats allowed/prevented

Application services

- SLA attainment
- Frequency of problem-solving events
- IT staff engmt in business process *kaizen*
- Application maintenance frequency
- Technical and process debt reduction
- Enhancement backlog size reduction
- Development WIP reduction
- Customer & ops testing involvement
- Cadence of ERP/COTS changes
- Staff retention/churn in critical areas
- Business customer productivity

Customer services

- Customer self-service app usage
- Service desk time and quality trends
- Service desk repeat call incidence
- Customer satisfaction feedback
- Consumer device app support
- Voice of customer analytics investment
- Increase % of sales from new products
- New product time to market
- Distribution channel efficiency
- Website and social network hits
- Lost sales trend
- Product return trend

Figure 6.2   Three primary value streams and cascading box scores.

once removed from the end customer,* so the activities and measures of value for the end customer are more indirect and difficult to measure, particularly if these application support services are shared among several value streams.

To help maintain focus let's ask the *purpose question.* The outcome measurements to the business customers may be in terms of speed, productivity, and quality. But how do these outcomes translate into providing more value to the end customer? How do we correlate faster order entry time or friendlier internal sales support systems with increasing sales and improving the experience and satisfaction of the end customer? The business and technical colleagues, working together as a value stream team, determine through experimentation how the internal application support services activities drive customer value. The team should then visualize this cause-and-effect relationship as a box score, helping them monitor and improve those activities over time.

Now let's take a step backward to the underpinning technical services that help the applications run so that the business can serve the end customer: infrastructure, system administration, connectivity, security, and so on. Some of these technical services may be performed internally, whereas others are performed by external service providers. Some of these services may be dedicated to a particular application or value stream, whereas many more are provided as IT services that are shared broadly across the enterprise.

Here the box score should measure operational activities that lead to improved quality, cost, standardization, consistency, reliability, and price/performance of these technical services—according to the ITIL framework these are the result of good IT service strategy and design. Service catalog offerings should be presented in terms that are meaningful to those consuming them, explaining how the offerings work, what they cost, how they are measured, and with a simple means for subscribing to them.†

When it comes time to make IT service consumption and investment decisions, who can determine whether a particular technology or application service is performing properly and delivering the right price performance to help serve the end customer? Is it a cost accountant at corporate headquarters, working through complex cost allocation spreadsheets? Is it a division manager, looking

---

* Exceptions to this include customer self-service applications, customer-facing transactional interfaces such as B2C, B2B, and electronic data interchange (EDI). Even in these cases the business customer often acts as a proxy for the end customer when defining requirements and testing, although the team should seek real end-customer input and interaction whenever possible.

† For good examples of service catalog presentation, visit the University of California Santa Cruz at http://its.ucsc.edu/services/index.html and the National Institutes of Health at http://www.cit.nih.gov/ServiceCatalog.

over the P&L, trying to meet quarterly financial objectives? No, they don't have the perspective to see value drivers; they can only see cost outcomes.

With a line of sight to the entire value stream, the team can understand cause and effect and thus eliminate unnecessary steps, redundant and disconnected systems, unnecessary handoffs, data errors, and other forms of waste. And because it has a relationship with the customer, the team can make informed prioritization decisions on what needs to be improved first to serve the customer while at the same time supporting enterprise strategic objectives.

STABILIZING THE CHANGE REQUEST PROCESS

Tom Knutilla

*Group Director of Applications Management
Ryder Systems, Inc.*

Ryder Systems, Inc. is a Fortune 500 provider of leading-edge transportation, logistics, and supply chain management solutions. The freight bill audit and payment (FBAP) team began its Lean IT journey in 2010. This was a combined effort of both the FBAP business and IT teams. The teams are co-located and work on most efforts in a joint, collaborative manner. After an initial "waste walk," the IT team chose the management of change requests (CRs) as the first area for improvement. The backlog was high, and the turnaround from request to delivery was more than a hundred days. Discussions with the affected business teams revealed several potential opportunities to reduce waste, including standardizing the initial evaluation and prioritization of CRs, reducing the number of end-runs around the formal CR process, and establishing better collaboration among business and technical colleagues on the team.

To correct these issues several activities were established:

■ More detailed change-request metrics were established and captured. Examples of metrics included actual cost to estimated cost, actual delivery date to estimated delivery date, average time to complete, average time from CR submission to acceptance, and quality rejection rate. From this data, targets were established and tracked. Targets were created based on a theoretical rate of improvement. Targets were periodically modified based on achievement and reasonableness.

■ A daily shift-start meeting was started to review progress from the previous day, establish targets for the next day, and identify any roadblocks. Shift-start meetings were organized around a visual presentation that contained tasks, accomplishments, and statistics on performance. Shift-start meetings improved communication and collaboration significantly. If issues were identified that involved other teams, they were invited to the shift-start meetings to discuss and resolve the issue.

■ A ticket process was established to address the informal work requests that came from the business team. These tickets were identified as assistance requests that did not require a programming change. Ticket examples included requests for explanations of system logic, data extracts, data correction, and training.

Ryder Systems, Inc. realized several measurable benefits from this pilot Lean IT initiative. One was labor savings [increased capacity] of more than $230,000 in one year for reducing the amount of time required to work on a change request. In addition, there was a reduction of turnaround time for a change request from more than one hundred days to approximately thirty days. This allowed the team to complete 110 more CRs in 2011 than were completed in 2010. Surprisingly, the improved responsiveness and reduced cost led to an increase in the volume of change requests from our customers.

The next step in the Lean IT journey is to roll out these practices to other IT teams. Additionally, a *kaizen* activity has been started whose goal is to reduce the number of tickets/assistance requests.

Real Value Is at *Gemba*

As useful as it can be, the Lean box score is still an abstraction: data and information arranged to portray reality maintained by those closest to the work and the customer. Although the box score is an important visual management tool, each team must intuitively grasp that reality is far richer and more complex than these abstractions can portray.

H. Thomas Johnson* first encountered Toyota management practices in 1987, and he spent the next ten years in intensive study at the invitation of Toyota president Fujio Cho. As one of the founding fathers of activity-based costing (ABC), Johnson eventually came to realize firsthand the harmful consequences of invasive management accounting systems and renounced his support for ABC. "I came to understand how [Toyota] designed its operations so that it *avoided the indirect or overhead activities* so prevalent in American business. Toyota had no use for management accounting and control systems to control, motivate, and assess operations."[6]

According to Johnson, "traditional" managers cause harm because they believe they can run operations mechanically by chasing financial objectives rather than by nurturing and improving the *underlying system of human relationships* from which such results emerge:

> You don't rely on secondhand reports or tables and charts of data to get true understanding of root cause. Instead you go to the place (*gemba*) where you can watch, observe, and ask *why?* five times. It shows a deep appreciation that results (and problems) ultimately emanate from and are explained by complex processes and concrete relationships, not by abstract quantitative relationships. In other words, all the information needed to control operations is in the work.[7]

Reality is only found at *gemba*, where the work is done, and the moment the box score becomes a greater focus than how the work is actually being done, who is doing it, and why, the abstraction begins to dominate the reality. I see this occasionally with overly zealous Lean teams that become enamored with elaborate visual management systems and lose sight of the purpose and the need to find the simplicity of the underlying flow of value.

The Lean management system must ensure that people are connected with their work (and the value created by it) in a very intimate and intuitive way. This leads to a fundamental truth of Lean thinking: *sustained outcomes*

---

* Over his long career H. Thomas Johnson has authored many books on this subject, including *Relevance Lost: the Rise and Fall of Management Accounting* (Boston: HBS Press, 1987; coauthored with Robert Kaplan) and *Profit beyond Measure* (New York: Free Press, 2000), which resulted from many years of research deep inside Toyota. He is the recipient of the Shingo Prize for his pioneering work on Lean accounting and the Deming Medal recognizing his contributions to the theory of managing for quality.

result from the informed decisions and actions of individuals and teams with a shared purpose. At first this seems so obvious, but do we truly grasp what we're saying here? If we really took this realization to heart, would it direct our effort and investment to the right places?

One tool that may help to shift from financial to value thinking is the balanced scorecard, which introduces four interdependent measurement dimensions that must be kept in balance for the enterprise to remain healthy. If any one of these aspect is weak, it leaves a flank exposed for a competitor to exploit:

1. Financial measures
2. Operational excellence measures
3. Customer satisfaction measures
4. People engagement, learning and innovation measures

But like all other measurement tools, this too has its limits. H. Thomas Johnson, whose early work with Robert Kaplan led, in part, to the development of the balanced scorecard, insists that if we're not careful, the balanced scorecard can actually reinforce this disconnect between measurement and the work itself because it is yet another abstraction that leadership and management often use not just to assess enterprise performance but to *control* it.[8] Brian Maskell, Lean accounting pioneer, agrees, saying, "I have found the balanced scorecard method often leads to too many measurements and too little continuous improvement."[9]

There is a danger of using a good measurement system in the wrong way, so we must be vigilant to avoid measuring for measurement's sake. Nevertheless, the balanced scorecard is my preferred abstraction because it counteracts the powerful and often exclusive focus on financial outcomes. Don't get me wrong. It's *essential* that we measure financial outcomes for a variety of valid reasons, and Lean can definitely move the needle on these outcomes: reducing costs, increasing revenue, profit, the percentage of revenue from new products, customers, regions, and so on. But it doesn't do that by focusing only on those financial outcomes; they're simply lagging indicators. Trying to run operations based upon them is like driving down the road while looking through the rearview mirror.

Lean drives positive outcomes by focusing on the *activities and behaviors* that produce them,[*] removing the obstacles that stand in their way. This is

---

[*] This is why the fishbone cause-and-effect diagram is such a useful problem-solving tool, because it helps a team determine those behaviors that produce and/or inhibit the results it is looking for.

what it really means to be a learning organization, understanding cause-and-effect relationships. This requires people who are able to watch and learn, paying special attention not to what goes according to plan but what *doesn't*. "Most of the time, things do not turn out as we expect," says Peter Senge. "But the potential value of unexpected developments is rarely tapped. Instead, when things turn out contrary to our expectations, we go immediately into problem-solving mode and react, or just try harder—without taking the time to see whether this unexpected development is telling us something important about our assumptions."[10]

Many enterprises on the Lean journey fall into their own trap, pursuing measures that have somehow lost their connection with how the work creates value for the customer. According to Jim Womack, teams often focus on questions such as the following:

> How many *kaizen* events have been done? How much has lead time been reduced? How much inventory [physical or virtual] has been eliminated? At best, they are performance measures for the Lean improvement function. What's really needed instead, are *purpose* measures for every value stream. These measures must be developed and widely shared by a responsible value stream manager and understood and supported by the entire value stream team.[11]

It all comes down to that really. Value is created at *gemba*, where the work is done, by those doing it.

Notes

1. Chris Murphy, "Innovation Atrophy," *InformationWeek*, May 30, 2011.
2. Paul Desmond, "Esselte Group Does More with Less by Embracing Lean IT," *ERP Executive*, August 16, 2011.
3. David Almond, interview, June 3, 2011.
4. Eric Ries, *The Lean Startup* (New York: Crown Business, 2011), 138.
5. Stephanie Overby, "IT Value Is Dead: Long Live Business Value," *CIO Magazine*, May 12, 2011.
6. H. Thomas Johnson, "Lean Accounting: To Become Lean, Shed Accounting," *Cost Management*, January/February 2006, 9.
7. H. Thomas Johnson, "Lean Dilemma: Choose System Principles or Management Accounting Controls—Not Both," in *Lean Accounting: Best Practices for Sustainable Integration*, Joe Stenzel, editor (Hoboken, NJ: John Wiley & Sons, Inc.), 7.

8. H. Thomas Johnson, interview, November 15, 2011.

9 Brian Maskell, interview, December 4, 2011.

10. Peter Senge, *The Fifth Discipline* (New York: Doubleday, 1990), 289.

11. Jim Womack, *Gemba Walks* (Lean Enterprise Institute, 2011), 8.

Chapter 7

Lean Leadership and the Lean Management System

Steve Bell

Leaders don't create followers; they create more leaders.

Tom Peters

WHAT YOU'LL LEARN IN THIS CHAPTER
- How Lean leaders guide the enterprise utilizing a Lean management system
- How a Lean management system utilizes an iterative, cascading, visual communication framework to do the following:
  - Provide teams with a clear vision of true north
  - Connect enterprise strategy with daily operations, projects, and improvement efforts
  - Equip everyone with near real-time information and communications, enabling rapid, adaptive, and informed decision making close to where the work is done
  - Foster teamwork, idea exchange, collaborative learning, and innovation

Long ago great thinkers, craftsmen, and laborers came together to build a grand cathedral. It would require generations to complete. As mathematicians, stonemasons, and other artisans worked around him, a man swept the floor. When asked what he was doing, the man replied, "I'm helping to build this grand cathedral." A similar story is often told about a man sweeping the floors at NASA, saying that he was "putting a man on the moon." Whether either story is true, or just a familiar parable, the meaning is clear.

One of the greatest differences between a Lean enterprise and a traditional one isn't how it is organized, or what tools are employed, but how it is led. Embodied in the Lean leadership philosophy is the conviction that cross-functional value stream teams with a shared purpose and respect for all perspectives and ideas can make great things happen. Together, they can build cathedrals. They can put a man on the moon.

Whether one is leading engineers, nurses, factory workers, or technologists, the core questions are universal: How can leaders engage the hearts and minds of everyone in the enterprise and facilitate alignment of a collective, coordinated effort toward a clear true north vision? Such alignment requires a skillful combination of *purpose, process, and people*[1] enabled by an effective management system.

The Role of Lean Leaders

According to Warren Bennis,* "Leaders are people who do the right thing; managers are people who do things right."[2] Senior leaders set direction, the true north of the enterprise; they're responsible for communicating and reinforcing this shared purpose (strategic intent) throughout the enterprise. Managers are responsible for execution and for guiding performance to support the strategy. But describing the roles of leadership and management in this way, it seems that these roles belong to different people, yet everyone can and should be a leader in every situation.

In the archetypal command-and-control management system, managers tell people what to do, reward them when they do it, and punish them when they don't. In the Lean approach, managers help teams understand the purpose and the strategic targets; then they help them achieve those targets by overcoming obstacles through a never-ending journey of experimentation, continuous improvement, and learning. The team owns the work, its outcomes, and the efforts to overcome the obstacles that stand in its way. The manager plays the role of coach,

---

* This quote is usually attributed to Peter Drucker. However, I located this original statement in Warren Bennis's 1994 book *An Invented Life: Reflections on Leadership and Change* (New York: Basic Books). This statement, and variations of it, appear in several of Bennis's subsequent publications.

facilitator, and coordinator across the vertical and horizontal dimensions of the enterprise.

The word *empowerment* is often used in association with Lean leadership, but it can be misinterpreted as suggesting an overly permissive approach. According to John Shook, who learned management practices at the New United Motor Manufacturing, Inc. (NUMMI) joint venture with Toyota and General Motors (GM) in the early 1980s (which in a very short time transformed GM's worst plant into one of their best):

> What changed the culture at NUMMI wasn't an abstract notion of 'employee involvement' or 'a learning organization' or even 'culture' at all. What changed the culture was *giving employees the means by which they could successfully do their jobs.* It was communicating very clearly to employees what their jobs were and providing the training and tools to enable them to perform those jobs successfully.[3]

As we discussed in Chapter 1 when exploring the topic of managing uncertainty, traditional leadership emphasizes "knowing"—those with a bold "follow me, I know what I'm doing" confidence are often rewarded. The problem, particularly in a complex and dynamic environment, is that leaders don't always fully understand the problem or know what changes are needed to most effectively resolve it. Indeed, according to Snowden, complex situations by their very definition are not knowable. In contrast, Lean leaders don't exert authority. They ask questions. They are "learners" rather than "knowers." They make space for the ideas from the workforce to emerge and evolve. In this climate, the enterprise utilizes the extensive collective knowledge and experience of those doing the actual work; everyone feels valued and respected, which leads to greater motivation and loyalty. It is this spirit of respectful and participatory leadership that enables the enterprise to leverage its greatest asset: its people. As Shook explains:

> Leadership and the management system need to facilitate a shift from debate about who owns what (authority) to a dialogue around what is the right thing to do [purpose]. As one of my bosses in Japan told me, "Avoid telling your staff exactly what to do." Whenever you do that, you take responsibility away from them.
>
> However, while good Toyota managers would rarely tell their people exactly what to do, it is equally true that they would never

say, "I don't care how you do it." We see this all the time: "You are 'empowered,' but you're on your own. If you are successful, good for you—your bonus will reflect it. If you are not successful—your lack of a bonus will reflect that, too." Contrast that with the Lean manager who says, "I care deeply to hear what you want to do, and how you want to do it." Avoidance of command and control does not have to mean laissez-faire abandonment.[4]

The transition to a Lean way of thinking can be a significant change, both for organizational cultures and for individual management styles. Such a transition should be expected to evolve gradually and unevenly; some will adapt more quickly and easily than others. It's up to each individual to engage in continuous self-reflection and to help peers observe their own behavior, coaching and encouraging each other as everyone develops new habits. It is through this self-awareness that everyone in a Lean enterprise learns to lead in a new and respectful way, as suggested by the personal reflections of Agile thought leader Alan Shalloway:

> Some people are natural managers. I am not one of them. Historically, I have always micromanaged. I knew that this behavior was inhibiting the team's growth, so I tried delegating—letting the team figure out how to do things on their own—often with very poor results. I was really abdicating via delegation. I needed to find a way to let the team figure out the solution but remain involved enough to ensure that it would be a good one.
>
> Fortunately, Lean management provides a way to do this. With visual controls, I can see the team's process—I can see how the team is doing at any time—and I can see the team's outcomes. If the team gets into trouble, I can actively coach them to improve their results without telling them what to do. Lean gives me a way to become a better manager without resorting to old habits.[5]

The Lean Management System

> An empowered organization is one in which individuals have the knowledge, skill, desire, and opportunity to personally succeed in a way that leads to collective organizational success.
>
> **Dr. Stephen R. Covey**

The Lean management system employs the principles of Lean in its design: elimination of waste, with an emphasis on simplicity, speed, visual management, and collaborative learning. Just as Lean emphasizes standardized work for frontline workers, it also encourages consistent and repeatable behavior of the management system itself. David Mann, organizational psychologist and author of *Creating a Lean Culture*, emphasizes the four basic elements of a Lean management system:

1. *Leader standard work* for consistent focus and behavior
2. *Visual controls* at the *gemba* so that everyone is in tune with process performance
3. *Daily accountability* with respect for everyone's time and contribution
4. *Discipline*—consistent behavior that reinforces good work habits and process stability, establishing a culture of quality and accountability[6]

Here are a few basic principles to remember about the Lean management system:

■ The value stream is the primary organizational unit that aligns resources and activities with purpose and delivers value to its customers.
■ Leadership clearly communicates purpose (strategic intent) and sets strategic targets, while managers help value stream teams achieve the targets, overcome obstacles, coordinate cross-functional behavior, and improve processes.
■ Leadership and managers emphasize systemic reduction of overburden (*muri*) and unnecessary variation (*mura*), whereas frontline workers reduce waste (*muda*).
■ Managers help to coordinate and synchronize the cadence of change across the enterprise.
■ Everyone makes the pace of work, workload, status, priorities, and problems visible.
■ Everyone continuously monitors operational and strategic targets and actual performance, searching for gaps, problems, and opportunities for improvement.
■ Interactions among all vertical and horizontal dimensions of the enterprise occur on a regular cadence to promote organizational learning and agility.

I like to describe the Lean management system as a "three-layer cake," as shown in Figure 7.1. Senior leadership communicates strategic intent and the underlying thought processes to management, who share this knowledge and insight with frontline workers, helping them to achieve strategic targets. Feedback from the daily work flows back through management to senior leadership, with lessons learned from the field (what is working, what appears not to work, what new situations they should know about), which leads to reflection and potential strategic course correction. This continuous macro plan-do-check-act (PDCA) cycle integrates strategy with daily action, and it requires standardized work and discipline from all participants if it is to work effectively.

In my experience, it's not difficult to inspire senior leaders to support a Lean transformation, although getting them to actually demonstrate (rather than just delegate) Lean behavior is often another matter. Leadership has the long view; senior leaders can see the strategic horizon and the opportunities and dangers lurking there (often called the "burning platform"), and they understand clearly the compelling need for transformation.

Often it's not difficult to get the frontline workers to be enthusiastic about the Lean journey because they are the ones who deal with the frustrating waste, variation, and overburden on a daily basis, and they hear the voice of the customer more clearly than anyone. Usually, all it takes are a few pilot *kaizen* events for a team to recognize the opportunity it has to own and

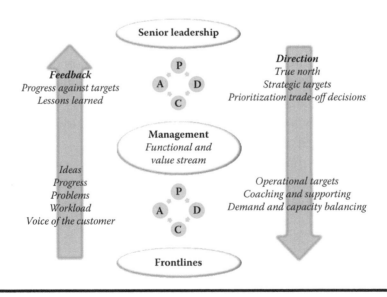

Figure 7.1 The three-layer cake.

improve its processes, and it becomes highly motivated and eager for more time and coaching to make more improvements.

But middle managers often present a serious challenge; they can easily derail the transformation before it gathers momentum. The mental model of what it means to be a manager changes dramatically: how they manage people, how they manage their functional area, how they interact with peers, how their performance is measured, and—in some cases—how they are rewarded. In a Lean enterprise, the purpose of the organization is realized through cross-functional value streams that are no longer focused on the performance of particular functions or departments. So the functional manager must now coordinate with several value stream managers and other functional managers whose people support cross-functional value streams in a matrix of responsibility, accountability, and collaboration to enable the flow of value. They must also "manage" people differently, shifting from control to coaching. To many traditional managers, these changes may feel disorienting and threatening. If the existing management, governance, performance measurement, and compensation frameworks are not changed, this will likely cause strong undercurrents of resistance.

Such resistance can be especially harmful because it may go unnoticed and lead to business as usual. All a manager must do to impede the transformation process is to hold the team accountable to its ordinary (prevalue stream) work goals and methods, supporting the Lean activity *only as long as* the team meets its monthly numbers, which are likely to conflict with desired value stream behavior. In other words, managers can throw a wrench into the Lean transformation *just by doing their job the way they've always done it.*

Issues of management roles and responsibilities are often given the least emphasis in the initial stages of a Lean transformation, when focus is on building momentum through localized improvements. But as the transformation begins to address broader cross-functional value streams, the conflict between functional and value stream management and accountability builds, creating confusion and friction. Only later, after significant resistance is encountered, is attention turned to management alignment, but by then, deep patterns of resistance and doubt may have set in. In my opinion, the delay in anticipating middle management-related obstacles is a primary reason that many transformation efforts ultimately fail.

The countermeasure is to get managers on board early, helping them to understand the nature of the value stream transformation: how their role, responsibility, and leadership style will change, and, most importantly, *why* it is important (purpose). This can be threatening for many who thrive on the traditional management role; the transition requires education, patience, courage, and trust. Senior leadership must work with managers (individually and collectively) to develop new ways to measure performance tied to value, serving as a role model for Lean leadership for everyone. In this way, senior leaders support the transformation journey by demonstrating commitment through their own actions, a willingness to challenge the status quo, and continuous experimentation with new approaches—always asking *why*.*

The Value Stream Manager

As we have learned throughout this book, the value stream plays an essential role in the Lean enterprise: it is the way value is delivered to the customer. So it follows that the role of value stream manager is very important and responsible for the overall flow of value across all organizational functions and departments.

It is easy to underestimate the scope of this role. According to Brian Maskell:

> Some make the mistake of thinking a value stream manager's job [is primarily an] operations function. A value stream manager is a business person with responsibility for the sales, delivery, and support of the company's products to the customer. The value stream manager—and the value stream team—have clear line of sight to the customers. This leads to a deeper, first-hand understanding of customer needs and responsibility to fulfill those needs better than any competitor.[7]

In *The Toyota Way*, Jeffrey Liker describes the role embodied in a particular individual—the chief engineer:

> Traditionally, the importance of a person at a company directly relates to how many departments or direct reports he or she has. Although thousands of Toyota associates work on a new vehicle program, the Chief Engineer (CE) has perhaps only a half-dozen people formally reporting to him. The CE controls the vehicle

---

* In *The Toyota Way to Lean Leadership* (New York: McGraw-Hill, 2012), Jeffrey Liker and Gary Convis describe in depth how Toyota continuously develops *every* employee's leadership skills through a commitment to lifetime learning and mentoring.

program and is responsible for the results, but not the people who work on the project. While it is an American adage that managers must have authority commensurate with their responsibility, the CE system works contrary to this belief and the role would be uncomfortable for most US managers.

This forces the person responsible, who has no formal authority, to defend his or her ideas, work through other people, and convince the person with formal authority that the ideas are correct. The only defense for taking action is to present the real facts of the situation to the formal authority.[8]

The role of value stream manager requires an individual with strong and respectful listening, problem-solving, and conflict-resolution skills. The key to effective value stream leadership, according to John Shook, is that "the responsible person or owner is not authorized to make decisions so much as made responsible to get the decision made."[9] Most of all, this role requires someone who makes a case based on facts and holds to a sense of conviction, but also demonstrates both receptiveness to new ideas and the humility to quickly admit he or she is wrong when proven so, shifting quickly and decisively to the new position and keeping the team focused on the next challenge.

Principal responsibilities of the value stream manager include the following:

- To ensure the right stakeholders are represented on the value stream team and that appropriate executive sponsors remain actively engaged
- To focus the value stream team members on customer value and keep them aligned with strategic direction and targets
- To facilitate the actions of the value stream team and ensure that the visual management system reflects daily reality, that the right things are being measured, and that the right problems are being attended to in a disciplined manner in alignment with strategy
- To attend regular team meetings, listen attentively, ask questions, and show respect
- To nurture an environment of respect, transparency, open communications, and management by fact
- To actively mentor individuals and to help them develop leadership and problem-solving skills (this also requires managers to actively engage in their own mentoring)
- To reach out to customers and to create opportunities for team members to visit *gemba* to engage with and observe their customers directly

■ To manage demand and balance with capacity, promoting conditions that will create a level schedule; to avoid spikes and dips in demand that cause the value stream team to be alternately overburdened and starved for work

■ To ensure that planned slack exists so that teams can (1) stop the daily work to swarm and solve a problem when it surfaces and (2) consistently invest in continuous improvement

■ To coordinate with other value stream managers to resolve shared resource and cross-functional issues

■ To help prepare and communicate the business case in relation to enterprise strategy for improvement initiatives

This last item often includes making a business case for IT consumption and investment. However, many business people feel anxiety or insecurity when facing such decisions; they may not have the experience or the understanding to make a confident, informed decision on technical issues. Nevertheless, value stream teams must take more responsibility for learning, understanding, and guiding fundamental IT capabilities to achieve business objectives. The *Wall Street Journal* article "Put IT Where It Belongs" suggests the following:

> Business units and their teams become responsible for satisfying their day-to-day needs on their own. IT shifts to more of a support role. It empowers business unit self-sufficiency by providing education, coaching, tools and rules, which allow for individuals to meet their needs in a way that protects the overall needs of the enterprise—for example, ensuring accurate and safe data, integrating business processes, and promoting collaboration. The trick is getting from here to there, to move from a world where IT is delivered *to* the business to one where IT is delivered *through* the business.[10]

To accomplish this, the value stream manager looks to the technologists on the team as well as to center of excellence (COE) advisors to offer guidance and education on technology-related matters of importance to the value stream. Over time, the team will develop basic proficiency and self-sufficiency on IT issues related to its common activities. With this transition, IT capabilities become part of, and are delivered *through*, the value stream.

When viewed like this, it's clear how vital this role of value stream manager is in overseeing and being accountable for the value stream, yet in practice I don't see the formal role of value stream manager as often as I expect. Not investing in the creation and support of value stream managers may be a root cause of why so many enterprises fail to achieve a sustained transformation. If you don't have someone responsible for its performance—monitoring, guiding, coaching, coordinating—the value stream is not going to get the attention required to realize its potential.

The development of the value stream manager role can be especially difficult in a highly verticalized (siloed) enterprise where the culture may actively resist the new role. If you're not careful, in such a situation the value stream manager role may become just another dimension, a perceived silo that can complicate rather than simplify matters.

Developing this role is an experiment like everything else in the Lean transformation. As enterprises begin sorting out the many fractal relationships among core and supporting value streams, I usually suggest that they choose one or two core value streams and experiment with the role.* Start slowly, make sure functional managers understand the purpose and nature of the experiment, and learn together.

Everyone Knows Everything

One of the most significant challenges of Lean leadership is effective communication and coordination of the many core and fractal value streams as they adapt to changing conditions. In their influential 1999 *Harvard Business Journal* article, Steven Spears and Kent Bowen refer to the *DNA* of Toyota. In a subsequent *Harvard Business Journal* interview on Toyota's approach to leadership and decision making, Spears states:

> [O]rganizations must have some mechanism for decomposing the whole system into sub-system and component parts, each "cognitively" small or simple enough for individual people to do meaningful work. However, decomposing the complex whole into simpler parts is only part of the challenge. The decomposition must

---

* This approach is often called a *model line*, where an end-to-end value stream is used as an ongoing prototype for experimentation and learning to lead the rest of the enterprise along. For a comprehensive description of this approach, see *Leading the Lean Enterprise Transformation* by George Koenigsaecker (New York: Productivity Press, 2009).

occur in concert with complementary mechanisms that reintegrate the parts into a meaningful, harmonious whole.[11]

The Lean management system establishes a framework to integrate the various functions and value streams together through *operations, projects,* and *improvement activities.* The interrelationships among layers of leadership and management and among strategy, organizational functions, and value streams can be complex. To connect all the levels (vertically and horizontally) in a regular cadence of back-and-forth communication creates an iterative communications process called *catchball.* It's a simple version of a neural network, where the ideas from the customer-facing processes cascade regularly and frequently through management to the executive level and laterally across the value streams, functions, divisions, etc. In response, strategic direction, performance targets, and improvement guidance feeds back to the process level.*

Catchball is a back-and-forth discussion and collaborative learning process, a set of continuous, interlocking PDCA feedback loops or "connected checking" both vertically and horizontally, where senior leadership, management, and frontline workers together discover how to achieve their goals while overcoming obstacles that stand in their way.

According to Thomas L. Jackson in *Hoshin Kanri for the Lean Enterprise*, leadership first proposes a set of strategic targets. "The chartered teams then respond by stating *how* they intend to hit those targets." This pattern of interaction is repeated at every level of the enterprise; leaders set targets and encourage their managers and teams to develop an approach to meeting those targets. "Catchball gets people invested in strategic intent, which motivates them to achieve the set of targets that you want, rather than merely stating the targets and then punishing teams if they fall short."[12]

Another important element of communication within the Lean management system is the practice of visual management at every level of the enterprise. Teams manage their daily activities and value stream flow visually, while each level of management rolls up the view to a higher level to see the systemic conditions and larger trends. This often culminates in a large

---

* "From my experience working with executive teams I typically find a significant imbalance of (human) resources required to execute all planned projects vs. resources actually available. There has to be a high level of trust in the enterprise, otherwise one is considered to be disloyal or 'not a team player' to admit one doesn't have the resources to do one more project so we heroically take it on, which perpetuates overburden (*muri*)." —Dr. Michael Rowney

room (which Toyota calls an *obeya*) where leadership meets on a regular basis to monitor operations, projects, and strategy deployment. An *obeya* is a manifestation of the entire multitiered PDCA process visually displayed within a single room. This is a highly interactive space, where leaders and managers are encouraged to meet whenever an issue must be discussed, which eliminates the communication gaps and delays that usually slow down problem solving and decision making. In an *obeya* room, or other highly visual environment, participants physically interact with the artifacts and each other, attaching sticky notes to displays, contributing to issues lists, writing questions on charts, having spontaneous whiteboard discussions, and so on. Such an integrated, holistic, full-body experience helps participants to cognitively engage visually, audibly, and tactilely, intuitively grasping the situation, stimulating discussions and ideas, and accelerating problem solving and decision making.

Consider the weekly management cadence found in the executive offices of Ford Motor Company, where in recent years CEO Alan Mulally has led the company on a dramatic turnaround. Mulally meets with his 15 top executives for 2½ hours every Thursday at 7 am. The heart of Mulally's data operation is located near his office. The walls are covered with color-coded tables, bar charts, and line graphs. They represent what's going on in every corner of Ford's operation—China, Russia, South America, Ford Motor Credit, and so forth.[13] He requires his direct reports to post more than 300 charts, each of them color-coded red, yellow, or green to indicate problems, caution, or progress. He is known for applauding those who candidly bring him bad news; the faster issues are uncovered, the more proactively they can be addressed. Mulally praises the system, saying, "You can't manage a secret. When you do this every week, you can't hide."[14]

This approach of visual management may be utilized at every level throughout the enterprise, supporting not only senior leaders but also managers and frontline workers. As this management system framework builds out, senior leadership and managers must make a deliberate effort to encourage communication and decision making as close to the work as possible. As we mentioned in Chapter 5, Jim Womack insists, "The Lean manager realizes that no manager at a higher level can or should solve a problem at a lower level; problems can only be solved where they live, by those living with them."[15] There is no one-size-fits-all approach to creating such a framework; it must grow organically, depending on the enterprise structure, operating model, and culture.

When starting out on the Lean transformation, many fear that such interlocking, cascading catchball sessions will create an endless death march of meetings. This is only natural because often people have become frustrated with endless, useless meetings that accomplish little. When practiced in a simple, disciplined manner, the Lean management system becomes self-organizing and self-directing. "As work habits change, meetings become short, regular, vital and productive," insists Toshio Horikiri, former CEO of Toyota Engineering Corporation. "They have a rapid, exciting cadence. Before each meeting, project members update all charts and action items. Agendas are very detailed and pertinent, with strict control over time. Individual accountability includes a weekly report of the current situation, and as issues are raised, the meeting generates clear decisions and agreements. Cutting waste from meeting time is a relief to everyone."[16]

The idea of "meeting waste" itself is a curious one. Most will agree that many meetings are wasteful—their purpose is not clear, they are not supported by facts, they are not well facilitated, they revisit the same topics again and again, and they often attempt to make decisions without clear decision rights or rules. Clearly there is much that Lean thinking can bring to the improvement of meeting efficiency and effectiveness.

But let's reconsider the notion of wasteful meetings from another perspective. In the *Harvard Business Review* article "The Contradictions That Drive Toyota's Success," authors Takeuchi, Osono, and Shimizu observe:

> Toyota's operations are efficient, but it uses employees' time in seemingly wasteful ways. You would be amazed to see how many people attend a meeting at Toyota even though most of them don't participate in the discussions. The company assigns many more employees to offices in the field than rivals do, and its senior executives spend an inordinate amount of time visiting dealers. When making presentations, they summarize...on a single sheet of paper. Toyota insists internal communications be simple, yet it builds complex social networks. Communication is viral and knowledge is diffused in all directions. Toyota fosters a complex web of social networks because it wants "everybody to know everything."[17]

There is clearly something going on here that contradicts our traditional notion of "efficiency." Recall our earlier explorations of the productive and creative forces of Lean. There are certainly productive aspects of the Lean management system: rapid cadence, short meetings, and tightly focused agendas. But the Lean management system must also be creative, emphasizing enterprise-wide communication, innovation, and collaborative learning.

Not only does this knowledge spread vertically throughout the tiers of management, it also spreads horizontally, which is represented by the Japanese word *yokoten*. According to Jim Womack,

> [t]he trick to *yokoten* is to be sure that someone is responsible for accumulating the knowledge where it has been developed. (The A3 reports prepared for Lean implementation can be an excellent resource.) In addition, the person responsible for accumulating the knowledge must be available to help share it with others in the organization with a need. At the same time, managers elsewhere in the organization must understand that most learning occurs horizontally (whatever those at the top of the organization may think) and that they need to "go see" and "ask why." Direct observation on the *gemba* is always the best way to learn.[18]

In traditional models, many senior leaders and managers spend most of their time troubleshooting and engaged in reactive behavior. But when a Lean management system takes hold, with an emphasis on process improvement, the environment stabilizes, and everyone can invest more time in proactive behavior. In *The Toyota Management System in the Executive Office*, authors Tanaka, Horikiri, and Flynn explain the value of such leader standard work:

> By visualizing their work and taking immediate countermeasures, executives can increase the proportion of improvement activity. More time comes free for improvement as the daily work is made smoother and more routine. Troubleshooting is reduced by creating new work routines. This enables more than 50% of the executive's time to be devoted to improvement.[19]

Lean leadership and management are social activities; they emphasize interaction and shared learning. With the focus on process improvement, an entire organization may become stabilized and visualized over time so that everyone can focus on the "vital few" things that require immediate attention.* This is how a "fractal" management system—comprised of simple, interrelated patterns of communication and decision making across many dimensions—develops into what Spears refers to as "the mechanisms that reintegrate the parts into a meaningful, harmonious whole."[20]

In this way, the Lean management system acts as a quasi-organic structure of synaptic pathways, providing senior leaders, managers, and teams with the ability to quickly sense and respond to changes and to align all activities with strategy. When this management system is working effectively, teams and individuals at the lowest level of the organizational hierarchy should be able to clearly relate how their daily actions support the strategic goals of the enterprise—hence the popular metaphor of the person sweeping the floor who sees himself as a vital part of sending a man to the moon.

THE POWER OF SELF-DIRECTING TEAMS

My first encounter with a self-directing team occurred in a factory in the mid-1980s. This plant ran continuously in three shifts. During each shift, the outbound and inbound teams in each work cell would gather for a brief session to discuss the following questions: What did they achieve on the last shift? What problems did they encounter, and what was being done about them? Was there anything unusual expected to happen during the coming shift that they should know about and prepare for? And what were the targets for the coming shift, and how could they meet them? In less than half an hour, three times a day, shifts would transfer knowledge and maintain continuity. (Little did I know then that I had witnessed my first *stand-up meeting.*) This bears a close resemblance to shift change meetings in hospitals, where the value stream (care of the patient) requires a very high degree of continuity and coordination.

But the most powerful story I've ever heard about self-directing teams comes from Jeffrey Liker, relating Toyota leadership's swift response to the devastating 2011 earthquake and Tsunami in northern Japan:

---

* As senior leaders and managers emphasize "go see" behavior, this may actually mean attending more, not fewer, meetings. They are, after all, where their teams are often solving problems and making decisions. The emphasis on meeting waste reduction thus shifts to improving meeting quality rather than reducing meeting quantity.

The general managers actually run operations, and those above are managing the general managers and making more strategic decisions, going around checking and coaching. On the day of the earthquake Akio Toyoda called together all of the general managers in Japan in a room and said, in essence: You need to solve this. I cannot from my position. You are on the ground running the actual operations. This will require rapid decision making and action. So I am going to ask that you do not report anything you are doing upward to the executive level. You have to make the decisions together. Reporting up will be a distraction. I only have three requests. You focus in this order of priority: (1) help our team members and those in the supplier plants who were affected by the disaster, (2) help people in the community, and (3) get the plants running and parts flowing.

This general manager was shocked. Never in his thirty years with Toyota had a president asked them not to report upward, which they usually do constantly. He said that Akio Toyoda met with each board member to explain that the general managers would not be reporting on their work and they should not ask for reports. Instead he said there was a big meeting room (*obeya*) and they could go down and see it at any time and listen to the discussions but not disrupt the process. That same day the team sent tankers of water, supplies from a company run store, and a team of engineers up north to assess the situation [Genchi Genbutsu—"go and see"].[22]

Self-Directing Teams

social (*adj.*): tending to form cooperative and interdependent relationships with others

Merriam-Webster's Dictionary

Throughout this book one theme that has appeared consistently is that cross-functional teams must own value stream performance. While this sounds like a noble ambition, the proof is in the execution: how teams interact on a daily basis; how they maintain a line of sight to customer value; how they plan their work, manage their priorities, measure their results, and address their problems. To be effective at self-directing, teams must be guided by clear communication with leadership, with interrelated value stream teams, and with each other.

The four elements of the Lean management system—leader standard work, visual controls, daily accountability, and discipline—are enacted as a cadence of meetings that cascade throughout the organization. The foundation of catchball is the daily meetings of teams engaged in the daily work.

These daily catchball sessions are often called *stand-up* meetings, or huddles, because they are short, focused, and energetic. Daily stand-ups are indeed often conducted standing in front of visual management displays, with all team members *actively* participating, writing on sticky notes and applying them to the boards. Stand-ups are primarily for team synchronization and thus are intentionally kept short, usually no more than thirty minutes (and often much less). Weekly or monthly meetings that cover a broader scope should be no less focused, but they're typically longer in duration, and usually people are sitting down.

Let's explore the basic approach to this communication framework, but understand that these are not prescriptive guidelines to be copied; they are merely suggestions for an approach that each enterprise must adapt to its individual organization structure, operating model, and culture.

Daily Frontline (Stand-Up) Meetings

Each team focuses on what is important to maintain the flow of work. Operational teams may focus on measures of stability, quality, and rate of throughput, whereas project/product teams may focus on learning cycles and customer interactions. In addition to scheduled daily meetings, the team may swarm and solve a sudden problem at any time.

A typical daily stand-up creates a space for each individual on the team to quickly understand what the teams goals are for the day and how his or her work aligns with them. The meetings occur at the team's visual management area. Whenever possible, the team should use manual (noncomputerized) visual techniques to communicate the work. There is something cognitively different about a physical display in a work area compared with reviewing data on a computer. Individuals are asked to write on a whiteboard or move a sticky note on a *kanban* board when a task is complete, a question arises, or a problem occurs; the physical act of getting up, picking up a pen, and writing on the board creates an opening for reflection, for the individual to look around thoughtfully and ask, "Why did this happen?" When someone puts up a new color-coded sticky note, the team is naturally drawn to the visual.

The visual display contains key performance measurements (box score), work in process, new opportunities, problems, and the team's issues list. It's a visual display of what the team should focus on *now* (for example, a sudden change of priority or a serious problem) as well as measurements to let the team know if it's on track or heading in the wrong direction.

This visual display helps the team intuitively understand the work and workflow and immediately spot deviations and problems when they arise. This serves as the focal point for the agenda. When everyone comes together, everyone can see and learn what's happening, and this informs the focus for that day.

While standing in that visual field all team members quickly communicate the following:

∎ What was accomplished yesterday
∎ What they hope to accomplish today
∎ What obstacles they are facing

If a new problem is identified, those involved take it offline for analysis, or if it does not need to be solved immediately, it can be recorded on the issues list (Chapter 5) for later consideration. And if a new priority is identified, the team as a whole becomes aware of it and adjusts its daily work accordingly.

The manager may attend—but does not run—the meeting; the role of the manager is to monitor the situation, ask questions, and provide support when needed. Many enterprises rotate the stand-up meeting leader assignment to ensure every team member takes a turn facilitating the group. Often a second person is assigned to keep time. Rotating the leader role helps keep the pace fast and the meetings fresh; it also cultivates stronger team bonds and leadership.

Ideally, the team is physically located together and able to gather for daily stand-ups. However, many enterprises are geographically dispersed; those working on different continents, or even different buildings, may not have line of sight to the entire value stream. So it may be necessary to create an online visual management and team collaboration environment that is *both* physical and virtual. But the important point is to focus teams on the product and the process, not the technology tools.

Weekly Frontline Meetings

Here, each team goes more deeply into challenges and problem solving. Managers generally attend this session, but it's their job to listen and ask questions (go see, ask why, show respect). They are also there to answer questions and to escalate issues as needed either laterally to other functions or teams or up the management hierarchy. They also work to ensure that the team is moving in the direction of strategic alignment and in support of company policies. Weekly meetings are often visited by managers and members from other teams to learn and cross-pollinate ideas.

The questions the team asks may include the following:

■ Where are we now?
■ Where do we want to be?
■ What obstacles are keeping us from getting there? Are there new issues to be recorded in the parking lot? Do existing issues need to be assigned a higher priority?
■ What experiments shall we try next to test our understanding of how to overcome these obstacles?
■ What are our targets for this experiment so that we can measure the results against our hypotheses?
■ What did we learn from the last PDCA cycle that we can apply to the next?
■ How do we share what we've learned with other teams across the enterprise?

The emphasis on visual management for the weekly frontline meeting is upon tracking targets versus actual operations performance, progress on product, project and improvement efforts, and review of the issues list.*

Weekly Manager Meetings

Value stream managers take what they have learned from attending daily and weekly frontline team meetings and review target and actual performance of overall operations, projects, and *kaizen* to address issues requiring

---

* If you are familiar with the practice of Scrum then you may notice the similarities described here; Scrum is a Lean project and workload management methodology that is not limited to just software development. According to Jeff Sutherland, cocreator of Scrum, "Most of the team dynamics, the role of leadership, and the dilemma of middle management you write about in this book sound exactly the same as in a Scrum transformation. There is very fertile ground here for creating value by linking Agile/Scrum and Lean more explicitly so that companies don't think that they need to choose one or the other."[21]

cross-functional problem solving or coordination; they also monitor demand and capacity balancing within and across value streams. They may ask questions such as the following:

- Are team priorities clear and aligned with strategy?
- Are we experiencing communication problems?
- Are our metrics the right ones? Are we confident in the data? Are we getting the right signals?
- Is there unnecessary variation in the work content or flow?
- Do teams have a level demand? Do we have any sudden disruptions to our planned demand and supply that need to be addressed?
- Do we have the right skills on the teams?
- Do we need to coordinate cross-functional activities or projects that span multiple teams?
- Do we have any overloaded resources? If so, why? (Management needs to perform an honest and transparent root cause analysis here.)
- Are there any new or existing items on the issues list that require our immediate attention?

Weekly Executive Catchball Meetings

The interfaces between value stream management teams and senior leadership depend on the organizational structure. The enterprise should strive for simplicity, keeping the number of layers and interfaces to a minimum, because the goal is rapid catchball communication that fans out across the entire enterprise. A standardized agenda at the executive level is used to ensure that the meeting focuses only on specific strategic targets, trends, and exceptions that require executive visibility and "a vital few" issues escalated for a decision. Visual management should focus on consolidated views, using dashboards and scorecards, with the ability to drill down to lower levels of detail as needed.

Aligning Strategy with Action

There will always be more opportunities for improvement than there are time and resources to pursue them. So senior leadership must establish a process for prioritizing improvement efforts to align with enterprise goals and strategies. However, the Lean transformation usually starts in a more opportunistic fashion, focusing on specific areas of waste rather than on the overall value stream flow and its alignment with strategy. Most often it begins with great enthusiasm, a supportive executive sponsor, an eager team, and a series of *kaizen* pilots chosen because of the likelihood of early and visible benefits.

As success stories and lessons learned are shared and interest in Lean grows, other parts of the enterprise create a pull for more improvement activity. As momentum builds, it's important to attach a steering wheel to this vehicle; otherwise it can become counterproductive if the *kaizen* continues to be focused on local optimization and not overall value stream performance. In *Lean Thinking*, Jim Womack and Dan Jones describe these as

> Kamikaze Kaizen, [with] lots of commotion, many isolated victories…widespread initial enthusiasm on the basis of early results, impressive amounts of consciousness raising, and…loss of the war when no sustainable benefits reached the customer or the bottom line. The solution [requires] looking at the big picture, including the most important business needs, and determining the overall plan of march before conducting process kaizen on the individual steps.[23]

Developing such an overall plan, guiding deliberate change within the complex fractal value stream architecture of an enterprise, is not an easy undertaking. But it is necessary if the transformation is to be self-directing and sustaining. *Strategy deployment* helps guide improvement efforts toward strategic goals. Known by other names such as *Hoshin Kanri* and *policy deployment*, strategy deployment defines a vital few *breakthrough* strategic change efforts and sets improvement targets that cascade throughout the fractal enterprise.

Organizational efforts to address significant weaknesses and exploit strategic opportunities are translated into a limited number (usually just three to five) of *strategic themes*. Examples of strategic themes may include faster delivery time, increased customer referrals, or environmental sustainability. A *strategy theme team* is assembled that is made up of individuals chosen from several value streams who are collectively responsible for developing and promoting the improvement targets for that particular theme. Each theme team assesses the current state of the enterprise related to that theme, sets improvement targets, formulates an action plan, and then meets with value stream managers and teams across the enterprise, translating enterprise-wide strategic theme targets into localized value stream improvement targets. On a regular cadence, each value stream team then compares actual performance with its strategic targets, adjusting improvement efforts accordingly.

For example, an enterprise may determine that it is losing customers because of poor customer service speed and quality. So a customer service improvement strategy theme team is formed. The team conducts a current state assessment and, using a *strategy A3* process,* identifies enterprise-wide future state targets and potential countermeasures to get there. Theme team members then meet with individual value stream managers and their teams,† helping them develop their own strategy A3s that align with and support the overall enterprise strategy for customer-service improvement, engaging in their own root cause analysis and countermeasure development. In this way, the enterprise is synchronously directing itself through catchball, team by team, experiment by experiment, flying in formation toward shared strategic objectives.

Strategy deployment also provides each team with guidance to help it prioritize and select among the many problems and opportunities it has identified. Each value stream team periodically plays catchball with representatives from the strategy theme team to review performance and gather input and lessons learned. The strategy theme team then compares the feedback from all value stream teams and interacts with senior leadership to explore the progress and challenges relating to their improvement efforts and to understand the realities in the field, which in turn enables leaders to make adjustments to the strategy or resource allocation in light of what they have learned.

It should come as no surprise that technical colleagues play a vital role in the attainment of strategic improvement targets. Consider Southwest Airlines, where leadership created seven strategy teams. These strategy teams, with names like Low-Cost Carrier, Best Place to Work, and Best Customer Experience, meet twice a month to define enterprise priorities for

---

* The strategy A3 differs from the more familiar problem-solving A3; it focuses on strategic problems and opportunities and charts a course of experimentation that cascades throughout the enterprise. The interrelationships between the strategy and the problem-solving A3s are often visualized with a tool called an X-Matrix. The strategy deployment process is illustrated through story in *Getting the Right Things Done* (Cambridge, MA: Lean Enterprises Institute, Inc., 2007) by Pascal Dennis. To download strategy and problem-solving A3 form templates visit http://www.lean.org.

† In most cases a strategy theme team won't meet with every core and supporting value stream team but rather will focus on those whose activities relate to the theme. This is where capability mapping (see Chapter 3) may be helpful to identify which individual value streams support a chosen strategic theme.

implementing the strategy. Approximately 80% of Southwest's technology projects are aligned with one of the strategy teams.[24] Southwest recognizes that IT capabilities play an important role in meeting each of these goals. In today's IT-enabled marketplace, most enterprise strategies will require IT involvement and vision. So each strategy theme team should include a technologist with knowledge of the organization's technology architecture and strategy.

STRATEGY DEPLOYMENT IN ACTION

Bruno Guicardi

Chief operating officer and cofounder
Ci&T

Sixteen years after Ci&T, our software development company based in Campinas, Brazil, was founded by three college friends, we have grown to more than 1,500 employees. For five years now we have been among the top one hundred best companies to work for in Brazil, selecting the best and brightest students who come from our many technical colleges. We now have offices and customers around the globe. Our experience applying Lean practices and our value engineering-driven Lean software development approach (see Appendix C) have helped to grow our business.

As we prepared for the next stage in our growth and evolution, we decided to apply Lean thinking to our strategic planning and management process. So we called the Lean Institute Brazil and asked for their help. I said to their senior consultant, Flávio Picchi, "We're having a two-day strategic planning session in a few weeks, and we're bringing our eleven directors in from around the world. As we have done before, we will formulate a plan for the year and document the plan, and our directors will share it with their managers, who will share it with their teams. We'd like your help formulating this plan."

"It doesn't work that way," said Flávio. "In order to produce a meaningful strategy, you need to engage more than just your directors in the learning process. And you need more time...a lot more time. Before you decide what you need to do to achieve your goals, you must understand where you are now and the obstacles to achieving your goals. This is a learning process, not a weekend event."

"Ahh, he's talking about the A3 problem-solving process," I thought to myself. That makes perfect sense. "But we don't have time for that," I said. "Then I can't help you," said Flávio.

That was two years ago. Needless to say, we asked for Flávio's help and agreed to his conditions. In the past, our eleven directors would present the "weekend plan" to our managers and their teams, and they would follow it on trust because they didn't understand the thinking process behind the plan. Our new strategic planning process has engaged our directors and managers in the strategic intent behind the plan, which has led to the development of a clear understanding of the targets and obstacles we're trying to overcome—working together as a complete organization.

We scheduled six weeks for the initial planning process and anticipated spending three weeks on the left side of the strategy A3 (problem analysis) and three weeks on the right (action plan). We began by defining our true north, understanding the current condition, gathering data, doing root cause analysis on the most critical gaps, and defining our vision for the future. Because we are all engineers, there was a temptation to jump quickly to a solution for every problem. Flávio helped to discipline us, keeping us focused on understanding the problems. In our root cause analysis, we used fishbone diagramming, and often we had to go three or four levels down before we finally came to the root causes because they were buried deeply within our behaviors, thought processes, and management systems.

In the end, we completed the initial plan in six weeks of hard work and profound discovery. But the problem analysis consumed five of those weeks. Once we reached consensus on the problems, the plan came out easily and naturally in the final week. We gradually started to change our culture of decision making and planning toward a more data-centric one. Since that first planning session, the top management has made many discoveries about the business. We have found that our most profitable line of business had a much greater potential for growth than everyone in the sales frontlines believed. We have also discovered many opportunities for waste reduction among our development centers.

While it looks easy on paper, strategy deployment is a tremendous change effort, and it takes years to get it really incorporated into the culture. We have run the annual cycle twice now, and as we cascade the strategy A3s to every business area, we have all managers involved in the process and producing their own A3s. In this second round we have already increased the number of managers (to a total of thirty-five) and involve them earlier in the process, which results in even more profound analysis and quality plans.

We have learned many important lessons so far, such as the importance of "CA" in PDCA. Although the CA lacks the "coolness" of the P, managers need to be focused and fully supported by the senior management to thoroughly analyze the situation. In addition, catchball needs to be carefully structured in terms of the frequency and synchronization with lower-level PDCA cycles, and as often as possible executives and managers need to go on *gemba* walks rather than sitting through endless PowerPoint presentations.

We are aware that we have a long road ahead; there is still much to improve. However, we are very optimistic—we have already achieved important results, and we have a new appreciation for PDCA discipline at the strategic level.

The Lean Management System as a Neural Network

"Survival learning," or what is more often termed "adaptive learning" is important—indeed it is necessary. But for a learning organization, adaptive learning must be joined by "generative learning," learning that enhances our capacity to create.

Peter Senge
The Fifth Discipline

In this chapter I have referred to the linkages of the Lean management system as synapses within a neural network. Is there more to this notion than merely a curious metaphor? Consider how learning occurs in the human being. The brain has a remarkable characteristic called *plasticity*: the ability to quickly adapt and learn by physically restructuring itself. Information is communicated to and from the brain through decentralized networks of synaptic pathways. These pathways are coated with a chemical substance called myelin, which increases the speed of transmission. The brain signals the building of more myelin for the pathways used most. This is how skill—both physical and mental—is deliberately created; the brain is self-organizing, continuously optimizing its own performance based on how it's being used.

Does this sound familiar? Pathways are established to communicate information, reinforcing those utilized most often to optimize a specific purpose.

As Daniel Coyle describes in *The Talent Code*, great performers—athletes, musicians, and professionals across many disciplines—have demonstrated that they can achieve deliberate, sustained breakthrough performance by reinforcing these learning pathways with iterative practice (PDCA). By concentrating on specific problems, such as a difficult passage of music or a physically challenging golf swing or tennis stroke, and practicing it over and over and over, the individual is unknowingly building myelin pathways, which make it faster and easier for the brain to signal execution of the refined action in the future.[25] This is how habits are formed and skill is deliberately created.

This is how enterprises can become great performers too—through disciplined and repetitive *practice* of the most difficult tasks. As everyone in the organization adopts the Lean management system as daily practice, it becomes habitual and, eventually, part of the culture. The entire organization stabilizes and shifts from reactive to proactive behavior. This is what Lean practitioners mean when they use the word *transformation*.

Notes

1. John Shook, "Purpose, Process, People," http://www.lean.org/shook/DisplayObject.cfm?o=899, March 30, 2009.
2. Warren Bennis, *An Invented Life: Reflections on Leadership and Change* (New York: Basic Books), 1994, 78.
3. John Shook, "How to Change a Culture: Lessons From NUMMI," *MIT Sloan Management Review*, Winter 2010, 68.
4. John Shook, "We're All Connected and Nobody Is in Charge," http://www.lean.org/shook/DisplayObject.cfm?o=907, January 26, 2009.
5. Alan Shalloway, Guy Beaver, and James R. Trott, *Lean-Agile Software Development* (Indianapolis: Addison Wesley, 2010), 190.
6. David Mann, *Creating a Lean Culture: Tools to Sustain Lean Conversions* (New York: Productivity Press, 2005), vi.
7. Brian Maskell, "Why Create a Value Stream Organization," http://blog.maskell.com/?p=244, November 26, 2011.
8. Jeffrey Liker, *The Toyota Way* (New York: McGraw-Hill, 2004), 179.

9. John Shook, "Lessons from Toyota for Healthcare Management," Lean Healthcare Transformation Summit presentation, July 5, 2007.

10. Susan Cramm, "Put IT Where It Belongs," *Wall Street Journal*, April 25, 2011.

11. Sarah Jane Johnston, "How Toyota Turns Workers into Problem Solvers," interview with Stephen Spear, *Harvard Business Review*, hbswk.hbs.edu/item/3512.html, November 26, 2001.

12. Thomas L. Jackson, *Hoshin Kanri for the Lean Enterprise* (New York: Productivity Press, 2006), 81.

13. Alan Mulally, *The Outsider at Ford*, *BusinessWeek*, March 5, 2009.

14. "The Happiest Man in Detroit," *BusinessWeek*, February 3, 2011.

15. Jim Womack, "The Mind of the Lean Manager," http://www.lean.org/womack/DisplayObject.cfm?o=1083, July 30, 2009.

16. Takashi Tanaka, Toshio Horikiri, and Craig Flynn, *Lean for Leaders: Toyota Management System in the Executive Office* (Rochester, NY: QV System, Inc., 2010).

17. Hirotaka Takeuchi, Emi Osono, Norihiko Shimizu "The Contradictions That Drive Toyota's Success," *Harvard Business Review*, June 2008.

18. Jim Womack, "Yokoten across the World," http://www.lean.org/womack/DisplayObject.cfm?o=758, March 6, 2008.

19. Takashi Tanaka, Toshio Horikiri, and Craig Flynn, *Lean for Leaders: Toyota Management System in the Executive Office*.

20. Sarah Jane Johnston, "How Toyota Turns Workers into Problem Solvers," interview with Stephen Spear, *Harvard Business Review*, November 2001.

21. Jeff Sutherland, interview, April 12, 2012.

22. Jeffrey Liker, interview, January 9, 2012.

23. Jim Womack and Dan Jones, *Lean Thinking*, 2nd ed. (New York: Simon & Schuster, 2003), 315.

24. Peter Weill and Jeanne Ross, *IT Savvy* (Boston: Harvard Business Press, 2009), 93.

25. Daniel Coyle, *The Talent Code* (New York: Bantam, 2009).

Chapter 8

The Lean Learning Enterprise

Steve Bell

> The only sustainable competitive advantage is the ability to learn faster than the competition.
>
> **Arie de Geus**
> *The Living Company*

Who are your customers?
What do they want now?
What will they want tomorrow, and the day after that?

You can temporarily capture the market's attention with a great innovation, but can you profit from it? Can you keep it? What will you do next? How will you remain at the front in a marketplace that has become accustomed to, and perhaps even expects, constant change?

True competitive advantage arises from the ability to continuously offer what customers value, in new and better ways, and then to capitalize on it through effective operations while simultaneously preparing your next wave of improvement and innovation. It's a continuous balancing act of development and operations, operations and development, in this highly collaborative, always-connected world. Run. Grow. Transform. Every day, in a continuous cycle.

But just changing quickly isn't good enough. As the technology visionary Geoffrey Moore observes, many companies waste their innovation effort on being *different* but not *differentiating*.[1] Ask your customers; they know the difference.

Learning what really matters to your customers requires continuous experimentation, collaboration, and interaction with them. Delivering what they want requires the ability to execute what is learned by internal employees and external partners across organizational lines, time zones, languages, and cultures—from the front lines through middle management to senior leadership and back again. According to John Shook, collaborative learning is not just an individual, but a *social* act.[2]

Throughout this book one theme remains constant: leadership and management should establish a strategic vision and shared purpose, engage people with respect, encourage them to form cross-functional and cross-disciplinary teams, and create conditions where they can succeed. A Lean learning enterprise encourages and enables everyone to communicate, collaborate, experiment, solve problems, and innovate with a focus not on profit but on *purpose*.

Steve Jobs was one of the greatest product visionaries of our time. His personal eccentricities are now legendary, and some say that he could have been even more effective if he had practiced a little more "respect for people." According to Walter Isaacson, the author of his biography, Jobs was passionate, even fanatical, about his product and what his customers could do with it. Shortly before his death, Jobs told Isaacson: "My passion has been to build an enduring company where people were motivated to make great products. Everything else was secondary… the products, not the profits, were the motivation. It's a subtle difference, but it ends up meaning everything."[3]

How People and Purpose Are Driving a Lasting Transformation

In many organizations financial measures dominate decision making. This focus is only natural, many will say, because making a profit is necessary for survival. But what is the driving force that produces those financial outcomes? Think back to the balanced scorecard we discussed in Chapter 6. The four elements, in increasing order of importance, are as follows:

1. Financial measures
2. Operational excellence measures
3. Customer satisfaction measures
4. Employee engagement, learning, and innovation measures

But wait a minute—how can employee engagement be more important than customer satisfaction, because it is the customer that defines value, and it is the customer who creates financial return for investors?

Consider the two pillars of Toyota's enduring philosophy: *continuous improvement* and *respect for people.*[4] Beyond Toyota's extraordinary six-decade experience, can another enterprise demonstrate this causal relationship of employee engagement as the driver of customer value and profitability? Let's revisit Southwest Airlines, which has been making money while most other airlines have been losing it. In 2011, Southwest marked its thirty-ninth consecutive year of posting a profit.[5] Clearly they have demonstrated the ability to sustain impressive financial outcomes in a continually troubled industry. How do they accomplish this?

"You put your employees first and if you take care of them, then they will take good care of you," says Herb Kelleher, the airline's legendary cofounder. "Then your customers will come back, and your shareholders will like that, so it's really a unity."[6]

One of the key success factors in the airline industry revenue model is aircraft utilization. For Southwest, achieving one more flight per day from its fleet translates to an approximately US$1 billion increase in annual revenues.[7] Southwest doesn't accomplish this by flying faster. They do it by reducing the nonvalue activity while the plane is on the ground.[8]

Most airlines require sixty to ninety minutes at the gate to service and turn a plane around. Southwest's average is half of what their competitors require.[9] Southwest goes through the same servicing and safety inspection, the same unloading and loading of passengers, luggage, and fuel. How do they do it?

Recently, Tom Foco, a Lean Enterprise Institute faculty member, flew Southwest. The plane he was scheduled to fly arrived late due to weather. He worried that he might not make his next connection. But twenty minutes after docking at the gate, the plane pushed back on schedule, clean, fully loaded, and ready to fly again. Astonishing! Arriving early at his destination, he remained onboard for a few minutes (*gemba*) and watched as the crew prepared the plane for its next flight. He describes what he saw as choreographed motion with little waste, similar to what you see with a racecar pit crew.[10]

Recognizing that the people doing the work knew the daily challenges of turning a plane around, Southwest asked ground and flight crews what slowed them down at turnaround and what would help them to do their jobs faster and better. Ground crews reported that one of the most significant causes of delays involved technicians searching for information when an equipment issue arose. "There's nothing more frustrating for a mechanic than to have to stop what he's doing to chase something down," says Dave Boyer, manager of maintenance projects at Southwest.[11] Southwest chose to make a significant investment in aircraft maintenance automation. Their inspectors pioneered the use of wireless tablet computers to communicate with maintenance crews. Southwest estimates technicians used to spend 30 to 40% of their time searching for information, and the new systems reduced the waste introduced by those delays.

The need for information also played a role in delaying the pilot checklist process. Working together as a cross-functional team, they quickly arrived at a simple countermeasure. With a better understanding of the pilot checklist, ground crews adapted the order of their inspection and servicing checklists to synchronize with the pilot checklist to eliminate wait times. There's a great lesson in this: not all information-related problems require technology solutions. But what every problem requires is teamwork, respect, a shared focus on purpose, and the skills and leadership support to invest in finding and fixing problems every day.

Fundamentally, it's not about IT; it's about serving the customer. IT doesn't get the planes off the ground faster—the people on the ground do. IT merely helps them do their job better and faster. The development of appropriate aircraft maintenance automation was driven by the people doing the job, with a clear understanding and thoughtful examination of the processes required to accomplish it.

At Southwest, employee engagement results in more than just a great place to work; it means sustained profits. Ground crew engagement, innovation, and continuous improvement lead to faster ground turnaround, which leads to more on-time flights, lower prices, better value, and happier customers. This leads to increased revenues, lower operating costs, and higher profits. This series of cause-and-effect relationships (shown in Figure 8.1) illustrates how innovation and improvement—led by people—cascade throughout the enterprise, improving productivity, increasing market share, and creating a healthier business with more jobs and a greater long-term valuation.

Where are the value-adding capabilities within your enterprise? Where could an improved focus on purpose, fueled by the knowledge and insights of your employees and partners, create breakthrough performance and substantial market differentiation? How will that translate to your bottom line? Are you and your shareholders willing to patiently invest in this transformation of behavior, capability, and culture to realize the long-term benefits as Toyota, Southwest Airlines, and many others have done and continue to do?

This recognition that engaged people are at the heart of a successful business is not new—but it is now more important than ever before. The global economy is in the process of rewiring itself. Like the Italian Renaissance,

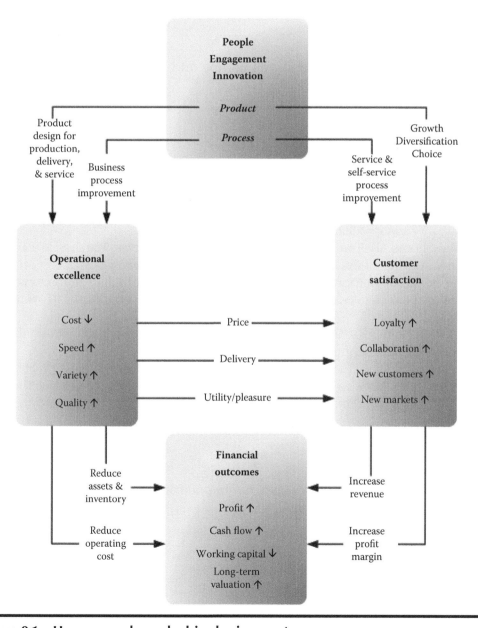

Figure 8.1   How engaged people drive business outcomes.

creative thinkers across countless disciplines are collaborating in new and interesting ways, redefining the rules and questioning the basic assumptions within their industries and in many cases changing the way we live.

Even when these innovations are enabled by emerging technology, the focus is not on IT—it's about creating a steady flow of value for the customer and producing an experience that leaves them satisfied and wanting more. The path for sustaining success is *purpose, people, and process*; in this way you and your enterprise can run, grow, and transform.

> The way to get started is to quit talking and begin doing.
>
> **Walt Disney**

Notes

1. Geoffrey Moore, "The Future of Enterprise IT," http://www.youtube.com/watch?v=P5zWZagA4ps&feature=related.
2. John Shook, LEI Transformation Summit keynote address, March 8, 2012.
3. Rana Roroohar, "What Would Steve Do?" *Time*, February 27, 2012.
4. Toyota Motor Corporation, "The Toyota Way 2001," April 2001, http://www-personal.umich.edu~mrother/Materials_to_Download_files/The%20Toyota%20Way%202001.pdf.
5. Southwest Airlines, "Fact Sheet," http://www.southwest.com/html/about-southwest/history/fact-sheet.html.
6. "Something Special about Southwest Airlines, *CBS News*, February 11, 2009.
7. Dan Shunk, "Back to the Future—Applying Lean Principles to the Healthcare Community," presentation, Association for Manufacturing Excellence "Measure Up for Success" conference, Calgary, Canada, June 8, 2011.
8. Ibid.
9. "Something Special about Southwest Airlines."
10. Tom Foco, interview, November 14, 2011.
11. Tony Kontzer, "Wings of Change," *Information Week*, March 28, 2005.

INTEGRATING THE LEAN IT COMMUNITY

Steve Bell – Editor

Now that we've developed a framework for Lean IT integration throughout the enterprise, let's turn our attention to how the different subspecialties of IT integrate with each other to realize this vision.

As Dan Jones insists in the Foreword, for Lean thinking to truly deliver on its promise, we must adopt a process-centered view of the entire enterprise. This means understanding how *all* the functions, capabilities, and people deliver value to the customer, so everyone can strive for a shared purpose and eliminate the waste that stands in their way.

While we don't need to become an expert in all the technical disciplines, we do need a basic understanding of their relationships and interdependencies so that we can fully engage IT capabilities in value stream improvement and innovation. Part II helps us gain that understanding. Here we learn from the experience and perspectives of thought leaders from within key IT subspecialties as they share how their respective disciplines join together in the broad context of Lean IT. In the spirit of an Italian Renaissance *salon*, during the development of this book we have talked, debated, and engaged in each others' writing and have collectively arrived at many insights about how our disciplines can more effectively think and act together to create value.

In the first two chapters in Part II you will learn about two disciplines—enterprise architecture and business process management—presenting systemic, architectural perspectives of the enterprise that are seldom seen or heard within the Lean community. In Chapter 9, Charles Betz explains how the many architectural elements of enterprise IT form the underlying "technical stack" of enterprise value streams. Then, in Chapter 10, Paul Harmon and Sandra Foster illustrate how the practice of business process management can help leadership understand, organize, and measure the enterprise along value streams.

With an understanding of how the overall system fits together, we then move to IT service management. In Chapter 11, Troy DuMoulin leads us through an examination of how organizational culture and awareness develop through various stages of maturity and how this development helps us see beyond the technical considerations toward value streams and, ultimately, toward the end customer.

In Chapter 12, I examine enterprise resource planning (ERP) systems and other commercial off-the-shelf enterprise systems (COTS). These massive systems are often at the heart of enterprise transactional computing and analysis. And for many enterprises, these complex systems act as a dragging anchor—resisting change, slowing the Lean transformation down. But a Lean approach to ERP and COTS systems can improve value, speed, and agility.

In Chapter 13, we shine the Lean lens on product and application development. Mary Poppendieck, who for the past ten years (along with her husband and business partner Tom) has advocated the merits of a broader vision of Lean thinking to the Agile software development community, examines how many of the fundamental Lean principles apply to the end-to-end development value stream in order to drive innovation and speed to market.

To ensure this large gathering of interconnected elements we call "IT" has integrity, in Chapter 14 John Schmidt makes the invisible visible, helping us to understand the value of quality data underlying every process, and the vital importance of a Lean view to enterprise-wide data management and governance.

Finally, in Chapter 15, I investigate the "virtual voice of the customer" with an exploration of the vast opportunities for listening to and communicating directly with the marketplace and our customers. We peer into the crystal ball and consider the increasing role that big data, social media, mobile computing, and other emerging capabilities that are now possible in an always-connected society play in engaging and serving the end customer in new and often disruptive ways.

With the systemic view provided by this gathering of Lean IT thought leaders, we are far more capable of utilizing the boundless potential of IT to help the enterprise run better, grow more effectively, and—ultimately—transform.

Chapter 9

Lean Enterprise Architecture
An Architectural View of IT Value Stream Flow

Charles Betz

> Architecture: The fundamental organization of a system, embodied in its components, their relationships to each other and the environment, and the principles governing its design and evolution.[*]
>
> **International Standards Organization**

Enterprise architecture (EA) emerges in large information technology (IT) organizations over time as the need for coordination and a systemic vision increases with the size and complexity of IT services. In general, this is the highest-level, most long-range work in establishing the principles and long-horizon objectives of the IT organization in its service to its customers.

Supporting long-term objectives remains a challenging topic in enterprise IT. Information technology is continually presenting new opportunities for adding business value, opportunities that may be well justified but that can also introduce redundancy and complexity into the IT environment. Architects seek to support new IT functionality by simplifying and optimizing its introduction into the existing IT landscape, seeking economies of scale and efficiencies of reuse.

---

[*] ISO/IEC (2007).

Lean and enterprise architecture are "twin sons of different mothers" (to borrow from the 1978 Dan Fogelberg and Tim Weisberg album). Both are oriented toward a systems perspective, and both abhor waste. We can look at EA from a Lean light, and EA techniques can be applied to Lean IT. Finally, in building such an architecture, we can help answer the central question of this book: What is an IT value stream?

Lean EA, or EA for Lean IT?

This chapter has two sides, both of which reflect the other. First, there is the influence of Lean on traditional EA practices. Second, there is the application of EA techniques to understanding the Lean challenge to traditional IT management.

Influence of Lean on Enterprise Architecture

Enterprise architecture and Lean come from very different origins. EA traces its roots back through structured systems methodologies originating in the first generation of software engineering practitioners such as Ed Yourdon and Tom DeMarco, the concepts of computer-assisted software engineering, the Zachman framework, and the work of the Object Management Group. Lean's antecedents, on the other hand, lie with the thought of Taiichi Ohno in his development of the Toyota Production System, in turn influenced by W. Edwards Deming, Shigeo Shingo, Henry Ford, and others. Both of these histories are well documented elsewhere. But if we consider the intersection of the two, there are both comparisons and contrasts.

Lean/EA Comparisons

In *comparison*, both are systemic approaches. Both seek to view a problem area as an integrated whole and understand overall objectives and the interplay of parts toward some greater purpose. Both serve as a critical counterweight to local optimization at the expense of the whole.

The definition of enterprise architecture for this chapter draws on TOGAF (The Open Group, 2009) and is seen to encompass business, data, application, and technical architecture. Process and capability analysis are key components of business architecture in this approach. And as discussed in Chapter 10, the Lean concept of value stream mapping is well understood within the broader world of business process management (BPM).

The actual missions of the architecture capability may include the following:

■ Strategic planning for IT.
■ IT portfolio management—target and gap analysis, recommendations for investments, and promotion of shared services.
■ Technology standards governance—controlling for redundancy and fitness.
■ Internal analysis—"first line of defense before calling Gartner."
■ Solutions design standards and patterns for nonfunctional concerns (security, availability, etc.).
■ Continuous improvement of systems availability and capacity management.
■ Data architecture—establishing master data standards, data quality approaches, and systems of record.
■ Project governance—assessing project proposals and early deliverables for architectural impacts and redundancies. For example, is the new system consistent with the existing approach to master data management? Is the proposed system duplicative with an existing system?
■ High-level configuration management, e.g., tracking services, systems, and their relationships.
■ Center of excellence for data, process (BPM), and systems analysis and modeling.
■ Consulting "bench"—"first line of defense before calling Accenture."
■ IT ombudsman.

In many ways, IT architects habitually practice Lean in their everyday work. Computers provide endless opportunities for performance optimization and waste reduction. Even without using the term *Lean*, IT architects, developers, and engineers are continually seeking to improve throughput, data quality, availability, and other performance indicators. Some intuitive examples:

■ Any programmer who figures out (by cleaning up the design or improving the code) a 50% faster way for a system to run is practicing Lean IT.
■ The architect who reconciles two competing systems of record by establishing one as the master is similarly practicing Lean IT by reducing the waste of inconsistent data.
■ And IT portfolio management, including the systematic reduction of redundancy in technology, asset, and service portfolios, predates the concept of Lean IT by many years and yet is essentially Lean in its goals.

And as we look more systematically to the traditional views of enterprise architecture:

■ Business architecture
  – Business processes
  – Business capabilities
■ Data architecture
■ Systems architecture

We see that each of the following four examples embodies some Lean-like goals and methods.

1. ***Business process thinking*** is all about flow and end-to-end value. It pays particular attention to handoffs between organizations or individuals, where value can easily be lost. It also is attentive to questions of cycle time and optimizing throughput. Many architects spend time as process analysts, which is a useful broadening of experience beyond data and technical concerns.

2. ***Business capability architecture*** is the steady-state, ongoing functions that perform work within value streams. Even in a Lean world of flow, it is still important. The "structure of the silos" can influence value delivery deeply. It's hard to understand flow without understanding what it is flowing *across*.

3. ***Data architecture*** is about the structure and management of information. Data, when unmanaged, proliferates wastefully. Redundant data lead to uncertainty and ultimately poor execution and service (the bank that can't seem to get your address change right). Increased operating costs, redundancy and rework, and exposure to audit risk all result from poorly managed data.

   Data architects serve Lean ends every day by improving this key aspect of IT service design and delivery. The data architect "goes to *gemba*" with those needing an IT system, listening carefully to their language and translating it into structures a computer can manipulate. They reduce waste by seeking opportunities for reuse and consolidating duplicate data repositories.[*]

   Data architects also work with concepts such as "constraints" and "business rules," which are a form of *poka-yoke* (a Lean term for mistake-proofing) IT systems at a transactional level:

---

[*] See also Chapter 14.

- A U.S. address must have a zip code.
- An invoice must have at least one line item.
- Products are either in the consumer or industrial line but not both.

4. Finally, ***systems architecture*** is the systematic management of the numerous tradeoffs between utility (what the system *does*) and warranty (how well the system *runs*) in the design of systems and services. Is the gorgeous new user interface scalable? How to achieve 99.995% uptime on a budget? Can the service consumer accommodate a day-to-day recovery period in case of a disaster? EA must be attentive to all aspects of the complete system. Current trends toward cloud computing and outsourcing only increase the importance of such a systems view, as now multiple service providers must be integrated into a seamless whole.

Taken together, these four views are the basic foundations for the practice of EA. But delivering value from EA requires far more than just correct application of architecture techniques. The architectures, as deliverables, are used to do the following:

■ Inform business strategists as they consider the operational and technical aspects of operating model choices for the enterprise
■ Inform business leaders and managers (including value stream managers and teams) as to the various options for service designs supporting business units
■ Help individual value stream teams understand the linkages among the various processes, capabilities, and systems

Lean/EA Contrasts

It should be clear from the above that architecture often embodies Lean goals without necessarily using Lean terms. However, there are contrasts as well. EA (in my view) remains biased toward the world of computing and its operational implications for the enterprise.

As noted earlier, there is a concept of "business architecture," but this is still usually limited to an operations perspective, such as enterprise value streams, processes, and capabilities—the aspects of business that call for automation. In other words, EA is IT-centric even when it is trying hard not to be. Missing in particular are core marketing and sales strategies, alliances, and non-IT risk management and enterprise finance, legal, and human resource concerns—essential parts of the business model. And even the most advanced expressions of enterprise architecture typically don't address culture, organizational change management, psychology, and similar matters. These deficiencies can lead enterprise architects into ivory tower isolation and irrelevance.

Lean on the other hand has as fundamental tenets "respect for people" and "going to *gemba*," that is, going to the heart of matters and understanding the problem in a thorough, bottom-up manner. The related work of Eli Goldratt started by posing the basic question (in *The Goal*): "[W]hat is the purpose of this factory?" The purpose almost always transcends the narrow perspectives of IT, which can easily become insulated and inwardly focused.

If we apply Lean thinking to the enterprise architecture practice itself, we might see further waste:

- Attempting to dictate design and engineering at too detailed a level, producing models and designs that are ignored by implementing teams
- Preoccupation with new technologies that become "solutions in search of a problem"
- Too much attention to documenting "as is" state (work that should be shifted to a configuration management capability)
- Standards that are poorly defined; difficult to understand; difficult to interpret, apply, and enforce; and liable to introduce needless delays to projects or generate nonvalue-added work in and of themselves
- Rigidity toward project-team-driven innovations ("not invented here" attitude)
- Artifacts created with no clear receiving process—architectures and designs that have no formal relationship to other IT processes
- Lack of engagement with key IT value streams (ivory tower syndrome)
- Standards that are too rigid (perhaps optimizing locally) and governance processes that don't allow for rapid escalation

The end result of such EA mismanagement is to inhibit innovation, locking in arbitrary and often obsolete standards, with one result being that the most creative teams go rogue.

Another aspect of Lean that is not well understood by many enterprise architects is the principle that too much information, and unnecessary information complexity, are forms of waste. More is not better in information systems design. Information must have a clear business use in terms of an operational model. This again gets into the issues of human factors, problem solving, decision making, and organizational change management.

Finally, leading-edge Lean thought emphasizes the need for a learning organization. Although EA may represent some of the most intellectually curious individuals in an organization, this does not mean that EA understands how to systematically support a learning culture. Systems thinkers and continuous learning advocates such as Peter Senge (*The Fifth Discipline*) are recognized by many Lean practitioners as fellow travelers while being relatively unknown in EA circles.

Nevertheless, despite these contrasts, there is a natural affinity between Lean and EA, as perhaps indicated by the fact the middle two letters of Lean are "EA"!

AN ARCHITECT'S PERSPECTIVE ON THE IT FRAMEWORKS

Enterprise architecture is a method for managing conceptual complexity by using multiple views on a problem and establishing traceability across those views. Although there are different approaches, many enterprise architects use some combination of processes, capabilities, data, and systems to model difficult domains.

IT service management is a complex domain and can be better understood through architectural techniques. It's possible to create process, capability, data, and system models for IT service management just as it's possible to do so for financial services, supply chain management, and indeed any major industry or operational function.

Frameworks such as ITIL and COBIT can be useful inputs into such a model. They reflect years of industry experience gained by multiple subject matter experts in the business of IT. However, the act of architectural modeling and analysis can illuminate ambiguities and problematic concepts in those frameworks, challenges that in turn may limit their potential application.

For example, *process* as an architectural concept has become relatively well defined over the past fifteen years or so through the work of thought leaders such as Roger Burlton, Paul Harmon, and Alec Sharp; it is event-driven, countable, and provides a clear output of value to some stakeholder. The "verb-noun" naming standard is well accepted as a heuristic for determining whether something is or is not a process;

"Originate Mortgage" is a clear process with a beginning and end, whereas "Loan Servicing" is a function—it never ends.

By this criterion, many, if not most, of the "processes" listed in ITIL and COBIT are not actually processes. There certainly are clear, true processes in IT, such as "Resolve Incident" or "Deliver Release." But concepts such as IT financial management or capacity management, although called "processes" in ITIL for example, are in reality functions, that is, ongoing steady-state activities with no beginning or end.

This basic distinction between event-driven/countable versus ongoing/uncountable pervades much business management and architectural thinking—and for good reason. Countable processes are measurable, amenable to well understood improvement techniques, and typically serve as critical coordination signals for a wide variety of stakeholders. *It's my view that IT value streams are better understood as countable, large-grained processes and not as functions.*

Similar insights can be gained through the application of data architecture and systems architecture techniques to the IT service management (ITSM) problem domain. From a data architecture perspective, the very concept of "service" as called for by ITIL is highly ambiguous, as is the concept of "configuration item." The system-level concepts of configuration management database, configuration management system, and service knowledge management system also encounter fundamental challenges when subjected to architectural scrutiny.

In sum, practitioners who find themselves implementing ITSM in an environment of any complexity are well advised to seek advice from architects and BPM professionals who have learned many lessons in their years of applying their tools to a wide variety of problem domains in modern business.

An Enterprise Architecture for Lean IT

Now let's turn the mirror around and reflect the Lean/EA relationship the other way. How can we apply Lean to the large-scale enterprise IT organization? How would the Lean imperatives of systems thinking, flow, and waste reduction translate via EA practices to a better-run IT organization: agile yet stable and of clear business value to its sponsors?

It starts with the long-established "business of IT" thought experiment, the idea that the conception, development, and operation of IT services is itself a value stream. This can be controversial; however, it is a forty-year-old thought experiment used by many authors.* Lean pioneers Jim Womack and Dan Jones note that enterprise value streams often contain miniature versions of themselves; that is, they are self-similar at different scales, or *fractal*, an insight that also supports the "IT as a business" model.†

However, in understanding the business of IT, a singular value stream won't do. It's also well established in the Lean literature that it is helpful to view the product lifecycle as distinct from the transactional lifecycle (Figure 9.1). That is, "concept to production" (or the product portfolio lifecycle) is distinct from "quote to cash" (which in this representation includes manufacturing as well as selling, also known as "make and sell"). From the Lean Enterprise Institute's *Lean Lexicon*:

> All of the actions, both value-creating and nonvalue-creating, required to bring a product [or service] from concept to launch (also known as the development value stream) and from order to delivery (also known as the operational value stream). These include actions to process information from the customer and actions to transform the product [or service] on its way to the customer.‡

This basic "dual-axis value chain," as I call it, translates readily to enterprise IT: the service lifecycle is distinct from the actual delivery of the service on a moment-by-moment transactional basis (Figure 9.2). In terms of the value streams proposed in Chapters 2 and 3, the service lifecycle and professional services are seen along the horizontal, whereas transactional service delivery is tightly coupled to the daily human-to-human support needed when new use is to be provisioned or when delivery is interrupted. Chapter 10, Figure 10.9 identifies the two processes of "develop/change/ retire application" and "deliver application," which equate precisely to these two axes.

The transactional service is fundamental to understanding what IT services are and are not. Business services are owned by business units and

---

* The concept of considering IT as a business within a business was conceived as early as A. E. Ditri, John C. Shaw, and W. Atkins, *Managing the EDP function* (New York: McGraw-Hill, 1971) and IBM Corporation, *A Management System for the Information Business, Volume I, Management Overview*, 2nd ed. (1981).
† Jim Womack and Dan Jones, *Lean Thinking: Banish Waste and Create Wealth in Your Corporation* (New York: Free Press, 2003), 322.
‡ Lean Enterprise Institute, Inc., *Lean Lexicon* (Cambridge, MA: Lean Enterprise Institute, Inc., 2008).

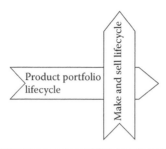

Figure 9.1   Two lifecycles.

may or may not require the application of computing. IT services may be provided in a variety of organizational models but *by definition involve automated computation* (computing either as the basis of delivery or computing as the subject of professional services or consulting). The "value" of an IT service at a "moment of truth" experiential level is transactional: some predictable state change is executed with a high degree of confidence, such as a balance transfer, an online purchase, an e-mail sent and delivered, or the viewing of a streaming movie.

This fundamental transactional "value stream" is highly complex, involving elaborate stacks of technology: data centers, power and cooling, racks, networking, computers, operating systems, middleware, databases, and the final visible layer of the application as encountered by the end user. Maintaining the flow of value across the intricate, myriad failure points from top to bottom of this stack is the work of IT service management, and a number of supporting processes surround transactional delivery.

It's also helpful to see feedback loops from both axes (Figure 9.3). The act of continuously sustaining the sequential lifecycles and feeding back information (the "lessons learned") to the next lifecycle instance is the role of ongoing functional management and cross-functional value stream improvement teams.

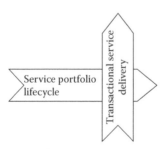

Figure 9.2   IT portfolio versus delivery.

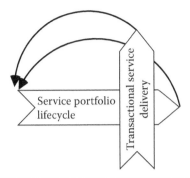

Figure 9.3 Feedback loops.

Incident and change management are typically the first processes to be formalized, with project, release, service request, continuous improvement (including problem), demand, and retirement eventually following (Figure 9.4).

The processes are not strictly sequential, and they interact, decompose, and overlap in complex ways. However, each concept can be treated as having its own clearly bounded lifecycle with definite start- and endpoints. Notice that the vertical process naming all follows the established BPM verb-noun standard.

It is also misleading to show them as equal in size. A project may be where initial functionality is developed and may encompass releases, changes, service requests, and much ongoing iterative development of the product. Demand may be an even broader construct, front-ending all of the other processes.

As an IT organization matures, it may define processes for all of Figure 9.4. (Many process maturity models emphasize the formal definition of a process as a key early step.) Of course, this does not mean that the IT organization itself is effective. If the processes are poorly integrated, they may act as silos.

Furthermore, the service lifecycle itself can be broken down into four major components:

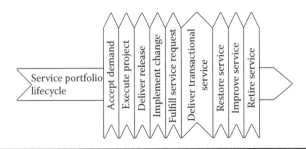

Figure 9.4 Processes supporting transactional delivery.

1. Application service
2. Infrastructure service
3. Computing asset
4. Technology product

1. ***Application service lifecycle***: This is the cradle-to-grave existence of a direct application of computing technology assets to a business problem, such as a payroll or supply chain management system. This lifecycle view deliberately encompasses both the "development" and "operations" components of the service lifecycle.
2. ***Infrastructure service lifecycle***: This is the cradle-to-grave existence of an IT service that supports other IT services—not business services. Examples include networking, hosting, storage, and other technical services. These are not directly used by the business but rather indirectly support the business via their support for applications such as payroll systems. This equates to the support process "provide infrastructure services" in Chapter 10, Figure 10.13.
3. ***IT asset lifecycle***: The forecasting, acquisition, operation, and disposition of a tangible IT asset (e.g., a *specific* server with a distinct serial number or a software license).
4. ***Technology product lifecycle***: The specification, choice, operation, maintenance, and retirement of a *class* of assets (e.g., a server model or a version of database software).

If we combine these lifecycles with the supporting processes, we derive the final process architecture* (Figure 9.5).

This may seem complex, but the reality of IT management often reduces to "lining up the lifecycles" (the horizontal flows). The lifecycle timings and complex dependencies among foundational technology products, the assets that embody them, and the services upon which they are built are a never-ending source of effort and innovation in IT. Figure 9.6 graphically illustrates the interplay of the asynchronous lifecycles.

For example, let's say that a well-known provider of database software (a technology product) decides to retire version 8, forcing customers to upgrade

---

* This overall process architecture was derived using a software engineering technique known as "entity lifecycle analysis." The detailed derivation is to be found in Charles Betz's *Architecture and Patterns for IT: Service and Portfolio Management and Governance,* 2nd ed. (Amsterdam, the Netherlands: Elsevier, 2011).

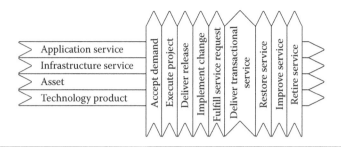

Figure 9.5   Lifecycle and process architecture.

their licenses (assets) to version 9, 10, or 11. (Since version 9 will be the next to retire, sensible customers will go to 10 or 11 if they can.) However:

1. When the technical requirements for version 11 are reviewed, it is found that it requires a newer version of the server operating system (another technology product, again licensed as an asset by the customer).
2. When the requirements for that server operating system are examined, it is determined that the current physical servers (assets) are not capable of running it.
3. The current servers must be upgraded for the new operating system for the new database software.

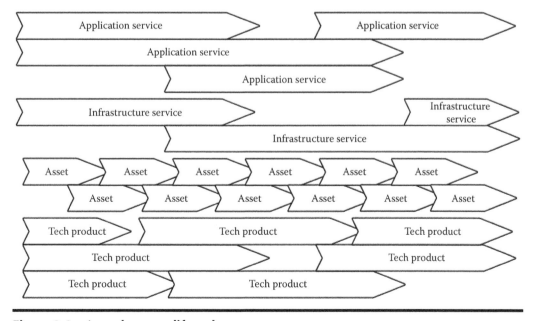

Figure 9.6   Asynchronous lifecycles.

4. The ripple effects continue; the new servers force a premature conversion to new power standards in the data center, a new monitoring infrastructure, or myriad other possibilities.

And all of these concerns might be considered internal to the infrastructure services of hosting and data management.

That's not all. Version 11 of the database software must be regression-tested against all the application services that use it. It is quickly determined that at least two applications from a packaged software vendor do not yet support version 11 of the database software and so cannot move to a hosting service based on version 11.

And so it goes. All of this work is typically analyzed during a project cycle, but in some cases some of these problems may not be understood until just weeks before a change is planned. The sequence of demand, project, release, and change serves as a form of defense in depth that prevents these kinds of complexities from resulting in service outages. However, the degree of control exercised by such processes is endlessly controversial, as they easily are perceived as bureaucratic overhead—at least until the next major outage.

What does this all mean from a Lean perspective?

The four lifecycles represent critical value elements. Although services are the primary concern in IT, *those services depend on assets and technologies*, which themselves have long lifecycles. The validated technology choices and delivery of the assets embodying the technologies provide the platform for the service value to be delivered. They themselves can be seen as long-lived value streams—subordinate to the service value stream, yet distinct.

Distinct? A given technology or asset may support multiple services, *and both its acquisition and disposition may occur on a timeframe distinct from the service.* As seen in our example, the retirement of database product version 8 is disruptive to a variety of services and lifecycles.

In summary, the IT value streams all have distinct customers:

■ Business sponsors requiring IT application services.
■ IT application teams requiring infrastructure services (IT supporting other IT, such as hosting, storage, and network teams).
■ IT service teams (application and infrastructure) requiring tangible IT assets (physical capacity and software license entitlements).
■ IT service teams and procurement support organizations requiring assurance that the technologies (of which the assets are instances) are not redundant and are fit for purpose in the enterprise. This service is

called "value engineering" in an industrial enterprise and in IT is typically handled by architecture.

By identifying the value-seeking "customers" for these lifecycles, we complete the value stream exercise for this decomposition, using a business-within-a-business paradigm to understand why these lifecycles exist and who gains value from them.

Value and Nonvalue-Adding Lifecycle States

It is helpful to think of the four lifecycles (which might be seen as fundamental "value streams" of the IT organization from an internal perspective) in terms of their value-adding versus nonvalue-adding phases. Traditionally, a Lean tool known as a "work/wait" diagram might be used; however, these lifecycles are too long and nondeterministic to use such a tool.

Instead, I propose a "4-O" model:

■ Obtaining
■ Operational
■ Outage
■ Obsolescence

A lifecycle object (application service, infrastructure service, asset, or technology product) is one of three nonvalue-adding* states (obtaining, outage, or obsolescence), or it is operational and adding value.

For example, if a need for additional server capacity is identified, the server is in an obtaining state, where the enterprise lacks its value. If a middleware product is found to have a serious security vulnerability, it is in at least a partial outage state until it is patched. An application that is currently being enhanced may be in a partial obtaining state.† And if an application is retired but residual responsibility for its electronic records

---

* This is not a strict Lean-style "VA/NNVA" or MUDA1/MUDA2 terminology. Presumably, all the lifecycle states are "necessary."

† Admittedly, this gets complex. As Steve Bell points out, "While that is NVA/NNVA from the delivery value stream perspective, it's VA from the product development value stream perspective since new software capabilities are being created with the customers involvement to increase their realized value." But replatforming, patching, and many other forms of application maintenance undertaken via a product development value stream could more easily be seen as NNVA. There is also the issue of enhancing existing systems, which are in a VA state but anticipating further functionality. I think these are all tractable problems.

and correct disposal of its associated hardware remains, it is in a non-value-adding state of obsolescence that may prove surprisingly costly.

The goal is to show the quantified operational value of the value streams as a percentage of the overall lifecycle time (a form of in-service reporting). For example, if a given asset requires eight weeks to procure, six weeks to dispose, and has an average of one week of outages over its life, the operational value ratio of the asset to the enterprise over its three-year lifecycle (156 weeks) would be as follows:

$$operational\ value = \frac{156 - 15}{156} = 95\%$$

If the processes are tied to the lifecycles they are interacting at a data level (e.g., this change affected this service), the overall performance of the IT organization starts to come into view. What do we mean by this?

Start by tracking an IT service's Operational value over time:

Year 1	Year 2	Year 3	Year 4	Year 5<
60%	90%	92%	93%	90%

For each year, we should know how many (1) demand requests, (2) projects, (3) releases, (4) changes, (5) service requests, (6) transactions, (7) incidents, and (8) improvement opportunities were affected by the lifecycle and whether the service as a whole is in retirement (obsolescence).

Consistently aggregated at scale, while all of these processes have inherent variability, we should be able to see some interesting possibilities in this data:

■ What portfolios have the highest operational value?
■ What portfolios have suffered the most from outages?
■ What portfolios have the highest obsolescence rates?
■ What is the correlation between nonoperational phases and the cross-cutting processes?
■ What can we infer about the performance of the cross-cutting processes based on the operational value of the lifecycles they are affecting?
  – What services have a high number of incidents?
  – Are projects related to a certain set of services chronically late?
  – Do changes involving a given technology product have a history of failure?

Many other analytic questions could be framed.

UNIFIED DEMAND MANAGEMENT

The 4-O model may be of use for the lifecycles but less so for the cross-cutting processes (incident, change, etc.). Although many attempts have been made to manage these processes in terms of their duration, it's not clear that true enterprise IT value is to be found by only trying to reduce process cycle time.

Instead, much current IT management thinking is turning toward better managing the aggregate demand represented by all of these processes. The following essay illustrates this.

Why IT Staff Work Seventy-Hour Weeks

Jane is a systems administrator in a large enterprise—or a database administrator, security architect, or any number of similar positions that provide shared services. There are three primary ways that demand for Jane's services appears.

Project managers come to her boss and ask for a percentage of her time. Once she is designated as a project "resource," she has deliverables: requirements and design assessments—perhaps even actual construction of infrastructure. She also finds herself responding to lightweight project workflow for "issues and risks" and "action items."

She is assigned incidents, service requests, work orders, changes, and the like through various enterprise workflow systems, especially the integrated IT service management system.

She also is tasked by her manager with responding to various "initiatives" that occupy a middle ground between projects and workflow: audits, compliance efforts, capacity assessments, root cause analyses, key system reviews, and more.

On Wednesday, she gets called into a Severity 2 incident involving the organization's supply chain system. On Thursday, she has a deadline of responding to a security audit finding for the organization's general ledger system. And on Friday, she has a critical path deliverable due for a strategic enterprise project. Fun life!

There is often no specific prioritization across these tasks beyond "who is screaming loudest." The Severity 2 incident may command her attention until it is resolved, but is this really the correct priority? What if it's only a partial outage and the project manager is ramping up the pressure for her deliverable? Jane may be attempting to do a little bit of each—switching her attention across the various tasks competing for her time, a very inefficient way to get work done.

Stories of such overburden pervade the IT industry. Ask yourself: How many people in my company accept both project and service request work (e.g., incidents, service requests, changes, and perhaps even "work orders" if distinct from service requests or changes)? And are they also assigned to the less-formalized initiatives (which we'll call "continuous improvement")? Do their line management and project manager at least have visibility into this aggregate demand and its consequences so they can make informed tradeoff decisions for the good of the whole enterprise?

It's scenarios like this that have made unified demand management an increasingly hot IT management topic lately. IT staff time is a precious resource, and there is always more demand than supply. Is Jane "working on the right thing"? Or is she just "working the thing right"—from the shareholder's perspective, doing perhaps the wrong thing efficiently and effectively?

The first step in answering these questions is understanding IT demand. Project, service desk, and continuous improvement have emerged for me as the three legs of the demand stool. And we, as an industry, are a long ways from having a holistic view of all these sources. Look at the historic walls between project management and the IT service management systems. It is only in the last few years that we have seen vendors addressing this problem. They are either building new integrated solutions supporting both project and service management as modules or they are integrating their legacy products together more tightly so that both kinds of demand are visible in a common view

What would unified demand management ideally look like? All project work would be integrated with all service desk work, and every continuous improvement initiative—every "bright idea"—would also be registered as a demand request. Project issues, risks, and action items would be captured using the same platform as service request management. Agile pipelines are part of the same mix—just more demand. And each individual would have a single pipeline for work, combining all these different flavors, and those individuals' managers would have much greater transparency into how their teams are supporting enterprise objectives and how to support them in setting optimal priorities.

It's going to be a culture shift. Those who are used to working in the old way may view unified demand management as an imposition—depending on how it is implemented. Lean philosophy, and modern *kanban* practice, would caution against an overly top-down approach. There are important questions of autonomy, morale, and motivation. It can't be about burdensome "dollars chasing dimes" time-tracking systems. But how can an enterprise ensure that resources are optimally allocated for value? How can we alleviate the ongoing overburden of IT staff?

It starts with cleaning house—for example, minimizing and centralizing your tracking systems. How many different workflow systems are you running for internal IT? Can you consolidate them? If you're not ready for a common platform for both your project management office and service desk, can you at least report after the fact on their combined demand and activity? Can you encourage the continuous improvement initiatives to either register as projects or as some appropriate IT service management work (e.g., problem)?

Then, if you want to really go to *gemba*, start thinking about your e-mail and calendaring system. It's the default queuing system and represents a vast variety of demand in any enterprise context. How can you get a better understanding of it? I'm not aware of any company offering demand analytics based on e-mail and calendaring, but with some creative application of text analytics, it would seem to be a possibility. (If you've got some thoughts on this, please contact me.)

And finally, demand management is only the first step. Once we consolidate the demand, how do we make better decisions about it? That is the role of execution management. Stay tuned…

Conclusion

It's all about flow, about the long horizon of value either spanning an intricate computing infrastructure traveling at the speed of light or spanning the years that a computing service may be in production and delivering utility.

The atomic IT value stream is the transaction, crossing all the IT resources and elements that support it and reinforced in turn by the change and incident processes on either side that put it into place and keep it running. These supporting processes are elaborated with demand, project, release, service request, improvement, and retirement as the organization grows in size and maturity. And as these processes each grow and take on more responsibility, the need to unify them under a governing demand-and-execution framework becomes critical.

The service as a product lifecycle can be seen as an orthogonal value stream in which value is fully realized when the system is finally retired. This longer value stream concept can be decomposed into a set of fundamental building blocks: application services, infrastructure services, assets, and technology products.

The object of this analysis has been to decompose high-level, inarguable fundamentals just enough to allow for analysis and eventual automation. The major value concepts outlined herein can all be *counted*, and this paves the way for measurement. Measurement, in turn, paves the way for management and continuous improvement, and so we can begin our journey to Lean IT.

STEVE BELL AND CHARLES BETZ ON MRP, ERP, AND LEAN FOR IT

Steve: Charles, we first met years ago when I responded to a post on your blog *ERP4IT* about how MRP might be useful for enterprise IT management. I'd like to reflect on our continuing discussions since then to see whether we've reached any useful conclusions.

In a traditional (non-Lean) manufacturing setting, a master production scheduling system (providing a unified view of demand and capacity, helping to make well-informed trade-off decisions) supported by a material requirements planning (MRP) system to manage detailed execution activities, intends to *help make daily decisions to manage the inherent chaos.* But it usually does little to fundamentally stabilize the situation in the long run. In fact, MRP often added complexity and caused production to be jittery as the system reacted to each sudden disturbance with rescheduling instructions. This explains why MRP was run out of town by Lean crowds wielding torches and pitchforks. MRP is a tricky and often disruptive intervention if the production processes are not designed to flow. And if they are designed to flow, then MRP is of limited use.

In much the same way, the traditional IT organization is a "job shop" arrangement, where work does not flow smoothly: similar skills are grouped together, projects are often one-off efforts, periodic or episodic activities with sudden demand spikes, sometimes big, sometimes small, and they usually share constrained subject matter experts and assets. In such a potentially chaotic, contentious, and interruption-prone environment, skillful planning and scheduling are needed so that reliable due dates may be committed and kept without resorting to continual heroic efforts. But as we know from years of experience with large-scale IT projects and operations, rigorous planning and control don't always yield successful results, both in terms of on-time delivery and budget.

Until workflows are separated and rationalized into value streams, no matter how well you expose the demand patterns and attempt to prioritize them, the fact is the work that you'll continue juggling leads to constraints, interdependencies, and interruptions. A unified demand view does not mean a *rationalized* demand view; it just means the patterns and dysfunction have been made transparent/visual. This provides input to planning and scheduling in order to attempt to manage the inherently chaotic behavior.

Charles: I'm thinking that the maturation process will start with people centralizing into a unified view and then realizing that (as you correctly point out) such a view is not "rationalized"—it's just a more transparent mess. Then what will they do? Well, I'm certainly not yet advocating the full master production scheduling approach to solve the problem of IT demand and execution management. Recent research into complexity theory causes me to seriously question how effective that can ever be.

But I do think it's inevitable that some vendors of IT management software will start to go down this path, and some companies will try it. It's a very well-understood response— we've got the problem more quantified, now let's throw some method, some math, at this madness. The big IT management vendors will start raiding the MRP software vendors. And I think this is a good thing. We'll learn from those experiences.

However, to your suggestion—I don't think it's feasible to dedicate certain kinds of skilled resources to each product value stream any more than it's possible in manufacturing for every line to have a dedicated electrician. Some of the solution comes in continuing to formalize services via catalogs, which we are seeing in cloud computing, for example—you don't need dedicated systems administrators because the infrastructure service offerings are standardized both in substance (what they are) and in process (how you get them).

But in large-scale IT, there will always be those resources (and in my experience, a surprising number of them) who may become constraints to flow. And I think that I'm starting from a very humanistic perspective—which is one of the things I admire about Lean—in describing the *gemba*, the day-to-day experience for Jane, our overloaded systems administrator. Whether it's full-blown scheduling, *kanban*, or some form of dispatch and tracking we haven't even considered, I'm going to keep coming back to the need to make her life easier. We haven't succeeded until we do this.

The examples of *kanban* I've seen work are in smaller shops. Perhaps that will become an industry discipline—to insist on keeping things small enough for daily rounds of the *kanban* boards. But I'm doubtful. There's too much of a coordination problem in IT shops of any real size.

And the MRP concepts are not dead yet—not by a long shot. In the third edition of *Orlicky's Materials Resource Planning* (just published), the authors come out swinging against Lean. "Brittle" is one of the nicer words they use. I've got other critiques here in some of the management textbooks I've picked up. As an outsider to such debates, I'm looking at it all with some wonder, and I fully admit to still being in a learning process in trying to apply these rich industrial principles correctly to large-scale IT management.

What if, instead of a prescriptive, heavy-handed scheduler, we had an automated system that served as more of an adviser, focused on clearly showing alternatives, tradeoffs, and recommendations as best the system can understand them at a given point in time? Kind of like the models a weather forecaster uses? They don't use just one "plan," they look at a variety of possible outcomes based on different approaches.

Steve: In the short term an effective finite-capacity scheduling (MRP-like) system for project planning and scheduling may help make well-informed due date commitments and scheduling, sequencing, and resource allocation and constraint management decisions. At the very least, the process of designing such a system requires you to identify and quantify the important moving parts, and that in itself is a useful learning process. And you're right, skilled master schedulers aren't "heavy-handed"; they are an advisor to the decision makers, helping them to make effective prioritization and tradeoff decisions. A skilled scheduler, with understanding of the environment and good command of the scheduling, modeling, and simulation tools, can be a virtuoso—but then you're relying on the singular skill of one individual to orchestrate the entire performance.

In the long term, the IT organization should strive to organize itself along value stream/product lines *when possible*. But there will always be shared resources, scarce technical specialists, and the occasional megaproject that requires coordination among many teams over a long period of time. In such a setting, flow is difficult. And the world of IT is becoming more, not less, complex, with the cloud, Software as a service, outsourcing, mobile microapps with lifecycles like fireflies, and more. So the transition toward value stream organization is bound to be a volatile journey with no finish line. In all this change and complexity, it helps to keep one thing in mind—as we continually emphasize clockspeed of iterations with smaller "batch sizes" this will naturally reduce work in progress and the complexity of managing it.

The world of MRP has much to offer when sorting out such complexity. But in the end, if you try to fight complexity with more complexity, then complexity naturally wins. Lean is about simplicity, learning, and continuous experimentation. There are plenty of tools and techniques with which to experiment, so keep it simple and try one thing at a time—learn from it, and try again. Look for patterns of flow-through simplicity and commonality. That's a vital insight that a Lean-minded enterprise architect can emphasize in guiding the enterprise forward.

References

Betz, Charles, *Architecture and Patterns for IT: Service and Portfolio Management and Governance*, 2nd ed. (Amsterdam, the Netherlands: Elsevier, 2011).

Ditri, A. E., John C. Shaw, and W. Atkins, *Managing the EDP function* (New York: McGraw-Hill, 1971).

IBM Corporation, *A Management System for the Information Business, Volume I, Management Overview*, 2nd ed. (1981).

ISO/IEC, *Systems and Software Engineering—Recommended Practice for Architectural Description of Software-Intensive Systems* (2007).

Lean Enterprise Institute, *Lean Lexicon, Version 4.0* (2008).

The Open Group, *The Open Group Architectural Framework (TOGAF),* Version 9 (2009).

Ptak, Carol and Chad Smith, *Orlicky's Material Requirements Planning* (New York: McGraw-Hill. 2011).

Ross, Jeanne W., Peter Weill, and David Robertson, *Enterprise Architecture as Strategy: Creating a Foundation for Business Execution* (Boston: Harvard Business School Press, 2006).

Ulrich, William and Neal McWhorter, *Business Architecture: The Art and Practice of Business Transformation* (Tampa, FL: Meghan-Kiffer, 2010).

Womack, Jim and Dan Jones, *Lean Thinking: Banish Waste and Create Wealth in Your Corporation* (New York: Free Press, 2003).

Chapter 10

Lean and Business Process Management
Seeing the Whole

Paul Harmon and Sandra Foster

The interest in Lean in the United States was initiated by the 1990 publication of *The Machine That Changed the World: The Story of Lean Production*, by Jim Womack, Dan Jones, and Daniel Roos.[1] Since then, those engaged in process change have not only learned a lot more about Lean, they have also explored a variety of complementary perspectives. The idea of process maturity, for example, has evolved as a popular way of describing the steps that organizations tend to go through as they learn more about processes and acquire more capabilities.

The best-known overview of the process journey that most organizations follow is provided by the Software Engineering Institute's (SEI) Capability Maturity Model (CMM), which is illustrated in Figure 10.1.[2] What research and assessments have shown is that organizations spend years developing their process capabilities and that they tend to acquire their capabilities by means of a rather consistent sequence of steps. For example, organizations new to process begin by focusing on core processes within specific departments. Only after they have developed some experience and success at redesigning departmental processes do they venture to try to (1) understand the broader issues involved in cross-departmental processes or (2) define a business process architecture for the organization as a whole. And, later still, only after organizations have even more experience in process change do they begin to

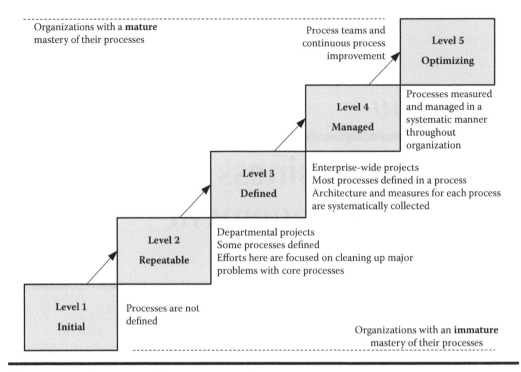

Figure 10.1 Steps toward process maturity.

create good process measurement systems and assign managers to manage processes. Only mature organizations create enterprise-wide systems in which processes are measured and managed and all employees know how their work fits into the enterprise-wide system.

In hindsight, we can see that Womack, Jones, and Roos, in describing Toyota, were describing practices and techniques being used by a CMM Level 5 organization. However, their initial emphasis on *muda* (waste) made good sense because that technique is particularly appropriate for CMM Level 2 and 3 organizations, which is where most worldwide organizations find themselves.

Business Process Management

Leaving Lean and process maturity for a moment, let's consider an alternative approach—business process management (BPM). Broadly defined, BPM has always been a part of process change initiatives, of course, but it has recently received much greater attention. BPM was probably given its first contemporary definition in 2001 by Roger Burlton in his book *Business Process Management*, which focused on how organizations needed to treat processes as assets that are managed in a centralized, systematic manner.[3] Business process management seeks to pull together all the various threads of process change into a single approach that can be managed; it has become increasingly popular as organizations focus on developing organization-wide business process architectures and comprehensive process measurement and management systems.

In 2003, a book by Howard Smith and Peter Fingar, *Business Process Management: The Third Wave*, offered an alternative way of using the term "BPM" and suggested that the Internet, Internet protocols such XML, and new software languages such as Pi Calculus made it possible to create a new generation of workflow software products that could not only model processes but also automate the execution of the processes and provide managers with detailed information about each process.[4] In essence, these new software applications provide a much more flexible way to approach the development and ongoing management of enterprise resource planning applications. After some confusion, the market seems to have reached a general consensus and has agreed to term these new software products as "BPM Software" (or BPM Systems–BPMS), leaving the shorter acronym BPM for the broader process management effort that embraces all aspects of process work.[5]

As it is currently used, BPM includes not only the work of managing an organization's process efforts but also the need to maintain various methodologies and technologies that managers use to monitor processes and to effect process change.

Today, many BPM theorists would say that there are three broad approaches to changing an organization's processes:[6]

1. *Top-down approaches*: Top-down approaches emphasize an organization-wide process architecture, process measures, and process management.
2. *Bottom-up approaches*: Bottom-up approaches emphasize specific processes or activities to be improved.
3. *Information technology (IT)-based approaches*: IT-based approaches tend to focus on using software applications to automate processes.

As a further generalization, top-down efforts tend to focus on projects that lead to major changes, whereas bottom-up approaches tend to focus on smaller, incremental changes initiated by employee teams. IT process automation efforts usually fall somewhere in the middle, alternating between major projects and incremental continuous improvement efforts (Figure 10.2).

There is, of course, no one correct approach to process change. As CMM has suggested, organizations evolve as they learn more about processes and their needs change. Similarly, Michael Hammer, in his talks on process reengineering, often used the chart shown in Figure 10.3 to emphasize that each specific business process, in the course of its lifecycle, required different approaches at different times.[7] When a process is created, or when major changes in technology are taking place, a concentrated top-down effort is often required to make many changes, quickly, or to assure that incremental changes to different processes don't cancel each other out. In between, incremental improvement becomes the preferred strategy.

Although BPM practitioners are interested in and support all process approaches, they often focus on top-down approaches because they are particularly concerned with understanding how all the processes and measurement systems can be managed in a holistic, systematic manner.

In this chapter we will provide an overview of the approach that some leading BPM process practitioners take when defining the processes in an organization. We will show how an organization can be conceptualized, from the top down, in terms of value chains, stakeholders, and value streams. Later we will consider how IT can be described in these terms.

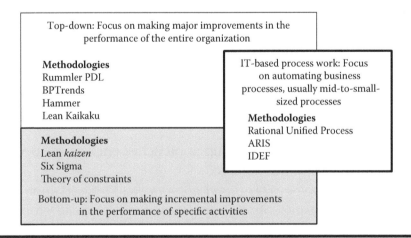

Figure 10.2   Three major approaches to process improvement and some examples of methodologies typical of each approach.

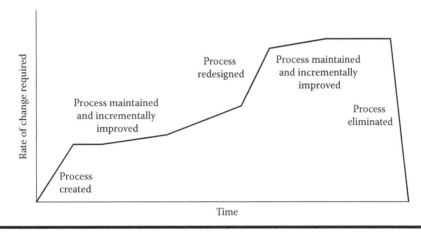

Figure 10.3   Hammer's process lifecycle model.

Value Chains and Value Streams

Lean practitioners have tended to focus on the concept of a value stream, which is an evolving concept. The best known definition of a value stream was offered by Mike Rother and John Shook in their book *Learning to See*.[8] Figure 10.4 provides an overview provided by Rother and Shook. A key feature of the value stream approach is that a stream is initiated by a stakeholder outside the organization, and the stream shows the steps the organization goes through to provide a response to the stakeholder. This is exactly how Steve Bell describes a value stream in Part I of this book.

BPM practitioners are more familiar with the concept of a value chain, as defined by the Harvard Business School professor Michael Porter in his popular book on strategy *Competitive Advantage*—published in 1985. Porter was focused on costing the production of a line of products or services when he created his definition; hence, he argued: "Every firm is a collection of activities that are performed to design, produce, market, deliver, and support its product. All of these activities can be represented using a value chain."[9] Figure 10.5 is taken from Porter's book.

Small organizations tend to have only a single value chain, so the definition of the company's goals and the value chain are essentially the same. Most large organizations, however, support more than one value chain. This means that they produce more than one product or service, which they sell to different customers. Figure 10.6 illustrates the situation at Michelin where the same organization produces tires and researches and sells restaurant guides.[10] The first step in defining the process architecture of any large

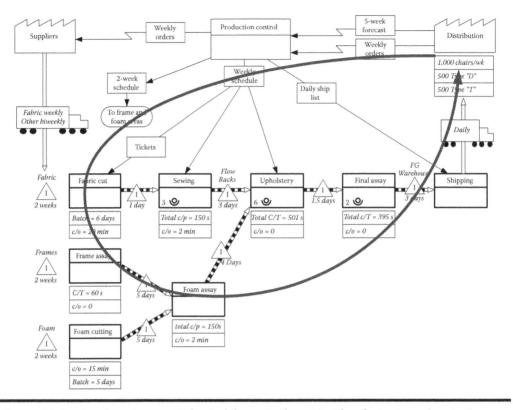

Figure 10.4 A value stream. (Adapted from Rother, M., Shook, J., *Learning to See: Value Stream Mapping to Create Value and Eliminate Muda*, Lean Enterprise Institute, Cambridge, MA, 2003.)

organization is to agree on the number of value chains the organization maintains and then analyze each one independent of every other.

A value chain is defined by a customer value proposition—a description of the value a group of customers expects to obtain from the value chain.[11] Focusing on the customer value proposition, which is abstract, rather than on specific products or services or existing lines or units of business makes it easier to assure that one is focusing on what customers actually want. Focusing on what customers actually want ensures that one won't be blindsided by competitors who might seem to be selling a different product or service but who are, in fact, satisfying the same customer need. For example, it is better to say that customers need information or entertainment rather than to imagine they need paperback books. If you focus on selling paperback books, you might be surprised to find that a digital bookseller is taking away your customers.

If we think in terms of value streams, we can define multiple customer value streams. Thus, for example, there is a value stream that describes how

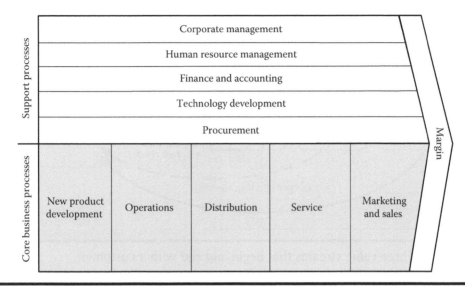

Figure 10.5 Porter's value chain. (Adapted from Porter, M., *Competitive Advantage: Creating and Sustaining Superior Performance*, Free Press, New York, 1985.)

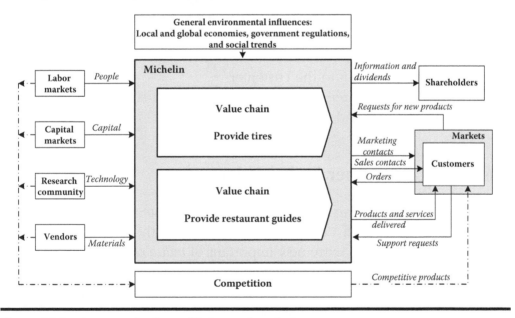

Figure 10.6 An organization with two value chains.

a customer decides to purchase a product/service and how he/she inquires, buys, and receives something in return. Assuming it's a service—say a checking account—the customer continues to interact with the company once the account is established. Thus, every transaction, from depositing a check, to writing checks, to transferring money from a checking account to a savings account online, is an instance of a second, transactional value

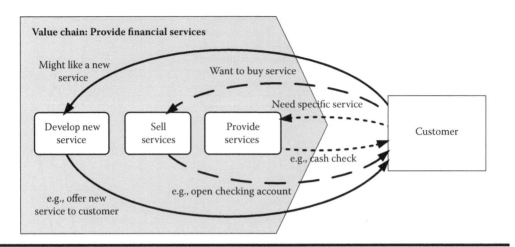

Figure 10.7 Three value streams that begin and end with a customer.

stream. Then there is a third value stream that occurs when a company monitors customer behaviors and new technologies and determines that a new product is possible. This is a more abstract value stream, but you can, in essence, assume that the stream begins with a customer need. The company figures out how to fulfill that need and then generates a new product or service. Then it offers it to the customer.

Figure 10.7 pictures three value streams all within a single value chain that would each begin and end with a customer.

Customers and Other Stakeholders

Note that in Figure 10.7 we have reduced each value steam to a process box. One way to think about a value stream is to consider the Level 1 process of the value chain, which is extremely important. *A value chain has in essence one major Level 1 process for each value stream it supports.*

Many have spoken as if the customer was the only stakeholder who had an interest in whether a value chain succeeded or failed. In fact, every value chain has multiple stakeholders. Shareholders who buy stock have a vital interest in the success or failure of a for-profit organization's value chains. Government regulators often have an interest as well. Similarly, employees, in deciding whether to continue to work for an organization or not, are key stakeholders. Figure 10.8 highlights some of the stakeholders who have an interest in a value chain. Figure 10.9 reformats the stakeholder diagram and suggests some of the value streams that exist to support the stakeholders

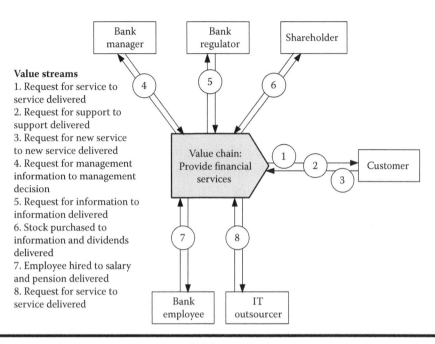

Value streams
1. Request for service to service delivered
2. Request for support to support delivered
3. Request for new service to new service delivered
4. Request for management information to management decision
5. Request for information to information delivered
6. Stock purchased to information and dividends delivered
7. Employee hired to salary and pension delivered
8. Request for service to service delivered

Figure 10.8   A diagram showing stakeholders who have an interest in a provide financial services value chain.

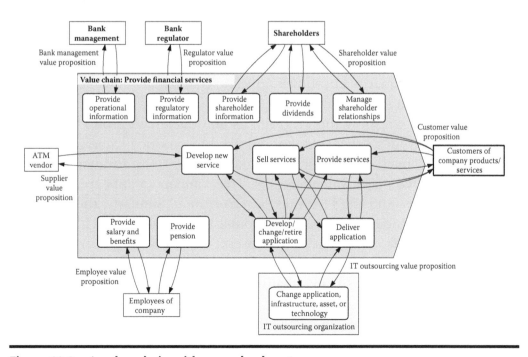

Figure 10.9   A value chain with several value streams.

of a value chain. In essence, a value chain should have one or more value streams for each stakeholder who has an interest in the success or failure of the value stream.

To clarify our vocabulary, value chains, value streams, subprocesses, and activities are all types of processes. *Process* is the generic term. Value chains and value steams are processes that have external stakeholders. Value chain theorists usually subdivide a value chain into Level 1 processes (subprocesses of the value chain) and then divide Level 1 processes into Level 2 processes ("fractal" *sub-subprocesses* of the value chain) and so on. It's not unusual in a large organization to find five to seven levels of processes. We argue here that the Level 1 processes of a value chain are value streams. The subprocesses that make up a specific value stream are, from the perspective of the value chain, Level 2 processes. Other authors in this book prefer to decompose value streams, and would, in effect, speak of a value stream as having sub-value streams, but we prefer to refer to subprocesses of a value stream as "processes"—simply to underline the idea that the subprocesses of a value stream do not provide outputs directly to external stakeholders— although we will see later in this chapter that support processes are an exception to this.

We realize that Figure 10.9 may look rather complex upon first glance. Keep in mind that this type of analysis would only be done when a team was trying to understand the process architecture of an entire organization— a situation in which complexity is unavoidable. Our approach has the advantage of defining a value chain in terms of value streams, thus reducing the complexity one ordinarily encounters in value chain analysis while unifying BPM and Lean in a systematic manner.

In Figure 10.9 we show the IT group as an outsourced group that nevertheless provides processes that are used to produce value for the organization. Thus, the IT group is a stakeholder—it has an interest in the success of two major value streams. The company wants applications and later changes, and the IT group provides them. Similarly, the company wants day-to-day support for customer transactions, which the IT group also supports. Note that in the case of these two value streams they originate with specific business processes that exist in the value stream. In essence, in these cases value chain processes are the stakeholders that need services from IT.

A slightly different situation occurs in the case of human resources (HR), where the stakeholders are employees who work for the company and expect pay and benefits in return. In this case it's helpful to represent the employees as stakeholders of the organization who receive pay for the work they perform as they undertake work for one or more processes within the value chain.

If we begin to define the subprocesses (Level 2 processes) in particular value streams, we often find that there is overlap. A subprocess that plays a key role in a "provide services" process value stream is monitored by finance and thereby also plays a key role in value streams that support management decision making and in regulatory and shareholder reporting. Thus, although each value stream can be conceived as a flow beginning with a need of the stakeholder and ending by satisfying the need of the stakeholder, the activities (Level 2 processes if you prefer) may be used in more than one value stream. In other words, once reaching Level 2 processes, one finds that a value chain is, in fact, a network and not a simple linear or even a simple circular flow.

This approach, as we suggested, is more complex than normal value stream representations usually suggest, but it actually clarifies a number of issues. First, Lean practitioners have always had problems with the distinction between value-adding activities (VAs), necessary but nonvalue activities (NNVAs), and nonvalue activities (NVAs). Considered from the perspective of the value chain and multiple stakeholders, NNVA activities vanish. All activities either add value for one of the key stakeholders of a value chain or are NVA and should be eliminated. From the customer's perspective, NNVA is nevertheless required to create value for regulators and shareholders of the organization. Similarly, other activities such as hiring new employees or accounting for their pensions, which are also of no value to customers, are value-adding activities for employees. And without the ability to attract and hold good employees, an organization's value chain will fail just as surely as if it fails to attract and hold customers.

An Aside on Support Processes

In passing, it's worth noting that support processes sometimes reverse the pattern normally found in the other value streams we have been discussing. Real support processes are recognizable because (1) they are not part of the direct flow of any value stream and (2) tend to support all or nearly all of the processes that are involved in every other value stream. The value of support processes lies in their support of core or value stream

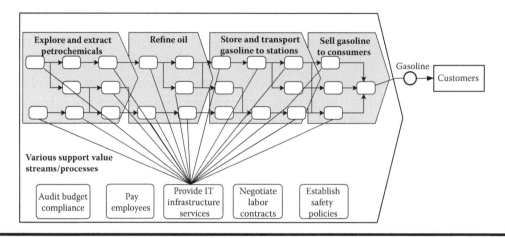

Figure 10.10   Support value streams are used by most or all other processes.

processes that could not proceed efficiently without them. In Figure 10.10, we have suggested some possible support processes for a set of core processes at a major oil company. We do not normally include support processes on process flow diagrams because they would turn the more-or-less clear flow into a tangled network that would be hard to read. When we try to create organization-wide process architecture, however, it is necessary to have a conceptual approach that can account for these complex interactions.

In many cases, the "stakeholder" for a support process is a process within another value stream. Thus, we have a value stream that sells financial services to bank customers. That value stream has a variety of Level 2 processes, including "plan sales call," "make sales call," "prepare offer," etc. At any time, the manager of this value stream might decide he/she needed a new salesperson and then contact human resources to initiate the "hire new employee" value stream. Similarly, any of the value stream processes might want to use corporate application services, such as e-mail, in conjunction with a process, and that service would, effectively, be provided by an IT value stream called "provide corporate application services" designed to provide corporate applications services to employees. Just as a regular value stream might service many different bank customers, the support value streams serve many different value streams or Level 2 processes throughout the organization.

This whole approach is easier to think about if you consider that IT and HR might be outsourced, in which case your organization would be the customer of the outsourcer and would pull services as needed.

Process Performance Measurement

So far we have focused on understanding the overall process architecture of a value chain and determining the stakeholders and the activities involved in providing value to each. We mentioned in passing, however, that this approach would also help systematize defining our value chain goals and measures—which we usually speak of as key performance indicators (KPIs).

Organizations capture KPIs in different ways. Unfortunately, too many capture KPIs only in the context of their functional departments and lack good measures of how successful they are in providing value to customers. Moreover, having captured KPIs using traditional departmental approaches, they lack a systematic strategy for working back from results to causes and thus identifying sources of problems.

This value chain/value stream architecture works well when one sets out to create a systematic process measurement system. Different organizations use different approaches, but one common approach is a scorecard system that monitors a mix of measures to ensure that an organization is serving all of its key stakeholders. Using this approach, it is common to divide a balanced scorecard into four cells: financial, customer, process, and innovation measures.[12] Trying to relate all of these measures to the creation of value for customers is not easy.

Once one determines that a comprehensive set of performance measures for a given value chain should satisfy all key stakeholders—then the problem becomes much clearer. One creates a matrix, lists each stakeholder on one axis, and asks what measure or measures the organization should track to determine whether the stakeholder is being satisfied. If you have three value streams associated with customers, you should expect three sets of measures (Figure 10.11)—one monitoring customer satisfaction with opening a new account; one (or several) monitoring customer transactions on a day-by-day basis as the service is used (e.g., check cashing, auto loan payments, withdrawals); and still another set of measures that monitor the organization's ability to introduce new products that please existing customers or attract new ones. In a similar way, there should be financial measures that monitor the organization's ability to provide a good return on capital acquired from banks or shareholders and still others that determine how well the organization succeeds in hiring and retaining key employees, and so forth.

Some stakeholders are more concerned with certain types of goals and measures than others. Thus, shareholders are interested in market share and customer satisfaction, but they are especially focused on the

Performance goals and measures

Stakeholders	Financial	Customer	Process	Innovation
Customers		Value from interaction 1 Value from interaction 2 Value from interaction 3...		
Shareholders	Value from interaction 1 Value from interaction 2 Value from interaction 3...			
Regulators				
Partners				
Managers				

Figure 10.11   Performance X stakeholder matrix.[13]

organizations financial position and return on investment (ROI). Similarly, regulators may be interested in financial issues, but some are only interested to know that particular regulations are followed in the course of specific activities (e.g., that milk is properly pasteurized or that prospects are notified of certain rights).

Working from a comprehensive description of the stakeholders in a value chain, a team can identify goals and KPIs for each key stakeholder and then use them to assemble a comprehensive set of scorecard measures.[14]

Once the scorecard for a value chain is defined, it can be used to determine whether the value chain is, in fact, working to maximize corporate goals and strategies (upward alignment), and it can be used to define the goals and measures for specific value streams and for the Level 2 processes that compose each value stream. This downward alignment focuses the organization on ensuring that Level 2 processes support value streams. Moreover, if the value streams have process managers, then the scorecards can also serve as a performance measurement system for the process managers (Figure 10.12.).

Lean, BPM, and IT

IT is usually conceptualized as a functional or departmental unit of an organization. In other words, IT is a source of capabilities and techniques. The head of the IT group is assumed to be an expert in hiring, training, and overseeing IT development and operations.

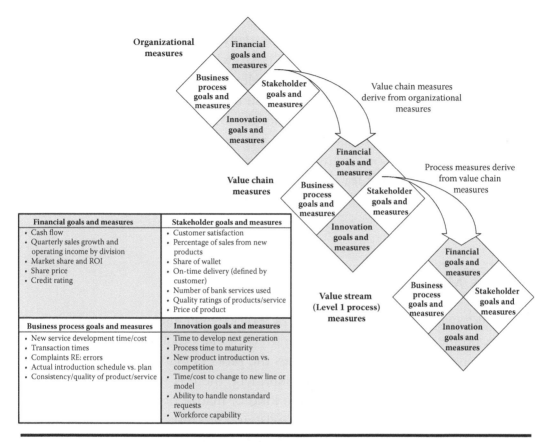

The following table appears within the figure:

Financial goals and measures	Stakeholder goals and measures
• Cash flow • Quarterly sales growth and operating income by division • Market share and ROI • Share price • Credit rating	• Customer satisfaction • Percentage of sales from new products • Share of wallet • On-time delivery (defined by customer) • Number of bank services used • Quality ratings of products/service • Price of product
Business process goals and measures	**Innovation goals and measures**
• New service development time/cost • Transaction times • Complaints RE: errors • Actual introduction schedule vs. plan • Consistency/quality of product/service	• Time to develop next generation • Process time to maturity • New product introduction vs. competition • Time/cost to change to new line or model • Ability to handle nonstandard requests • Workforce capability

Figure 10.12   Aligning process goals and measures with a scorecard system.

Until recently, IT has often been conceptualized as a source of support processes. There were the core processes of the organization that generate a product or service of value to customers, and then there were support processes such as IT and HR that provided support for core operations. Recently, it has been popular to outsource IT—or at least to conceptualize IT as if it *were* outsourced. In this case, one then reconceptualizes IT as a unique value chain (as an outsourcer does) that generates services that are sold to various clients. Neither of these options is really optimal when thinking about a process architecture in modern service organizations.

First, considering the example of our hypothetical bank, it's almost impossible to separate a bank service from its implementation as a software application. Imagine a new savings account service that will provide customers with daily interest on their balance. Talking about such a service is only possible because someone in IT has figured out how to create a software program that can monitor customer savings accounts and efficiently calculate and transfer interest to each account on a daily basis.

From a process management perspective, where the activities originate or where the employees reside is irrelevant. You manage a process to assure that the process generates the value required. Every activity involved in generating that value should be under the control of the process manager. Thus, if we have a bank manager who is in charge of providing financial services, and one activity is, in essence, a software application that manages the transactions for savings customers, that application is part of one of the key value streams and should be under the control of the process manager.

Process Management

We have touched on the importance of a process architecture and on defining a good measurement system. The third element that any BPM practitioner considers is how one organizes the process management system within an organization. As with measurement, there is no *one* answer, but most organizations end up with some kind of matrix organization in which departments or divisions continue to exist and are responsible for particular capabilities, while value chains and value streams are managed by other managers who are responsible for seeing that every activity involved in the creation of a specific type of value is considered as part of an overall process. Figure 10.13 suggests how one might organize a process management system.

As you can see, some software applications may be staffed by IT people, but the activity is also part of the "provide financial services" value chain and hence also a concern of the value chain manager. In this example, one process, "develop product/service operations," has two managers: an IT developmental manager and the manager for the provide financial services value chain. How the two managers divide control of reporting, salaries, and bonuses for employees involved in these activities varies greatly from one organization to the next.

Separately, however, you can see that real support processes, such as those that provide enterprise software and e-mail or that upgrade operating systems, are entirely under the control of the IT group manager.

For most organizations, creating a systematic process management system is something they approach only after they have an organization-wide

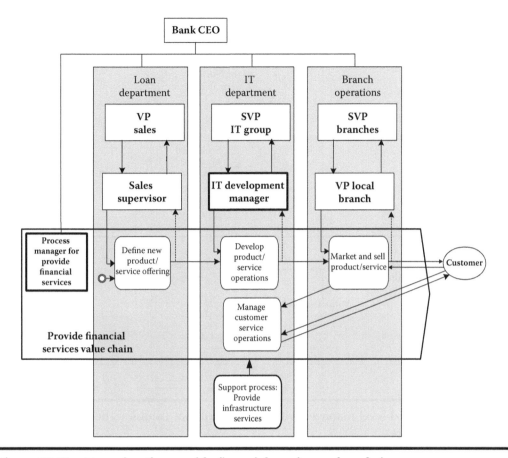

Figure 10.13 Managing the provide financial services value chain.

process architecture and process measurement systems in place. Most organizations focus on having value chain and, perhaps, value stream managers, but they rarely go below that. In essence, mid-level managers often wear two hats and function as both departmental and process managers.

If an organization has a balanced scorecard system that embraces both its departmental organization and its major processes, mid-level managers often find that they have goals and metrics assigned by both departmental heads and value chain managers, as illustrated in Figure 10.14. In effect, the organization scorecard has both process and departmental measures. They are subdivided for the different managers but come together again in the narrower and more concrete scorecards of middle managers.

Most organizations that undertake Lean projects are at Level 2 on the CMM maturity scale. In essence, they are focused on improving specific

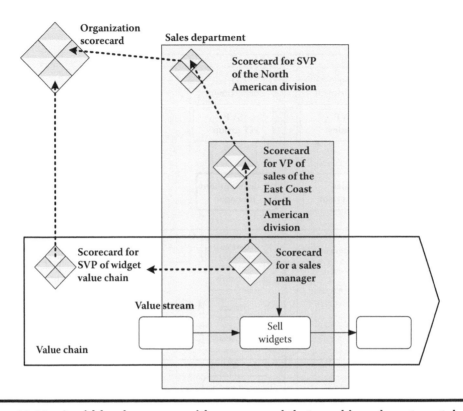

Figure 10.14 A mid-level manager with a scorecard that combines departmental and value chain measures.

projects. This is where most organizations begin the process journey. As time passes and projects are successfully completed, the organization becomes more knowledgeable and is capable of creating an enterprise-wide architecture. Some do this and then proceed to move on to the enterprise measurements systems and, ultimately, to enterprise-wide process management systems. Unfortunately, too many organizations, whether they use Lean or some other process approach, remain at CMM Level 2, focusing on specific projects and not developing an organizational awareness of how to integrate, measure, and manage processes throughout the entire organization. An awareness of BPM can help Lean practitioners think about issues they need to address if they want move their organizations toward a more comprehensive approach.

Although we don't have time to discuss it here, most organizations, when they reach Level 3 or 4 on the CMM maturity scale, set up some kind of group to coordinate process management work. In many organizations this same group may function as the coordination point for Lean and Six Sigma efforts. An effective BPM center of excellence depends on having a comprehensive organization-wide process architecture and good process metrics. If they are available, the center can be very systematic in monitoring which processes require improvements and in ensuring that changes to optimize one subprocess don't suboptimize other processes.

Summary

Figure 10.15 suggests some of the relationships between organization process maturity and architectural and process management activities. Level 2 organizations are just getting started on the process journey and focus primarily on fixing broken processes. It is only as organizations gain more experience in process work that they realize they need to think more broadly about processes. This usually occurs when people in one process or value stream complain that they can't do their job because they are getting the wrong or deficient inputs from some external processes. Once an organization begins to think in terms of value streams and proceeds to organize all of its processes in a systematic manner, it usually proceeds to define good metrics for evaluating the success of each value stream and the value chain as a whole.

Once senior managers have a clear picture of how processes define the work that the organization does to meet stakeholder expectations and have good metrics for evaluating value streams and chains, they naturally want someone to be responsible for achieving those metrics. Good process metrics are rarely the kinds of things that departmental managers want to be responsible for—from a departmental perspective there are too many things

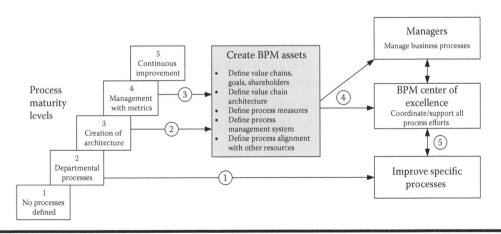

Figure 10.15   The development of BPM assets.

that are out of their control that happen in different departments—and this naturally leads to the idea that the organization needs a manager for the entire value chain—someone who is in a position to coordinate all the activities, no matter where they occur, that provide value for a particular group of stakeholders.

Consider Figure 10.15. SEI has been conducting studies of companies for over a decade. What they consistently find is that most organizations are at CMM Level 2. They have some core processes defined but do not have an integrated process architecture. In essence, they are (1) focused on improving specific processes. As companies run into problems that arise when specific processes are uncoordinated, they tend to move toward trying to understand how all of the processes in the organization fit together. This leads them to consider large processes, such as value streams and value chains, and, ultimately, (2) to begin to specify an organization-wide architecture. Once an organization has a reasonably good overview of its major processes, it (3) tends to define process metrics and to think about how to organize its management system to ensure that its value chains and streams achieve the metrics. We think of these two levels, which are approached rather differently in various kinds of organizations, as laying the foundation for serious business process management. In essence the organization creates the assets it needs for serious BPM. These assets, in turn, (4) are used by business executives and practitioners in a BPM center of excellence to manage, coordinate, and support ongoing process efforts in the organization.

Even when BPM *is* being practiced, there is still (5) the need for the continuous improvement of specific processes. The main difference is that before BPM was established, processes were chosen and improved upon in a somewhat random manner, and after the organization makes a commitment to BPM and developed resources, it is more systematic in identifying processes with problems and prioritizing its efforts. And, perhaps more importantly, it has metrics and management systems to follow through to see that changes are fully implemented and maintained.

We have tried in this chapter to discuss business process management in terms that will be more familiar to Lean and IT practitioners, although there have no doubt been places where a Lean or IT practitioner would have preferred a slightly different term. The fact is that there are a number of different types of process practitioners today—all from different traditions. Each of us, as we deal with the problems we face, gradually realizes that we have much to learn from those in other traditions. And each tradition is gradually expanding the concepts and techniques it includes within its boundaries. Hopefully a new, broader process profession is in the making.

It won't make much difference what we call the new approach, but it should embrace some top-down concepts; some incremental, bottom-up concepts; and concepts from other domains such as IT, business rules, process mining, and change management. We'd like to call this emerging big picture business process management, but, ultimately, it isn't the name that's important. What's important is that we create a comprehensive approach to improving the performance of our organizations and increasing the value our organizations deliver to our stakeholders.

Acknowledgments

We wish to acknowledge the major contribution of Roger Burlton to this chapter. He is an originator of many of the concepts we have discussed.

Notes

1. Jim Womack, Dan Jones, and Daniel Roos, *The Machine That Changed the World: The Story of Lean Production* (New York: HarperCollins Publishers, 1990).
2. Mark C. Paulk, Charles V. Weber, Bill Curtis, et al., *The Capability Maturity Model: Guidelines for Improving the Software Process* (Reading, MA: Addison-Wesley, 1995).
3. Roger T. Burlton, *Business Process Management: Profiting From Process* (Indianapolis, IN: SAMS, 2001).
4. Howard Smith and Peter Fingar, *Business Process Management: The Third Wave* (Tampa, FL: Meghan-Kiffer Press, 2003).
5. Celia Wolf and Paul Harmon, "The State of Business Process Management, 2010," http://www.bptrends.com.
6. See Paul Harmon, "The Scope and Evolution of Business Process Management," a chapter in J. Vom Brocke and Michael Rosemann, eds., *Handbook on Business Process Management, 1: Introduction, Methods and Information Systems* (Heidelberg, Germany: Springer, 2010).
7. Figure 10.3 is modeled after a figure used in a talk by Michael Hammer attended by the lead author ca. 1995.
8. Mike Rother and John Shook, *Learning to See: Value Stream Mapping to Create Value and Eliminate Muda* (Cambridge, MA: Lean Enterprise Institute, 2003).
9. Michael E. Porter, *Competitive Advantage: Creating and Sustaining Superior Performance* (New York: Free Press, 1985). Figure modified from Figure 2-2 on page 37.

10. This diagram is a variation on an organization diagram that Geary Rummler has popularized in his work. It puts the emphasis on picturing an organization as a system (or process) with inputs and outputs. See, for example, Geary Rummler, Alan J. Ramias, and Richard A. Rummler, *White Space Revisited: Creating Value through Process* (San Francisco: Jossey-Bass, 2010).
11. James C. Anderson, James A. Narus, and Wouter Van Rossum, "Customer Value Propositions in Business Markets," *Harvard Business Review* (March 2006).
12. Robert S. Kaplan and David P. Norton, *The Balanced Scorecard: Translating Strategy into Action* (Boston: Harvard Business School Press, 1996).
13. This and other diagrams from this article were originally created for and are used in the BPTrends Associates BPM. For a good overview of this methodology, see Paul Harmon, *Business Process Change*, 2nd ed. (San Francisco: Morgan Kaufmann, 2007).
14. When Steve Bell read this chapter, he noted, "In my experience, many organizations I see taking the Lean journey do so from a bottom-up perspective, lacking the systemic view to create a rational process orientation and ownership. I believe this is one of the key reasons why many well-intentioned Lean transformations fail! The fundamental premise of Lean is that organizations manage their activities along value stream alignment, but few seem to be able to work themselves through to the matrix management relationships that are part of a business process management and measurement system in a sustainable and rational way. There is a significant opportunity for Lean programs to leverage the power of BPM process architecture, process ownership, and measurement." We agree.

Chapter 11

Lean IT Service Management
Understanding and Navigating the Cultural Silos of IT Value Streams

Troy DuMoulin

Fundamentally the information technology (IT) function's reason for existence and right to ongoing funding is based on successfully performing the duties of a trusted service provider. As such, IT is charged with delivering outcomes customers want, value, and for which they are willing to pay. However, being a service provider does not make IT unique, distinct, or special within a business context. In a typical business, there are many support functions, such as human resources (HR), fleet management, facilities management, engineering, finance, accounting, and so on. Each of these support functions plays a key role (1) as a service provider to the line of business customers, (2) in external market value generation, and (3) in the larger business ecosystem. They all provide important services that are necessary for the overall business organization to grow and meet changing market demands.

At least this is how an academic or business school professor would describe IT's relationship with business. The challenge is that reality does not often reflect this textbook and even logical perspective. From experience, most readers will observe that the cultural reality is much more complex, disjointed, and often dysfunctional.

If you ask most business stakeholders if they believe IT understands their priorities and challenges, you will hear a uniform "no." In turn, the IT members will often see themselves as unique with separate goals (although somehow aligned) from the business customers they serve. This cultural perception of separation and distinction is not a one-sided view but is shared by the business units themselves. They often hold to the profound belief that IT is not part of the core business competency.

The fallacy of both views is that it would be difficult, if not impossible, in a twenty-first-century organization to identify a single major business process that is not highly automated if not completely dependent upon digital outputs. Information systems have in effect become as much a part of the business process as older technologies that have long been taken for granted. Information systems are not "nice-to-have" technologies but are simply part of the line or business value system. Point being: Business outcomes are wholly dependent on information technology and are very much part of the business core competency.

The false perception of separation represents a cultural gap that makes process improvement across business units and IT groups very difficult. To accurately map and improve a cross-functional value stream, it is important that all stakeholders involved in the improvement activities participate both willingly and in agreement on a shared goal. Effective value stream mapping depends upon understanding the linkage of the *who, what, when, where,* and *how* those goals are accomplished. For most business processes, the *how* is automated within information systems supported by digital data stores.

Attempting effective business value stream improvements without this acknowledgement and cultural acceptance is problematic at best and disastrous in a worst-case scenario.

As an interesting anecdotal example of business and IT separation, I once delivered a presentation on IT management best practices to a large-city transit authority. In attendance was a mixed audience. A number of the attendees were from the internal IT department, reporting up to the CIO. These attendees understood themselves to be part of the IT organization with such titles as network administrator, server administrator, database manager, and so on. This group of people spent their days focused on optimizing and managing networks, applications, and servers. In the same room was a group of people who reported to a business unit. These individuals were responsible for the systems related to scheduling and operating the trains and buses. However, they also managed their own separate networks, vendor-supplied applications, servers, databases, and so on, all outside the management and oversight of the IT function and the CIO. The business group had titles such as engineer, analyst, and scheduler and saw themselves as the business and the customer of the CIO organization. Both groups managed technology that automated the trains and bus transportation system. These two groups depended upon one other in regard to technology and data integration but did not share processes or priorities. One group thought of itself as IT and the other as the business.

- The question is which of the two groups had the more accurate view of its role within the business? (The CIO's group was in the business of technology management; the other was in the business of mass transit.)
- What risks does the lack of integrated management practices across the two groups managing interdependent technology systems pose to the business—not to mention the public using the transit systems?
- What impact does this perception of separation have on mapping and improving value streams that depend upon the participation of both groups?

In actual fact, the reality of artificial separation based on culture and organizational design goes much deeper than business and IT separation. Within the IT function itself groups are typically culturally fractured along technology lines—one of the most pronounced being the cultural divide separating development groups from operations. These separations and sometimes antagonistic relationships also challenge the improvement of value stream and IT management processes, which span departmental silos.

Understanding and working within this cultural maze rather than ignoring its existence is a critical success factor in applying Lean improvement principles to IT management processes.

To explore this topic fully this chapter will work through the following structure:

1. *Organizational separation*: What is it, and why is it a problem especially for Lean improvement projects?
2. *Two underlying causes of separation*: Organizational structural issues and cultural barriers.
3. *IT cultural maturity model*: A way to assess the organization's readiness for value stream improvement.
4. Practical advice on applying the model to support Lean improvement objectives.

IT Services and Underpinning Management Systems

The IT function is a service provider that receives demand for and delivers a variety of technical and professional services to support ongoing business needs. Underpinning this macro demand-supply value stream is an IT management system of interdependent and organizationally agnostic processes.

The IT management system in effect supports and underpins the basic enterprise IT value stream flow of demand → plan → build → run (DPBR) based on business requirements.

This generic value stream is defined and documented by various IT management frameworks such as The Information Technology Infrastructure Library (ITIL) and Control Objectives for Information and Related Technology (COBIT). Both frameworks use slightly different terms and provide different levels of detail for different goals, but the basic value stream is the same. For example:

- **ITIL** – service strategy, service design, service transition, service operation, continual service improvement
- **COBIT** – plan and organize, acquire and implement, deliver and support, monitor and evaluate

These two examples represent IT management frameworks that focus on the full DPBR value stream. It is useful to understand that there are also other frameworks that have a narrower but deeper focus on specific practice areas. For example:

- Capability Maturity Model Integrated (CMMi) for software development lifecycle management
- The Open Group Architecture Framework (TOGAF) for IT systems architecture
- Projects In Controlled Environments (Prince2) for project management
- Project Management Body of Knowledge (PMBOK) for project management

For the most part, technology functions understand and execute the various individual steps of this value stream with some degree of success or maturity (and suboptimization). The challenge and risk of the enterprise IT value stream is in the handoffs between these steps across the full DPBR value stream. For example:

1. Not understanding demand causes IT to deliver services that do not meet business needs.
2. Having limited-to-no input from demand into plan is a recipe for not getting the service design specifications correct.
3. Not understanding the plan or design specifications causes confusion in the identification of acceptance criteria for the building, testing, and promotion to production tasks.
4. Having nonaligned, poorly designed, insufficiently tested, and ill-coordinated service elements being introduced to the run/production environment delivers service outcomes that are unreliable and do not meet business needs.

The perception of separation discussed in this chapter is sometimes referred to as "silo mentality" and is by no means unique to IT functions but can trace its roots to early industrial organization design models focused on task specialization.

Since the early industrial revolution and the advent of modern manufacturing processes pioneered by men such as Henry Ford, organizational design has focused on breaking apart complex processes and value streams into the smallest individual tasks. One important reason for this approach was that at the turn of the last century the general workforce lacked highly skilled resources because most employees had recently moved from a rural cottage industry to an industrial model. In addition to the skills shortage, early industry was faced with severe challenges around general communication and collaboration tools. This created a need to simplify each person's task down to a set of focused and repeated activities.

However, still requiring the ability to maintain a larger picture of the entire process, the organization created a foreman or manager position to oversee a small set of related tasks performed by individuals, and then a middle manager to supervise that foreman and his related peers. Following this model, a senior manager was needed to oversee a set of middle managers that managed similar teams. The resulting organization was comprised of large vertically oriented management pyramids or silos focused on groups of like activities where communication was relatively efficient vertically through the pyramid but was extremely challenging when collaboration was required between silos. This management structure of task segmentation coupled with the need to create layers of management roles to hold the big picture together was the only practical way to accomplish large and complex objectives with the limitations facing the early industrial age. Thus was born our modern-day organizational design.

The unfortunate and undesirable cultural effect of this structure is to give individuals the false belief that they only have one task or specialty area with which to be concerned. This focus on task specialization and the typical supporting measurement and reward systems encourage individuals and groups to ignore the context or goals of the greater value system. For example, your job is to put brake pedals on the cars as they move past; you will do this as efficiently and as quickly as possible; this is what you are paid to do, nothing else; anything you do outside this task is someone else's job. These management structures are still used today, even though many of the reasons for their creation no longer apply.

In an IT context, this translates into management silos that are created around like-technology domains or platforms such as servers, databases, or applications. Today in IT you can see the culture of task segmentation clearly when the individuals in these entrenched silos, such as network administrators or application developers, believe fervently that they are doing the service desk a favor if they fix something. In their minds, responding to incidents is someone else's job. The inherent problem with task segmentation is that—by the very act of breaking down the complex processes into individual tasks or activities—those who perform the individual tasks do not always understand and accept their role in the overall picture.

We have lost sight of the forest by focusing on the trees!

The base premise of organizational design and corresponding HR job descriptions based solely on task specialization is that there is often an accompanying belief that by improving or optimizing each task the overall system will benefit. However, from the research and writings of Eli Goldratt on the theory of constraints (TOC), we know that no complex system or process can be more efficient than its limiting constraint or bottleneck.

So with this principle in mind it is critical to map out the entire DPBR flow of IT value creation to understand its limitations and constraints.

One of the critical success factors and deliverables that an IT organization must put in place to successfully battle a silo culture is the documentation and communication of the processes within the DPBR value stream. Process documentation is a tool or enabler to Lean goals but not the goal itself. By documenting and gaining agreement on expectations of policy, activities, and roles within the value flow, you remove ambiguity and subjectivity from improvement discussions

In this context, the IT function is like any factory where orders for goods and services are translated into results our customers want and for which they are willing to pay. The speed with which we translate capabilities and resources into customer value or in TOC terms "throughput" is also a key contributor to customer satisfaction. However, to improve throughput and speed it is critical to understand, map, and manage the flow of value from demand to supply—not just the individual activities. A successful service provider needs to manage how demand for a service (or product) is received and the means by which it assures that the services are designed according to specification and delivered into a stable operations environment.

The factory metaphor runs counter to the popular IT self-image. IT professionals often take issue with the concept of thinking of themselves in terms of a demand-based supply chain. Instead they prefer to focus on the role of research and development (R&D): running projects and developing software. Although R&D is certainly one aspect of the IT value stream (D, **plan**, **build**, R), it only produces the potential for value. The value of the project or new software is only fully realized when it is transitioned successfully into a stable and well-managed RUN environment.

So in that context, it is critical to IT's provider mandate that we need to understand the full sequence of processes for turning demand into valued outcomes. This means that we need to intimately understand and map the flow of work on the shop floor regardless of which functions or suppliers are performing the interdependent tasks.

To be successful at this objective, IT staff need to understand and accept their part in the macro process flows that tie together their specific capability areas as they relate to customer relations (demand), pipeline management (plan, build), operations (run), continual improvement, and governance activities.

This macro process model of the IT shop floor is often called an "operating model," and its definition and management are essential to plan, manage, and tune the flow of productivity through the enterprise DPBR IT value stream. In fact, referring again to the theory of constraints, understanding the full management system in terms of inventory, throughput, and cost is a critical step in determining the location of bottlenecks and applying Lean thinking to continual service improvement.

Operating Model Definition

An IT organization's operating model and its defined list of corresponding capabilities, objectives, and measures are an extension and deliverable of the IT governance's task of "Direct, Monitor and Evaluate," as described by ISO 38500. IT governance is responsible for (defining, establishing, and measuring) the enterprise IT (vision, strategy, policies, organizational structures, and capabilities) required to support business value generation and corporate governance requirements.

An operating model is also a logical representation or blueprint of the IT value stream architecture (Figure 11.1), and it is agnostic insofar as existing organizational structure and sourcing strategies are concerned. The operating model provides a framework to identify and define the major activities, capabilities, process dependencies, and critical success factors required to directly or indirectly convert customer requirements or requests into the expected service outcomes or deliverables.

The operating model initially provides an agreed framework against which to conduct a baseline gap assessment to determine which value stream activities should be a priority for Lean improvement projects.

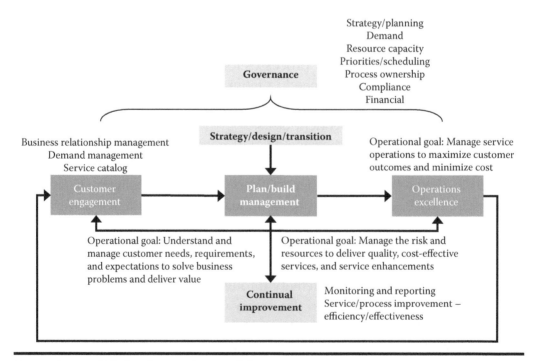

Figure 11.1 High-level operating model.

Outputs of the initial operating model assessment support management decisions related to the following:

1. Organizational structure, governance, and process ownership
2. Enterprise process/capability improvement prioritization
3. Creation of management dashboards and key performance indicators
4. Sourcing strategy
5. IT management tool and automation requirements

The operating model provides the basis for Lean value stream mapping and continual service improvement and is reviewed and adjusted as required.

The purpose of a clearly defined operating model can be summarized by the following assumptions:

- What is defined can be controlled and stabilized.
- What is stabilized can be measured accurately.
- What is measured accurately can be quantifiably improved.

Knowledge versus Acceptance

In the previous section we made the case for *understanding* the end-to-end DPBR value stream as a key dependency for Lean thinking at an enterprise IT or system level. Although it is true that to define is the basis for what can be controlled, measured, or improved, it is also true that the people involved in the full DPBR value stream have to *accept* that they are part of a larger system if they are expected to behave differently over the long term.

In fact, perhaps the most difficult constraint to overcome is the emotional acceptance of their roles beyond their specific specializations. For example, IT management frameworks such as ITIL and standards such as ISO 20000 have been around for two decades. However, it could be argued that global adoption has been limited. Is this the fault of the framework or the cultural readiness of IT to embrace or adopt the necessary cultural and process changes? And is the resistance to adoption an organizational or individual challenge?

Perhaps the most difficult constraint at play is not the head (understand) but the heart (accept). Professor John Kotter from the Harvard Business School describes the importance of the heart or emotional acceptance of change in his book *Leading Change*. Change efforts in their simplest form focus on the individual through education and awareness. Although one can improve knowledge of the larger change context, education and training alone do not assure final acceptance by those individuals or groups who must change how they work every day in order to achieve the desired end result, especially if there is no consequence for their noncompliance.

In essence, the first and most important step in a value stream improvement project is to reach the heart of the matter and to gain acceptance for the transformation goals. Changing attitudes, behaviors, and eventually culture starts with an understanding of the current state of mind/heart of those who will have to participate in and are affected by the change. In essence, to address value stream improvements across departments, individuals managing applications, servers, network devices, or databases must believe in and see the need for change. As a group they must share and value the broader goals that reside outside their silos and specialized task areas.

The silo mentality is further institutionalized by the fact that most HR job descriptions are limited to the activities and measurements related to an individual's specific functional area. Very few organizations have the insight to include in HR job documentation the expectations and measurements related to an individual's accountability and execution of the IT value stream processes that extend beyond a specific department or functional area. In other words, the concept of separation is built into the description of the roles and responsibilities used to guide and measure individual performance.

If you agree with the old saying that you "manage what you measure," then continuing to limit the focus of measurement on task specialization is a key contributor to the culture of silo or tribal mentality and a key constraint to value stream improvement. Measures must be aligned to focus on both individual and team behavior that drives desired outcomes.

Accepting a Common Management System

Because the culture of separation and its institutionalization by prevailing organizational structures and measurement systems can be strong, it becomes critical for the reader to understand the cultural context in which you are making changes.

Gaining the emotional agreement of the various groups (both business and IT) that a common management system is a base requirement for optimizing the DPBR value stream is often the first and most difficult task. Many companies that have invested significant time, energy, and resources in process improvement and costly automation have failed to realize any significant value from their efforts because of the inevitable collision with the hidden iceberg of culture, with resistance to change floating below the surface.

IT management frameworks such as ITIL, COBIT, CMMi, and TOGAF provide good practice descriptions. However, these frameworks only provide a definition of what can be achieved if they are introduced into a receptive environment. They do not in and of themselves create that environment.

IT Organization Culture Model

In this section I will present a cultural model that identifies the various shifts in belief and behavior that affect how IT sees its role within a business context and how those changes enable or block an organization's willingness to share a common goal and participate in cross-functional value stream activities.

The cultural model shown in Figure 11.2 is based on a model first published as part of ITIL's Planning to Implement Service Management.[1] This model represents how IT organizations evolve in both the perception of the IT purpose and their relationship to generating business value.

The key premise of this model is that IT strategy, governance, organizational structures, and measures change as organizations evolve from one maturity level to the next. The evolution is manifested in changes to the IT organizational role and the relationship to the overall business value stream introduced earlier in the chapter. The model progresses through the following stages:

1. Technology and project management focus
2. System and service management focus
3. Supplier/business customer focus
4. Business partner focus
5. Business value stream focus

Each of these levels has distinct characteristics in how IT views the following concepts:

External customer-focused External market flow	• Business revenue directly generated by the sale of IT services to external customers • IT-based services and their digital transactions perceived to be integral and synonymous with the business processes they support • Market share and stock price influenced by the market's perception of the quality and stability of IT capability
Business partner-focused Business process flow	• IT executives part of the strategic business-planning processes • The CIO has oversight and responsibility for other departments outside of traditional IT functions (e.g., facilities, processing, fleet management) • IT measures its success in terms of business transactional volume/availability
Business customer-focused Enterprise IT flow	• IT services are understood to support the business process • The IT organization is understood to be an enterprise function made up of both internal and external suppliers using common processes and tools • Enterprise governance mature enough to enforce standards across all IT groups • IT taking and fulfilling orders from its business customer
System/service-focused Application vs. infrastructure flow	• Shared services organizations establishing common services, tools, and processes • Service-level agreements based on services rather than technology • IT services typically defined as infrastructure- and user-based services
Technology-focused Departmental flow	• IT domains/departments (database, servers, desktop, etc.) • IT operations • Infrastructure organizations • Network

Figure 11.2   IT cultural model. (From Pink Elephant. With permission.)

1. *Value stream orientation*: Which processes or activities are deemed to be within the organization's scope or area of accountability and responsibility?
2. *Customer orientation*: Who does the IT function look to as its primary customer group and the focus of its value delivery?
3. *Measurement orientation*: Which measures will the IT group likely capture and use for management and improvement?

Level 1—Technology Focus

A technology-focused organization can be described as an IT function whose primary goal is the optimization of technology domains with a focus on performance and cost reduction. Each IT functional group (e.g., network engineering, help desk, application development) within its domain looks for ways to improve performance and technical throughput within its specific technology area and with an intense focus on cost reduction. The various functional groups conceptually understand that they don't manage independent technologies, but the reality is that decisions are made and priorities are decided by each group based on departmental goals.

Value Stream Orientation

IT processes are for the most part limited in scope to functional groups and primarily focus on technology tasks such as backup and restore, develop application, or new account setup. Management processes will often be unique to each technical group, which causes duplication of process functions and tools, e.g., multiple help desks based on geographic regions or technology types.

Customer Orientation

The concept of customer is vague and poorly defined. For the most part, a customer orientation is not a major concern at this level of the model.

Measurement Orientation

Measurement is focused on technology metrics such as storage capacity, CPU utilization, database performance, lines of code written, and domain-based cost reduction.

TECHNOLOGY SILOS

Quick improvements at this level will need to be focused at a functional or departmental scope. Time and effort are required to implement a management of change strategy to build awareness and acceptance of service and process involvement across silos.

From an ITIL perspective, the lack of system/service orientation limits the organization to improvements of basic support processes related to the service desk, such as incident management, asset management, and rudimentary change control, monitoring, and event management; these are performed at a device and application level with little to no understanding related to business impact.

Cross-functional improvements at this level will typically mean removing redundant processes and tools in favor of commonality across the organizational scope of the Lean improvement.

Level 2—System-/Service-Focused

Eventually, the risk, cost, and frustration of managing interdependent technology silos as independent groups becomes apparent, and the IT organization realizes the need for and makes the effort to develop shared management processes to support coordinated service delivery. Before an organization begins to think in terms of business outcomes, it must understand and manage systems, which are an integrated composite that consists of one or more of the processes, hardware, software, facilities, and people that provide a capability to satisfy a stated need or objective.

In other words, members of the IT organization begin to understand the need to manage technology solutions such as the SAP System or the MS Exchange System as a logical entity, which is made up of technology components from across multiple domains. System thinking is typically observed as each domain-based group captures and manages data about key technology relationships and other technology domains. For example, a server spreadsheet will have a new column added to track installed applications on each server.

A focus on the availability of business critical applications such as e-mail or enterprise resource planning applications are often a prime driver for managing system relationships. In these cases, business risk and regulatory requirements often dictate the need to understand and manage relational dependencies of the key technical and contractual objects that together deliver the full technology solution.

At this maturity level, infrastructure groups and data centers are often consolidated into the creation of a shared services/operation group. The structure of application groups can be much more varied in their organizational placement. Although it is common for there to be a single development function, it is also increasingly common to see development groups being managed and funded by business units outside the direct governance of the CIO (such as the transit authority case at the beginning of this chapter).

As a typical second phase of this cultural maturity level, various IT functions start to aggregate and to include related IT systems into service descriptions based on the business or IT outcome they deliver. For example, a shared infrastructure group will define collections of systems based on what they collectively accomplish or what business processes they support. Examples include collaboration, communication and messaging, desktop automation, and hosting services. Major business application groups begin to define the application-centric systems in terms of their business outcome: power generation, logistics, refining, online trading, and so forth. This grouping and naming of IT services, based on business outcomes, is the beginning of the group's cultural focus on service orientation.

Value Stream Orientation

With the beginning of system and service thinking, IT groups are willing to acknowledge and invest time in value stream and process improvements across functional groups. Examples of this are the consolidation of multiple help desks and the establishment of a common service desk that supports the incident and problem management processes across various IT groups or customer areas. Another example would be the adoption of a common change control and scheduling process across applications and infrastructure domains.

Customer Orientation

With the evolution of a larger system and service mindset, the concept of a customer begins to take definition and shape and requires a change in management focus. At a Level 2 of maturity, however, the customer focus is often not yet at a business unit level. Instead, typically the customer is another IT group or end user. For example, an infrastructure group focuses on providing hosting services to an application development function or the delivery of end-user services such as telephony and desktop automation.

Measurement Orientation

Building on technical and cost data, measurement now begins to take on a system and service aspect by looking at customer experience such as application availability/performance and the return on investment of business systems or technologies. A key focus of process metrics is on the results of technical support and change management.

APPLICATION VERSUS INFRASTRUCTURE

At Level 2 in the five-step maturity model, there is an openness to develop processes within those parts of the organization that are under a common management and organizational structure. In many cases, process frameworks such as ITIL are introduced by the infrastructure or operations group but are resisted by the application development group. This resistance often stems from the belief that the development group is distinct and different from the infrastructure organization and that the same processes do not apply.

Scope discussions at this level should take into account the willing participation (or the lack thereof) among the development and applications groups based on their perceived unity or separation with the infrastructure side of the organization.

ITIL processes that depend upon service definition such as service catalog, service asset and configuration, and service level management are now enabled by an understanding of and desire to manage against services as well as technology domains.

Level 3—Business Customer Focus

At this level of the cultural model, the IT organization is organized and managed as an enterprise function. The IT function encompasses both application and infrastructure groups regardless of whether internal or external providers supply them. In essence, the enterprise IT function is managed as a single business unit with a shared governance model and strategy. It is at this level that all aspects of the DPBR value stream are now part of the same organization and can align the priorities of each IT functional group to the end-to-end flow.

At this stage of evolution, all groups function as if they were part of a single IT factory or a single but multifaceted service provider. IT functions and individuals also culturally accept and embrace cross-functional processes such as those described in frameworks like ITIL. Examples at this level include the creation of a single service catalog and a configuration management system that catalogs all IT devices and application details.

Value Stream Orientation

The focus on enterprise IT principles results in a common management system. This system and organization enable and support the cultural acceptance by all groups of the various processes that support the mapping and improvement of the DPBR value stream. For example, application groups no longer claim to be an exception outside the general IT processes.

Customer Orientation

It is interesting to note that while the various IT functions begin to see themselves as a single distributed enterprise organization, the relationship with the business is still one of separation. The language of customer/supplier is predominate and promotes the perception that the IT function is separate and distinct from the business. Separation can be a challenge to IT as other internal service providers such as facilities, fleet management, human resources, and finance (as described earlier in this chapter) do not operate under this assumption.

Measurement Orientation

Building on the localized metrics listed in Phases 1 and 2, the focus now is on enterprise measures. Measurements emerge in a balanced scorecard format, and concepts of customer, innovation, maturity of operations, and finance become organizational key performance indicators. In essence, there is a move to develop holistic management dashboards based on agreed-upon service levels in the context of being a trusted internal supplier.

IT SERVICE PROVIDER

At this level the organization begins to move toward improving ITIL service strategy and design processes, which enable a customer/supplier relationship such as supplier management, business relationship management, IT service continuity, financial management, demand management, and so forth.

The risk at this level of maturity is that some IT organizations present themselves to the business units as an external managed service provider. I have seen examples where this has been done to the extreme and has damaged the trust relationship with their other business partners. In short, if you put yourself forward as an external provider, you will get treated as one rather than an internal collaborative partner working toward the same business goals.

Level 4—Business Partner-Focused

The cultural division and perception of separation between IT and the business units are not healthy for either party because they require decisions to be made by each group, which is not in the best interest of the overall business goals. Best-practice frameworks such as ITIL that use the term *customer* in referring to the business unfortunately inadvertently promote this perspective. There is a growing movement among IT professionals focused on cultural transformation that all internal business functions should be referred to as *partners*, believing that the term *customer* should be reserved for the external customer of the organization.

Consider the earlier example in which the transit authority has people who work with technology assets outside of IT and have titles such as engineer and business analyst. Just because they design, develop, manage, and administer information systems does not make them separate from the business they are working within.

Other examples of this collapse of separation based on my experience include the following:

- A major bank, which has moved all data management and transaction-processing functions into the same group that manages the information systems
- A power utility that has combined the traditional functions responsible for power generation and distribution with the IT function responsible for application development and operations tasks of the DPBR value stream

In both of these cases the organization has realized the fallacy of the false separation of business and IT.

Value Stream Orientation

With the cultural acceptance that IT does not function outside the business value stream, management focus is now ensuring that all IT projects, services, and policies are prioritized based on how improvements support business processes and business outcomes. At this maturity level, IT value streams and processes are seen as subsets or enablers to the larger business value stream context.

Customer Orientation

The focus at this cultural level narrows in on business partnership and enablement. IT leadership roles are part of business planning and strategy sessions, and senior IT leaders are included as key stakeholders in the decision-making process for business growth and strategy direction.

Measurement Orientation

IT begins to support its business partners by providing measures that relate to business results. For example, typical IT reports at this level might include the number of checks processed or the number of new users added to an online product line.

IT SUPPORTS THE LINE

At this level, processes such as strategy management and service portfolio management are focused on enabling business partnership and objectives. This laser focus on business objectives is due to the fact that there is a grounded realization that those are the only objectives that matter. IT has gotten out of the business of finding answers for problems that do not exist.

Level 5—Business Value Stream-Focused

The final level of this model describes an organization in which IT is considered to be an integral and critical success factor in achieving business goals such as profitability or expanded market share. There is no more discussion about information technology not being part of the business core competency. It is generally understood that information systems are as much a part of generating business value as are older or non-IT technologies. For example, the business cannot deliver banking, transport, and manufacturing capabilities without the inherent technology and business process automation supported and provided by IT capabilities.

Value Stream Orientation

IT organization and individual participation are now focused on external market goals. The IT function proactively suggests ways to extend market share or revenue through the use of technology, such as smart meters or new online business services.

Customer Orientation

At this level, IT now focuses on the external customer of the business (i.e., the external market and consumer of the overall business services). *Note:* As organizations mature from level to level in the model, customer perception and focus expands. In other words, there is not a replaced focus but rather an expanded one that takes into account various types of customers and their relative requirements and services.

Measurement Orientation

Building on the capabilities of previous levels, reporting is now focused on business measures and market intelligence through customer and external market data correlation using business intelligence technologies.

IT IS THE LINE

At this level of the model, IT processes begin to meld into business process with an IT focus or specialty. The following processes are consolidated as an example:

- Business risk management and IT risk management
- Business security management and IT security management
- Business continuity planning and IT service continuity management
- Business asset management and service asset and configuration
- Business finance and IT financial management
- Business call center and IT service desk

Where Are We Now?

So where is the IT industry today in the overall cultural model? In my view, most IT organizations are moving from a technology to a systems service mindset. Today's process improvement priorities typically concentrate on support, asset utilization, and processes related to transition to production.

However, one cannot oversimplify or generalize this assessment for any individual organization. Very often you will find various IT groups within an overall organization at very different levels depending on their current relationship with external customers and business units.

For example, in a telecommunications organization one part of the current IT organization may focus on the delivery of telecommunication services (cellular networks, messaging, data) to an external market such as other telecommunications or direct to the consumer. The primary focus of this group is on revenue and external service agreements. This technology group knows what it is to be either business value stream-focused or part of the line.

Within that same organization, you may find an enterprise resource planning group supporting key systems such as SAP or Oracle Financials. They often will report to or work very closely with the business finance group and are part business and part technology analysts. They have trouble separating in their minds the business process of accounts receivable and the financial system that supports it. This group is solidly in the business partner mindset.

Meanwhile, another application development group works very closely with several business units; they meet regularly and cultivate a close business customer/supplier relationship.

Finally, the IT staff living and working every day in the data center do not think frequently about the relationships between the devices they carefully manage and the business outcomes they support. This group is technology-focused.

The key cultural challenge here is that within the very same organization you may have different IT groups who understand their role in relation to business value in very different ways. Understanding and managing this complexity is one of the critical factors for successfully improving IT value streams and management processes.

Earlier in this chapter we referenced an old saying: "you manage what you measure." I think a more accurate saying would be "you manage what you *know*." I recommend that you use this chapter and the corresponding model to raise awareness and open up discussion so that individuals and teams can understand and work with the cultural disconnects that may naturally arise within their organization.

People at lower levels who are firmly entrenched in their attitudes, behavior, and culture often do not realize that there are other goals and a broader way for looking at how the organization works. For example, success for a technology-focused culture may be seen as optimizing each domain by making it faster and cheaper every year. Mission accomplished. IT strategy realized.

This is not to decry technology management. On the contrary—you need good technologists before you can manage service outcomes and participate as a partner with user business units. Try to involve a technology-oriented group within a business process value stream *kaizen* exercise, and you may struggle to even get them to agree to attend the meeting because they do not see the relevance or connection to their roles. However, if you work with the same group on mapping the value stream of a task within its cultural understanding, such as improving quality and performance of the server provisioning process, they may become willing participants.

So understanding this maturity model and how it applies to the scope of a Lean improvement project will help you to scope activities and deliverables with the best chance for success. For example, each group in the telecommunications organization example above can successfully participate in a Lean improvement initiative provided that the value stream scope being mapped and improved is understood within their individual and collective cultural context. Thus, the model presented in this chapter can be used as a tool for understanding how to successfully work within the cultural mindset of all value stream stakeholders.

In summary, improving value stream and process efficiencies needs to be understood in the context your organizational culture. Evolving a culture up the maturity scale is a long and deliberate journey requiring leadership and vision from senior leadership. A process or value stream project is at its heart a people project; process documentation, maps, role documentation, and so forth only serve as a means for defining and agreeing upon an accepted truth. The true task is changing attitudes, behaviors, and culture.

Note

1. "Planning to Implement Service Management," OGC, 2002, p. 26.

Chapter 12

Lean ERP
Combating Complexity and
Accelerating Change

Steve Bell

Many CIOs with whom I speak confide that their enterprise resource planning (ERP) system represents their biggest source of frustration, their largest single ongoing investment, and their greatest obstacle to agility and continuous improvement. Many say they feel trapped. If you're a CIO, you're familiar with the reasons. You know them well. They keep you up at night. You can probably skip to the latter part of this chapter where we explore ways to overcome these challenges.

But if you're working in the business, trying to do your job and serve customers, and are frustrated with an inflexible, unfriendly ERP system that resists your efforts for improvement, a system that feels like a ball and chain around your leg, then reading the first part of this chapter will help you gain an understanding that may allow you to more effectively partner with your technical colleagues to create positive change, as described later in this chapter.

This chapter is not just about the specific category of software suites known as ERP; it also addresses enterprise-scale commercial-off-the-shelf (COTS) software systems and suites in general, and the ecosystems of integrated applications that form around them. COTS include ERP, as well as sophisticated application suites such as Customer Relationship Management (CRM), Supply Chain Management (SCM), and Product Lifecycle Management (PLM), as well as industry-specific integrated core application suites such as

Fiserv for the financial services sector and EPIC for health care. So in this chapter we will discuss ERP-specific issues and COTS challenges in general.

Since this is one of the most costly, complex, and pervasive IT-related problems that many enterprises face, we'll use the A3 problem-solving approach to break it down into manageable pieces: What is the problem? What are the root causes? What is the current state? What is our desired future state? And what countermeasures can we experiment with to get us there?

The Problem: Accidental Architecture

Organizations purchase COTS systems for a reason: they provide one-stop-shopping for much of the core functionality and data management they need. But this comes at a huge cost. The complexity and total cost of ownership of such a system can be daunting, although it is often better than building or assembling it yourself (called a *best-of-breed* strategy). But such a system, which represents a collection of "best practices," never really does everything an organization needs. How could it? Best practices are common, and each organization invariably has its own unique processes that don't quite fit, so they often customize the core suite to meet their own needs and/or buy or build additional applications to meet these specialized needs. Then they attempt to integrate these customizations and add-ons into the fabric of the core system. This is where the real trouble begins.

In Lean manufacturing terminology, a *monument* is a large, inflexible piece of equipment that sits in the middle of the plant. Everything that moves through the plant must, at some point, go through this equipment (for example, a large oven used to finish a paint cycle or to cure adhesives). Such a piece of equipment has a long changeover cycle and runtime and acts as a huge bottleneck. No matter what else you might do to Lean-out the factory, if you don't do something about this hulking impediment, you haven't improved speed and flow of value to the customer. For all the value of a COTS system, if growth, change, and complexity are not managed carefully, it can become a monumental hurdle, a serious impediment to enterprise agility, and technical debt on a massive scale.

The typical COTS ecosystem is comprised of many applications that all somehow relate to each other. They support processes that flow across enterprise-wide value streams; they must be integrated with each other to present a unified (or seemingly unified) view to the user, and collectively they contain information to support automated workflow and decision making. Such a complex ecosystem is both a vital enterprise asset and often a significant liability because of its total cost of ownership, complexity, and resistance to change.

One client of mine, an executive of a Fortune 500 company, once told me, "We have over 4,000 known applications in our portfolio, and we suspect there may be another 4,000 we don't know about, spread across departmental servers and desktops." This is not a failure of the COTS system; it's the failure to manage change and limit unnecessary complexity— but with the proliferation of software and systems, large, distributed enterprises often find themselves in a bind. Every day it seems new software companies launch interesting products. This is the free market system at work, and it is, on the whole, a very good thing. With the popularity of service-oriented architectures (SOAs), software as a service (SaaS), and cloud computing, it continuously becomes simpler and cheaper to purchase and deploy new systems into an already crowded COTS ecosystem. And with the popularity of mobile computing to support individuals in their daily work, and the ability to quickly and inexpensively download apps, the pressure on IT organizations to embrace, integrate, and support these disparate point solutions has risen to a new level.

Some of these new applications may be integrated, either tightly or loosely, into the COTS ecosystem—complicating design, integration, maintenance, security, and compliance. Many others may simply be utilized by individuals and teams as "productivity enhancers," leading to greater end-to-end process and information fragmentation. From a Lean perspective, this is an example of local optimization, often at the expense of value stream integrity and performance. And from the perspective of an enterprise attempting to manage its application portfolio in order to provide stable and secure systems, quality data, and relevant business intelligence to the enterprise, the result is often just short of chaos. This emergent, accidental (nonpurposeful), fragmented enterprise architecture is what software development professionals call a *big ball of mud,*

> a haphazardly structured, sprawling, sloppy, duct-tape-and-baling-wire, spaghetti-code jungle. These systems show unmistakable signs of unregulated growth, and repeated, expedient repair. Information is shared promiscuously among distant elements of the system, often to the point where nearly all the important

information becomes global or duplicated. The overall structure
of the system may never have been well defined. If it was, it may
have eroded beyond recognition.[1]

This problem of accidental architecture isn't confined to a COTS ecosystem comprised primarily of commercially produced software. Any ongoing application development and maintenance effort can drift into fragmentation and unnecessary complexity over time. But because of the massive complexity of COTS ecosystems (and ERP in particular because it's at the very core of enterprise transaction processing and financial control), they have a strong tendency toward becoming an unmanageable and extremely fragmented legacy system unless deliberate preventative and counteractive steps are taken.

CIOs often list ERP as one of their most nonstrategic cost centers, the mundane but necessary automation of run-the-business transactions. But business colleagues are frequently clamoring for a new application that must be added and integrated with the already fragile ERP/COTS ecosystem. It's often these peripheral systems that provide the innovative capabilities that differentiate the business, driving growth and transformation. So we somehow need to learn how to manage the inherent complexity and frequent change of ERP and COTS more gracefully and cost-effectively. In order to do that, we need to better understand how and why the problem of complexity occurs.

ONE SIZE DOESN'T FIT ALL

There is so much sophistication and complexity built into ERP systems that they can be overwhelming for teams to grasp and apply at first. Thus, ERP implementations often lead to extensive and costly consulting engagements in which the users may lose control of their destiny.

For example, a large European distribution organization was making state of the art advancements in Lean supply chain design, and they decided to implement a new tier-one ERP system. The implementation partner (a prestigious tier-one consulting firm) was very resistant to learning anything new about Lean supply chain design and was firmly pushing traditional, non-Lean supply chain best practices onto the customer because it was part of their rapid implementation methodology.

After several rounds of contentious discussions, customer executives agreed to foot the entire bill for significant customizations that would enable their Lean strategy. I have to wonder: If the ERP vendor and consulting partner had been more willing to learn from and invest in this Lean supply chain experiment, could they have jointly developed and comarketed the enhancements to other customers, putting themselves in an advantageous competitive position? But by remaining in their comfort zone, a one-size-fits-all implementation mindset, they did a disservice to their customer and perhaps to themselves.

Root Causes

Why do so many enterprises become entangled in accidental architecture? Years ago, a senior executive of one of the largest ERP suppliers told me that automating your business processes in an ERP system was like "pouring concrete" over them. This is an example of *process debt*, where automation can make a process very difficult to improve later on. For example, a "single instance" of ERP,* while simpler and usually less costly to manage centrally, means that local business units must deal with the inflexibility of global standards. This also means that distinct business lines or regions, which may be on different business cycles and maturity stages, must all synchronize to the drumbeat of centralized ERP change management. This is not necessarily a bad thing; a steady cadence is helpful as long as it is fast enough to support the need for responsiveness to changing business requirements. But when the cadence is too slow (I have seen ERP release cycles as long as two years), everyone becomes tethered to the lowest common denominator of enterprise-wide change management and continuous improvement. This can become a chain gang that limits the flexibility of individual business units and value streams.

Then, consider that each individual application or extension that is integrated into the ecosystem may have its own change cycle of patches, enhancements, updates, upgrades, architectural shifts, tool and database version compatibility issues, data model changes, and so on that must be synchronized with COTS ecosystem change management. The intersections among these elements have been described as "shearing layers" and "stress

---

* *Single instance* means a single database running enterprise-wide operations, as is the case with some of the world's largest companies. This is compared to a multi-instance "hub and spoke" approach where local variations are more easily supported but which create additional design, integration, reporting, and maintenance challenges and costs.

fractures," fault lines that shift independently yet have global consequences to the entire system. Their accumulation acts like scar tissue that resists the flexibility of the entire system, causing high maintenance costs and data integrity challenges at the handoff points and, in general, slows the agility of the entire system.

Nevertheless, there is a natural tendency to add more external components to the COTS ecosystem based on individual business unit requirements.* But at the same time there is a significant enterprise-wide incentive to keep the number low. In the *Harvard Business Review* article "Exploring the Duality between Product and Organizational Architectures," the authors describe *propagation cost*, which "measures the percentage of system elements that can be affected, on average, when a change is made to a randomly chosen element."[2] For example, if a system has one hundred elements, each of which has the potential to be changed independently, then a 50% propagation cost means that half of the elements could be affected by a change to one element. (This means that risk and the amount of testing required can increase exponentially as the number of elements increases.) An architectural approach that results in a lower propagation cost is a more modular system that presents lower change-management risks, fewer delays, and a decreased need for a heavyweight release management process; 50% or greater propagation cost is common in tightly coupled architectures, whereas 10% is common in loosely coupled environments.[3]

In the case of a highly complex COTS ecosystem with heavy propagation costs, a rigorous change and release management process acts as both a necessary safety mechanism to mitigate the chaos and as a relentless and frustrating impediment to enterprise agility— with lengthy and chaotic testing cycles acting as an anchor dragging behind the ship of process improvement and innovation. Planned release cycles for ERP systems commonly range from six months to two years. This not only frustrates *kaizen* teams and dampens their enthusiasm, it inhibits the spirit of iterative experimentation we hope to achieve with Lean thinking. And worse yet, when teams are told the change can't be made in time to support their improvement efforts, they may "go rogue" in search of quick workarounds, creating isolated improvement but more technical debt with longer-term consequences.

---

* In a 2010 Forrester Research survey, 27% of respondents had a hundred or more packaged applications running in their data centers, and 27% spent between 10% and 24% of their IT budget on maintaining integrated point solutions.[4]

The Changing ERP Marketplace

Many CIOs feel trapped by their complex ERP ecosystems—stuck in the mud so to speak. It's important to note that this isn't a problem specifically caused by SAP, Oracle, or other enterprise-wide ERP vendors. After all, most business transactions worldwide run on these massive systems. In a way, however, these suppliers are victims of their own success and evolving complexity; many of these market-leading ERP systems have been around for two decades and have evolved through a combination of development and acquisition, with older technologies and designs deeply embedded within their architectures. Although these companies continue to invest heavily in modernization, they leave a crack in the door for competitors to exploit.

Emerging ERP vendors see the opportunity and are experimenting with new technologies and frameworks (e.g., SOA, SaaS, cloud) hoping to make it easier to customize, integrate, and manage change. For example:

■ Microsoft has invested heavily over the past several years, enhancing their Dynamics AX product family (while developing a network of industry-specific partners) in the hopes of overcoming many of the legacy architectural challenges of their market-dominating tier-one competitors. Several competitors in the tier-two space (serving midsize and smaller businesses and divisions of larger enterprises) have also been investing in new technologies; this list includes Epicor, Glovia, IFS, Infor, Intentia, QAD, Sage, Syspro, and UNIT4. Many of these competitors offer very mature capabilities and are starting to chip away at the underside of the tier-one marketplace.

■ Former PeopleSoft founders have established a new company called WorkDay, beginning in their familiar territory of human resource and financial management, with innovative capability and cloud-based technologies.

■ NetSuite, a cloud-based SaaS ERP and CRM company, has been steadily adding capabilities and proving viable in midmarket companies and is now breaking into divisions of larger organizations.

■ SalesForce, although known primarily as a CRM vendor, is chipping away at the fringes of enterprise ERP with an innovative application development and delivery platform (Force.com) that is gaining a large and diverse enterprise footprint.

■ Amazon.com, once known solely as an online retailer, is delivering a web services platform and ecosystem upon which many new companies are building their supply chain infrastructure.

■ Several emerging ERP vendors are targeting the emerging country markets, for example, Netsis, which has developed a cloud-based suite for Middle Eastern markets (see the case study in Appendix E), and TOTVS, which offers a portfolio of products for the Latin American markets.

■ There are also a large number of entrepreneurs trying to break into the next wave of cloud-based and open-source ERP systems while competing for market attention and funding in a variety of niches.

Similar investments are being made across many other COTS market sectors. In the end, however, much of the complexity of existing ecosystems is due to the growth of accidental architectures that resist replacement, and so this problem isn't entirely solvable by new piecemeal development and integration tools introduced by individual vendors.

Furthermore, even in the case where a replacement COTS system might be advantageous to the long-term enterprise and IT architecture strategy, the switching costs and risks suggest that many companies will not make dramatic changes unless they face a clear mandate, such as a merger or acquisition, or the necessary replacement of an obsolete legacy system. In some cases, this may be caused by the changing needs of the business that the legacy system can no longer support, whereas in other cases, the legacy system can no longer be supported because of technical issues or because of a lack of people with sufficient knowledge of the system and tools. No matter what brings it about, many fear that even if change is mandated they won't be able to react and that the new system may ultimately be no easier to manage than what it replaces.

Thus, many enterprises are motivated to better manage what they already have at the core, extending its useful life while continuing to deploy and integrate new, innovative applications around the fringes. In other words, entrenched COTS ecosystems are not leaving us anytime soon, so we need to learn how to deal with them. And we need to learn how to continuously improve them.

Future State: Lean ERP

Are Lean and ERP compatible? This is the question that began my journey of research and writing many years ago. There is a natural tension between continuous improvement and ERP best practices. This can be a healthy tension, but the value stream teams must understand that there is a balance that needs to be maintained between localized process optimization and total cost of ownership and enterprise complexity/agility.

Continuous improvement can be very helpful with ERP implementation and maintenance because teams develop an intimate understanding of their processes and how they want them to work. Standardized work means that the team determines "the one best way" to perform a process and then continuously improves upon the standard over time. Conversely, "best practice" from an ERP standpoint is prescriptive; it is the best (or most practical or economical) way the system can be configured to perform the work. Although some ERP systems offer tremendous flexibility and can be configured to perform a process in different ways, there often is still a gap between how the team might ideally want the system to work and how it actually works. At some point a team may come to the realization that a certain amount of waste is baked into the value stream by the system.

Is what the system offers good enough, or can the team justify altering the system? Experienced CIOs will put a premium on avoiding customization because of the significant total cost of ownership issues, says Barry Brunetto, CIO of Blount International. Originally known as Omark Industries, Blount was one of the earliest adopters of Lean practice in North America during the early 1990s, and Brunetto has learned to skillfully balance the complexities of a global SAP implementation with the rapidly changing requirements of a mature, growing, multidivision Lean enterprise. According to Brunetto, "Instead of letting a team design the process themselves, they should review the various ways the system can achieve the objective, and there are usually dozens of them. The team should pick the best one to meet their objective."[5]

However, the intention to limit customization is often more difficult than it sounds. "While the majority of organizations commit to an off-the-shelf ERP deployment," says Tom Jollands, Lean competency lead for Tata Consultancy Services, "the end result is inevitably bespoke [custom made to order] driven by the demands of the business for the system to map to their business processes, and the vested interests of the vendor to develop a long-term consulting and custom support relationship."[6]

Armed with appropriate awareness and caution to the many costs and risks of customization, a team should engage in value stream analysis to better understand the current state so that they can assess how well a COTS system will perform and the cost of the gap. And when an analysis suggests that the gap is very large, should the team argue for customization? The answer is *it depends.* The general rule of thumb is this: If the process does not differentiate the company in the eyes of the customer or provide some form of competitive advantage, then it may be in the long-term interest of the company to use off-the-shelf capability. After all, ERP best practices have evolved through the experience of countless companies, and they are usually adequate. Then again, if the process is a *critical differentiator,* one that is deliberately (not accidentally) unique and adds measurable value to the enterprise and its customers, then the team should be able to make a convincing business case (based on future state value stream analysis) to justify the long-term cost of ownership of the customization, integration, and change management. But be careful, because what the team may think is a critical differentiator may not be from an enterprise and an end customer point of view. "This is a critical point," insists Jollands. "[B]usiness value must be assessed end to end in the context of the enterprise, not in the IT context, which tends to focus on the systems and software of the ERP system alone."[7] This points to an important consideration that is often misunderstood: although it involves complex technology, ERP/COTS is a business investment, not an "IT project."

EMBRAER'S LEAN ERP JOURNEY

Alexandre Baulé
Vice President of Information Systems
Embraer

Embraer (pronounced "Em-Bray-Air") is headquartered in São José dos Campos, São Paulo, Brazil and is the third largest producer of commercial jets in the world. The economic turmoil since 2008 posed hard challenges for the aircraft industry, and Embraer responded with an aggressive enterprise excellence program. Based on Lean practices, the program delivered strong improvements in all business functions.

The Embraer IT organization participated in the effort, since nearly all *kaizen* events, particularly those related to office activities (e.g., engineering, supply chain, customer support), had significant IT involvement. In order to support the enterprise-wide Lean transformation, IT had to reinvent itself as well. In addition to assisting other business units, IT applied Lean principles to its own development and operations, establishing a value stream-oriented cellular organization. The biggest challenge for Embraer IT was to change its cost structure, which was approximately 70% for maintenance and only 30% for growth and innovation. This gap needed to change in order to support strategic growth targets, but increasing the overall IT budget was not an option.

Because approximately 50% of the recurring maintenance expenditures were ERP-related, this was the first improvement target upon which we focused. Embraer had invested in an ERP-centric architecture, relying on a single tier-one ERP supplier. But for a niche player in the high-tech aerospace and defense industry, IT innovation, agility, and flexibility are cornerstones that cannot be left to a third party. To respond to specific industry needs, a large degree of customization was necessary, making the ERP environment expensive, slow, and inflexible to respond to changes and, to a certain extent, less reliable.

To improve this situation, a threefold strategy was developed. First, we changed to a Java Enterprise Edition-layered architecture using business process modeling based on Enterprise Service Bus software for SOA interfacing/interoperability (loose coupling). The strong process-centric solutions design and open architecture enabled the use of open source software, which helped us alter the monolithic ERP structure, innovating around the edges using best-of-breed software in manufacturing execution systems, product lifecycle management, customer relationship management, and supply chain management, among others. This investment increased functionality while reducing total cost of ownership.

Second, we entered into negotiations with our ERP supplier, hoping to revise our contract to better align with our new business needs. Although some improvements in this arena were achieved, they were well below the targets for which we had hoped.

Third, we diversified our ERP ecosystem partnerships. Here we achieved tremendous success, as it was possible to sharply reduce maintenance costs while improving service levels. The master support and maintenance agreement with the ERP supplier was terminated, and a new contract with a third party was established with much better terms and conditions. As a result of those efforts, in the last three years our IT maintenance costs have been reduced by approximately 20% while our service levels have improved by more than 10% in average time to provide IT solutions, and systems availability has improved by more than 3%.

Countermeasures: How to Improve COTS Agility

Lean thinking can mitigate many of the problems described above both during initial selection and implementation and as existing systems continuously improve.

COTS Selection and Implementation

Lean thinking can clearly enhance the value (and mitigate the cost and risk) of COTS selection and implementation. At the start, cross-functional teams come together and identify the ownership and current state of their processes and define their target state. Then the teams engage in iterative plan-do-check-act (PDCA) cycles of improvement. These teams should initially emphasize creativity over capital, improving and simplifying processes while avoiding technology investments. In fact, they should take every opportunity to retire obsolete processes and legacy technology components. Finally, when each team understands the cause-and-effect relationships within their value stream and processes have become stabilized, visualized, standardized, and measured, the team will be in a position to clearly articulate where new technology investments add value.

Teams can then articulate their future state target and select a system based upon well-understood requirements, making them less likely to fall prey to a persuasive software sales proposition. Teams with keen process knowledge can make a strong business case by selecting the right system for the right reasons and then leading a rapid and iterative implementation that demonstrates the benefits realized within their value stream metrics. In my experience, the "alignment and integration" of business and IT stakeholders with ERP systems are often stronger than other areas of enterprise IT because of this intimate connection with the underlying business processes.

Improvements to Existing COTS Systems

Lean thinking can mitigate some of the challenges that arise when attempting to modify or add to an existing COTS ecosystem. According to Mary Poppendieck, in the traditional world of software development and maintenance, testing consumes a predictable one-third of the development lifecycle. So in a three-month project, testing requires one month. But by utilizing techniques such as test-driven development and continuous integration, Lean-Agile software developers incorporate testing within the development process so that problems are identified earlier, where they are easier to fix. Testing also becomes part of the iterative learning process and not merely a step to prevent errors from reaching the customer. As a result, high-quality software is delivered better, faster, and cheaper to the customer.

Can we use this same approach in a COTS environment, where there is proportionally less custom development and more coordination, integration, and configuration among multiple commercial applications and databases? We should certainly think this way whenever possible. But the very nature of COTS accidental architecture, the fact that the ecosystem is a quasi-random collection of many parts, makes testing automation difficult. I have seen many examples where testing requires more than half of the COTS change lifecycle simply because testing is a laborious and manual process that deals with many variables and unknowns. And when the day comes to push the button and go live, the team holds its breath, certain there are things they haven't tested—indeed factors they aren't even aware of that will break and need intervention. It is their hope that these explosions are minor and cause only a small amount of business disruption and risk.

Can COTS ecosystems themselves be designed to accommodate automated integration testing in the future? Are the leading vendors working on this? In short, I have found little evidence of it. Leading vendors in many COTS product categories appear to be making significant investments in SOA, Cloud, SaaS, and the automated and continuous testing and integration of their own internal development processes. Many feel they cannot maintain their competitive position otherwise. But in many discussions with COTS architects, designers, and engineers from these organizations, it seems that it is very difficult to design an off-the-shelf testing framework that would include the enormous diversity of tightly and loosely coupled components that exist in the typical COTS ecosystem. Nevertheless, COTS vendors (ERP in particular) could make a greater effort to expose application programming interfaces (APIs) and provide utilities that would aid their customers in automating testing to some extent.

COTS in Process Improvement

For a COTS system to support process improvement, those doing the work and making decisions on how to do it better must develop an understanding of the capabilities and limitations of the existing system as well as the economic implications of change discussed earlier. This means more investment in education, training, and ongoing learning and sharing among user communities. With this knowledge, teams will be better able to integrate existing but previously unused or underutilized COTS capabilities to support process improvements. This knowledge will also accelerate improvement initiatives, as teams don't waste time looking for technology solutions that don't exist—or are prohibitive to achieve. In this way, teams may more quickly arrive at simpler solutions, continuously asking what's really needed to accomplish their purpose and deliver real value—looking for less rather than more technological interventions. This was the emphasis of my first book, *Lean Enterprise Systems*, where I concluded that the focus must be on people, process, and technology—in that order.

COTS and the Lean Transformation

Once a COTS ecosystem is in place, how do we prevent it from deteriorating into a quagmire? How do we manage it to minimize unnecessary complexity and technical debt so that it is manageable, cost-effective, agile, and actively supports operational excellence, growth, and transformation?

As you might expect, this isn't a simple prescription. But it starts with discipline, and it requires everyone to make informed decisions in favor of overall enterprise value. Depending on the operating model, the decision may be in favor of local diversity, where the COTS system must manage greater complexity. In other cases, it may be in favor of standardization, which makes the COTS system easier to manage but requires often painful concessions at the local business level. Each decision must be made collectively by stakeholders and guided by a clear enterprise architecture strategy to optimize enterprise value.[*]

So with that in mind, here is a list of considerations to promote a Lean approach to COTS:

- *Establish a COTS/ERP center of excellence*: By taking a formalized approach to education and standardization, creating a clearinghouse for communication and collaboration, you can help establish the necessary

---

[*] In *Enterprise Architecture as Strategy* (Boston: Harvard Business School Press, 2006), Ross, Weill, and Robertson describe an enterprise operating model framework based on two dimensions: integration and standardization. I have found this model very useful in helping organizations to determine how to make strategically oriented COTS decisions that intentionally balance central and local concerns.

discipline to identify and remove many obstacles and risk factors. While the fundamental challenges of managing the ecosystem will remain, your ability to take a reasoned and deliberate approach, aligned with a thoughtful strategy, will pay dividends.

■ *Promote systems thinking*: Educate the business on the subtleties of total cost of ownership and agility and raise awareness of the many hidden costs to undisciplined, one-off technology interventions. Ensure that a transparent decision-making process considers the potential gains for local optimization weighed against the system-wide propagation costs.

■ *Focus on process improvement and simplification*: Emphasize the principle of *creativity over capital*. One reason that obsolete legacy systems are so difficult to replace is because they automate the tacit knowledge of the organization, undocumented assumptions and work processes that characterize how the organization really operates. Only as teams stabilize, visualize, standardize, and continuously improve processes can they release the grip of legacy systems and processes.

■ *Limit customization whenever possible*: Emphasize off-the-shelf functionality. The total cost of ownership for customization is far beyond the financial cost; unnecessary complexity and technical debt slow cycles of change and hinder agility on an enterprise-wide scale due to the propagation costs. When a customization or deviation from an enterprise standard is allowed, it should be backed by a solid business justification and demonstrated by measurable results, with provisions for ongoing maintenance factored in.

■ *Practice rigorous and transparent application portfolio management*: Reduce your portfolio whenever possible; this begins by establishing an architectural framework, taking inventory of all applications, and assessing each on the basis of cost, problems, risks, and necessity. Maintain a database to track all applications, databases, versions, and interdependencies.

■ *Create incentives for retirement*: Retiring technical and process debt is not going to happen unless you make it a priority. This means either requiring retirement or somehow rewarding it, but in either case, you should budget for retirement along with the other priorities (adding new "stuff") in your backlog.

■ *Standardize your data model*: Canonical (common) data models are useful to promote standardization and efficiency across value streams, making COTS integration and maintenance simpler, while ensuring "one version of the truth" is used by everyone for decision making.[8] (For more on this topic, see Chapter 14.)

■ *Loosely couple applications with a service layer*: When applications are tightly coupled they are essentially hard-wired and become extremely sensitive to changes (propagation cost). When too many applications are tightly coupled together it effectively creates a gridlock. Creating an abstraction service layer (middleware) makes it possible to independently change components (or even short-term architectural workarounds) with less risk of systemic disruption. Creating such a layer requires that all relationships and interdependencies be clearly understood. This promotes discipline when adding or changing components or the underlying process and data model.

■ *Encourage vendors to invest in APIs*: Most COTS vendors don't perceive a return on investment for creating APIs and utilities that help their customers automate testing. But the software industry is driven by free market forces, and if more customers start demanding these capabilities as part of their selection criteria, vendors may start delivering them.[9]

■ *Apply Lean-Agile software development thinking to the COTS change management process*: This requires some translation from a pure development methodology to one that involves proprietary systems, integration tools, and complex configurations, but the Lean principles and many specific Agile practices still apply:

– *Emphasize more real-time collaboration and user engagement*: System stakeholders should co-locate when possible and participate regularly in all team activities in order to maximize collaboration and rapid learning cycles. Conway's Law postulates, "Any organization that designs a system (defined broadly) will produce a design whose structure is a copy of the organization's communication structure."[10] This suggests that as each application may be managed by a separate intact development team, the quality of the whole system depends on the degree of coordination and communication among the teams. Thus, if large, complex, lengthy projects are executed, chances are that this complexity will cause the various teams to deviate, whereas if changes are kept small and in rapid cycles, with frequent communication among the teams, the likelihood that the outcome will have coherency and integrity increases.

– *Establish a lightweight project management footprint* (e.g., Scrum): The focus on smaller iterations with visual management (*obeya*) and frequent, cascading standup meetings helps to focus on the critical issues and eliminate much of the traditional project management overhead.

- *Manage your backlog*: Like any Lean-Agile effort, strive to keep the backlog small and highly prioritized and maintain a rapid cadence of continuous integration and delivery. Establishing transparent, visual, rapid processes for approving and prioritizing work across all business units will result in a more manageable flow of demand that can respond to market changes. Of course for this to be achieved, the overall application portfolio must first be normalized, consolidated, and carefully managed. By emphasizing backlog management and reduction, you manage the interface between demand and supply and can thus begin to regulate the balance based on facts and business strategies.

- *Practice test-driven development*: By identifying potential trouble spots and uncovering defects as early as possible, the team accelerates learning and compresses project timing while improving quality and safety. Evaluate test automation investments carefully. Although they're bound to be expensive and difficult to implement, they may pay significant speed and agility dividends in the long run.

- *Increase the velocity of change management cycles*: This is a time-tested Lean technique: By "lowering the water in the swamp" the team gradually (not too quickly) increases the velocity of each successive iteration. By exposing obstacles that are then removed through PDCA cycles, the team safely and incrementally increases speed and improves quality.

Notes

1. Brian Foote and Joseph Yoder, "Big Ball of Mud," Fourth Conference on Patterns Languages of Programs (PLoP '97/EuroPLoP '97), Monticello, IL, September 1997.
2. Alan MacCormack, John Rusnak, and Carliss Baldwin, "Exploring the Duality between Product and Organizational Architectures: A Test of the Mirroring Hypothesis," *Harvard Business Review* working paper, October 2008.
3. John Schmidt, http://blogs.informatica.com/perspectives/index.php/2011/01/31/release-management-is-waste, January 31, 2011.
4. George Lawrie, *Initiate Enterprise App Consolidation to Outmaneuver Your Competition!* (Cambridge, MA: Forrester, April 22, 2010).
5. Barry Brunetto, interview, November 7, 2011.

6. Tom Jollands, interview, November 16, 2011.

7. Ibid.

8. John Schmidt, interview, November 1, 2011.

9. Jez Humble, interview, November 3, 2011.

10. http://www.melconway.com.

Chapter 13

Lean Software Development
*Exploring the Principles of
Value and Flow*

Mary Poppendieck

Value

We held our first Lean software development class at Standard Life in Edinburgh in the fall of 2004. We spent two days with a couple dozen of the company's top developers, followed by a day-long workshop with the leadership team, which included chief information officer (CIO) Keith Young. To be honest, we didn't think we had made much of an impact until three years later, when we came upon an article in *Information Age*. It reported that Standard Life had generated 30% more business over the last couple of years while realizing a 70% leap in profit due to improved efficiencies—and this impressive performance was largely attributed to the information technology (IT) organization. The article quoted Keith Young saying that the light bulb moment for him occurred during our workshop when I suggested that over 60% of the features and functions in IT systems might be unnecessary.

> I thought that was astonishing, that there must be some terrible companies out there doing some really bad things. Then she said, "By the way, we have done a sample of Standard Life's projects and it's something like 64% for you guys."[1]

The leadership team was looking for efficiency, and efficiency was staring at them in the face: the current way of doing things generated quite a bit of code, but it was the wrong code. The first order of business was to make sure that everything being developed was adding value to the organization. They changed three things to make this goal a reality:

1. The way decisions were made about what to do was reexamined for every business. The ecommerce division, for example, took the radical step of moving the information systems and business staff into one department, with everyone sitting next to each other. When a business person had a problem, she simply talked to the IT person at the next desk, who saw to it that the problem was clarified and remedied in a matter of hours or days.

2. The size of projects was reduced from very large to as small as practical—a couple of weeks or a month became the normal project duration. This allowed decisions about what was important to do to be made very frequently and thus efforts were focused on the most important current issues. In addition, solutions were tested and validated (or not) very quickly before much effort had been expended. A side benefit of using small projects was that 90% were delivered on time.

3. A service-oriented architecture (SOA) had been under development for quite a while and was ready to go live. Deployment of this architecture made the first two steps possible. With services, it became easy to change code quickly, safely, and independently. Services were reused multiple times, significantly decreasing the amount of code that needed to be developed, tested, integrated, and supported.

In 2006, Standard Life won two of *Information Age*'s Effective IT in Action awards: (1) Most Effective Project and (2) Most Effective Use of IT in Financial Services. For years, Standard Life had sold financial services to small companies, but a newly developed application, GroupPensionzone, automated pension applications and pension information in a manner that delighted both plan administrators and plan recipients alike. This enabled Standard Life to attract a good number of large companies as its customers, whereas before it had served only medium-sized companies. The IT department's focus on understanding and delivering customer value paid off handsomely for Standard Life.

Tie Work to Value

Standard Life drove down IT costs dramatically during its move to Lean development, but it did not do this by focusing on costs. Instead, the IT organization at Standard Life focused on making sure that every project, every feature, every line of code was going to create value for the ultimate customers—the pension administrators and pension fund owners at their client companies. This focus on delivering value dramatically increased efficiency not just at Standard Life but also at its client companies. The 30% increase in revenue was delivered by delighted customers; the dramatic improvement in efficiency came mostly because the IT systems made it possible to handle the increased revenue without adding staff.

Most of the IT organizations we encounter—including Standard Life prior to our visit—lack a clear line of sight to customer value, making it difficult to determine what efforts will lead to improved customer and business outcomes. In one very large software product company, I was told: "Adding new features to our product is like pouring a cup of water into a swimming pool—we have no idea what impact our work will have on revenue or customer satisfaction." The problem with this is clear—the company had no way to make good trade-off decisions, no way to decide where to focus effort, no way to *tie work to value*.

The antidote for this problem is also clear: figure out how to structure work so that smart development teams can devote their creative energy to designing and implementing better ways of delivering superior business and customer outcomes. Make sure development teams are connected with the people who will derive value from their work—and recognize that this may mean restructuring the development team so that it includes people who understand the domain as well as the technology. Expect team members to focus on improving the value their systems deliver, making adjustments along the way as they discover better ways to deliver value. When you tie work to value, you do two things at the same time. First, you make it possible for the people most knowledgeable about the developing system to make appropriate trade-offs so as to improve delivered value. Second, development team members who clearly understand the impact of their efforts are much more likely to be deeply engaged in, even passionate about, their work.

Avoid Cost-Center Disease

A cost center is a unit of a company that adds cost without contributing directly to profit. The governance of a cost center is well established: plan what will be done and how much it will cost, then execute the plan. Good performance means that the plan is executed with little variance, while costs, if anything, come in lower than forecast.

We ran into an example of this governance approach some time ago as we were working with the IT leadership team of a well-known, very successful financial services organization. They sketched a value stream map that revealed constant multitasking and a serious work overload. The CIO asked us for help in figuring out how to decrease the overload. "Well," I asked, "how do you decide what to do?"

"Oh, that's easy," he said. "Once a year we develop a plan for what we will deliver over the following year."

"You plan for 12 months—so the end of the year is planned about 15 months in advance?" I asked skeptically.

"We have to," he said. "The organization has plenty of money, but it doesn't want to spend any extra on IT. To prove that we aren't spending any more than necessary, we have to commit to what every person in the organization will deliver over the year."

"Don't things change?" I asked.

"Of course they do," he replied, "so we add new things to the plan, but we still have to deliver what we promised in the annual plan."

It seemed clear where the work overload was coming from. "Couldn't you state the annual plan at a high-enough level that you could still deliver on it even if you didn't work on it full time? That would give you time for the changes."

"No," he said, "the plan has to be detailed to the individual level—remember it's a plan that justifies how many people we have, so I have to show a full year's work for each person."

"Well," I tried again, "couldn't you trade off new deliverables against prior commitments? I mean, if you have new things to do, couldn't you expect to do less of what was in the original plan?"

"Oh no!" He was emphatic. "In this company, you have to have a 'can do' attitude. Not delivering on the annual plan just isn't done. People just have to work overtime to accommodate the extra work."

We were at an impasse. The CIO knew he was driving his software engineers to work at about 120% of their capacity, and he knew that this overload was slowing things down and decreasing quality and that much of the effort went to developing things that were no longer wanted or valued. But every time I suggested a change in the governance system, he seemed almost afraid to consider the option; it seemed clear that the dysfunctional governance system was not going to change.

Software engineers are smart people; they can tell when they are spending their time on things that don't matter, when they are not given the time to do high-quality work, and when they are being pressured to reduce short-term

costs at the expense of long-term results. When these things happen, development team members often succumb to cost-center disease, a malady in which
people feel disconnected from the purpose of their work and lose interest in
delivering improved business outcomes and superior customer value. After all,
the governance system clearly signals that this is not their job.

Learn Rather than Predict

Recently a seasoned manager at a very large company called us for help.
The CIO's office was leading the development of a new and improved corporate customer relationship management (CRM) system; she had just joined
the project and had concerns about its viability. Could we teach the development teams some good Agile practices?

We starting asking questions: What is the purpose of the new system?
(Update a clumsy and expensive CRM system.) What is the expected payoff?
(Lower licensing fees and increased sales productivity.) How will that be
achieved? (The system would have a much better user interface.) What do
the sales organizations think of it? (Not clear they know about it.) How will
their processes be changed by the system? (Not clear.) How will the system
be deployed across the company? (Ireland will be first.) Oh! Is the development team in Ireland? (No, it's spread out all over the world.) Well, when
will the system be deployed in Ireland? (In about a year.) How long has the
project been going on? (Nine months.)

There are many red flags here, but the biggest one is the lack of involvement of the sales organizations that will be the recipients of the system
and will have to adjust their work practices if the financial benefits are to
be realized. The next red flag is the extraordinarily long time the project
expects to run before going live and obtaining real feedback from the sales
organization. We shared the manager's feeling of impending doom, but we
were pretty sure that training teams in Agile practices wasn't going to be
much help. Here is what we recommended instead:

> The most important step is to stop thinking about deploying the
> whole system in a year and start thinking about deploying part
> of the system in a couple of months. Select one or two CRM fea-
> tures that are simple yet widely used, and deploy a system that
> does just those things in Ireland (or any small location) as soon as
> possible—within three months at the outside. And then learn: What
> works? What doesn't? What changes are necessary? Adjust the initial

system until it works well—it's small, so this won't take much time. Then add a couple more features and get them working well. Next add another slightly larger location and get the two sets of features working there. At that point, if you want, you can think about making the proven features available across the company. But continue to add a few features at a time to the small sites and get them working before making them available company-wide.

It's time to abandon the idea that systems development—even (especially!) development of very large systems—should be done all in one big batch. We can just about guarantee that the guesses made about how a system should work will be wrong—they may be just a little bit wrong. They may be dead wrong. (We rather suspect the latter in this case.) Furthermore, any solution changes the context in which it is deployed and so changes the problem, usually in ways that cannot be correctly anticipated. It is these changes caused by the solutions that are a central part of what must be learned if you hope to evolve an effective solution. The winners will be those who deploy rapidly, learn fast, and adapt quickly.

"But," the counterargument always goes, "it will cost too much to do one small part at a time." If everything goes exactly according to plan with a big batch approach, then it may seem to cost more to work in small batches. But if we've learned one thing about complex systems, it's that everything will certainly *not* go exactly according to plan in a big-bang approach. Incremental deployment is the biggest risk mitigation technique there is for large system development, and you can be almost certain that the cost of failure of big-bang installation will be much more expensive than the seemingly higher cost of delivering in small steps and learning in the process.

Solve the Right Problem

In March 2010, the U.S. Army published a new manual on the operations process, FM 5-0,[2] and in it, three types of problems are described: well structured, medium structured, and ill structured (see Table 13.1). A well-structured problem is self-evident, and the solution is a matter of selecting a well-known technique and using it well. For somewhat harder (medium-structured) problems, there may be more than one right answer, and finding the best solution requires adaptive iteration. For ill-structured problems, there's an excellent chance that your efforts are not even aimed at solving the right problem.

Table 13.1   Types of Problems and Their Solutions

	Well-Structured	*Medium-Structured*	*Ill-Structured*
Problem structuring	The problem is self-evident.	Professionals easily agree on its structure.	Professionals have difficulty agreeing on problem structure and will have to agree on a shared hypothesis.
Solution development	Solution techniques are available, and there are verifiable solutions.	There may be more than one "right" answer; professionals may disagree on the best solution. A desired end state can be agreed upon.	Professionals will disagree on: • How the problem can be solved • The most desirable end state • Whether the end state can be attained
Execution of solution	Success requires learning to perfect technique.	Success requires learning to perfect techniques and to adjust the solution.	Success requires learning to perfect technique, adjust the solution, and continuously refine understanding of the problem.
Adaptive iteration	No adaptive iteration required.	Adaptive iteration is required to find the best solution.	Adaptive iteration is required both to refine the problem and to find the best solution.

It seems that most businesses have recognized that their problems are medium-structured—or worse. However, IT departments, governed as cost centers, often behave as if they are living in a world of well-structured problems. Businesses are comfortable with iterating solutions to problems as they arise, but cost-center governance tends to treat all problems as if they were well structured, where the solution is a matter of "plan the work, then work the plan." Although this might work adequately for well-structured problems, it spells doom for more challenging problems.

We have found that well-structured software problems are few and far between, even for IT departments that focus on infrastructure, not to mention those that address business problems. The typical cost-center governance model centers on making a good prediction about the future, assuming that the prediction is correct, and creating a plan to move toward the predicted future. If the prediction was correct in every detail, then measuring conformance to plan might be an adequate measure of performance. But this kind of governance system does not take into account the possibility (probability!) that the plan may be less than optimal, and it may even be aimed at solving the wrong problem.

A more useful approach to governance centers on measuring delivered value rather than variance from plan. For example, a business unit might start with a budget and a plan, but leaders are expected to adapt their decisions during the year based on unfolding events. They are expected to deliver good results rather than conform to plan. Of course, this requires that there be some results to measure. If a cost center cannot measure its contribution to business performance, it is often left with measuring conformance to plan. Most of the truly dynamic IT departments that we have encountered have figured out how to measure their contribution to business performance and measure development teams based on their ability to deliver improved business performance and superior customer outcomes.

Don't Separate Design from Implementation

I was a programmer for about fifteen years. Then I managed a factory IT department for a few years and managed vendors delivering software for yet more years. In all of those years (with one exception), software was delivered on time, and customers were happy. Yet I never used a list of detailed requirements, let alone a backlog of stories, to figure out what should be done—not for me, not for my department, not even for vendors.

In fact, I couldn't imagine how one could look at a piece of paper—words—and decipher what to program. I felt that if the work to be done could be adequately written down in a detailed-enough manner that code could be written from it, well, it pretty much had to be pseudocode. And if someone was going to write pseudocode, why not just write the code? It would be equally difficult, less error-prone, and much more efficient.

Software without Stories

So if I didn't use detailed requirements, how did I know what to code? Actually, everything had requirements; it's just that they were high-level goals and constraints, not low-level directives. For example, when I was developing process control systems, the requirements were clear: the system had to control whatever process equipment the guys two floors up were designing, the product made by the process had to be of consistently high quality, the operator had to find the control system convenient to use, and the plant engineer had to be able to maintain it. In addition, there was a deadline to meet, and it would be career-threatening to be late. Of course, there was a rough budget based on history, but when a control system was going to be used for some decades, one was never pennywise and pound foolish. With these high-level goals and constraints, a small team of us proceeded to design, develop, install, and start up a sophisticated control system, with guidance from senior engineers who had been doing this kind of work for decades.

One day, after I had some experience myself, an engineering manager from upstairs came to ask me for help. He had decided to have an outside firm develop and install a process-monitoring system for a plant. There was a sophisticated software system involved—the kind I could have written, except that it was too large a job for the limited number of engineers who were experienced programmers. He had chosen to contract with the outside firm on a time-and-materials basis, even though his boss thought this would prove to be a big mistake. The engineering manager didn't believe that it was possible to prespecify the details of what was needed, but if a working system wasn't delivered on time and on budget, he would be in deep trouble. So he gave me this job: "Keep me out of trouble by making sure that the system is delivered on time and on budget, and make sure that it does what Harold Stressman wants it to do."

Harold was a very senior plant product engineer who wanted to capture real-time process information in a database. He already had quality results in a database, and he wanted to conduct statistical analyses to determine which process settings gave the best results. Harold didn't really care how the system would work, he just wanted the data. My job was to keep the engineering manager out of trouble by making sure that the firm delivered the system Harold had envisioned within strict cost and schedule constraints.

The engineering manager suggested that I visit the vendor every few weeks to monitor its work. So every month for eighteen months I flew to Salt Lake City with a small group of people. Sometimes Harold came, sometimes the engineers responsible for the sensors joined us, and sometimes the plant programmers were there. We did not discuss "requirements" (there weren't many); we were there to review the vendor's design and implementation. Every visit, I spent the first evening carefully studying the current listings to be sure I believed that the code would do what the vendor claimed it would do. During the next day and a half, we covered two topics: (1) What could the system actually do today (and was this a reasonable step toward getting the data Harold needed)? (2) Exactly how did the vendor plan to get the system done on time (and was the plan believable)?

This story has a happy ending: I kept the engineering manager out of trouble, the system paid for half of its cost in the first month, and Harold was so pleased with the system that he convinced the plant manager to hire me as IT manager.

At the plant, just about everything we did was aimed at improving plant capacity, quality, or throughput, and because we were keepers of those numbers, we could see the impact of changes immediately. The programmers in my department lived in the same small town as their customers in the warehouse and on the manufacturing floor. They played softball together at night, met in town stores and at church, had kids in the same scout troop. Believe me; we didn't need a customer proxy to design a system. If we ever got even a small detail of any system wrong, the programmers heard about it overnight and fixed it the next day.

Bad Amateur Design

The theme running through all of my experience is that the long list of things we have come to call requirements—and the large backlog of things we have come to call stories—are actually the design of the system. Even a list of features and functions is design. And in my experience, design is the responsibility of the team developing the system. For example, even though I was perfectly capable of designing and developing Harold's process monitoring system myself, I never presumed to tell the vendor's team what features and functions the system should have. Designing the system was their job; my job was to review their designs to be sure they would solve Harold's problem and be delivered on time.

If detailed requirements are actually design, if features and functions are design, if stories are design, then perhaps we should rethink who is responsible for this design. In most software development processes I have encountered, a business analyst or product owner has been assigned the job of writing the requirements or stories or use cases that constitute the design of the system. Quite frankly, people in these roles often lack the training and experience to do good system design, to propose alternative designs and weigh their trade-offs, to examine implementation details, and modify the design as the system is being developed. All too often, detailed requirements lists and backlogs of stories are actually bad system design done by amateurs.

I suggest we might get better results if we skip writing lists of requirements and building backlogs of stories. Instead, expect the experienced designers, architects, and engineers on the development team to design the system against a set of high-level goals and constraints—in collaboration with their team, who may be product managers, subject matter experts or users, business analysts, quality analysis people, support and operations people, and so on.

A couple of my "old school" colleagues agree with me on this point. Fred Brooks, who led the development of the IBM 360 operating system and wrote the software engineering classic *The Mythical Man Month*, wrote in his recent book *The Design of Design*:[3]

> One of the most striking 20th century developments in the design disciplines is the progressive divorce of the designer from both the implementer and the user.... [As a result] instances of disastrous, costly, or embarrassing miscommunication abound.

Tom Gilb, author of the very popular books *Principles of Software Engineering Management* and *Competitive Engineering*, recently wrote:[4]

> The worst scenario I can imagine is when we allow real customers, users, and our own salespeople to dictate "functions and features" to the developers, carefully disguised as "customer requirements." Maybe conveyed by our product owners. If you go slightly below the surface of these false "requirements" ("means," not "ends"), you will immediately find that they are not really requirements. They are really bad amateur design for the "real" requirements. ...
>
> Let developers engineer technical solutions to meet the quantified requirements. This gets the right job (design) done by the right people (developers) towards the right requirements (higher level views of the qualities of the application).

The common thread in these quotes is the concept that *detailed requirements are design.* By the time a team encounters the level of detail found in most lists of requirements, someone has already designed the solution to a problem. This ignores the fact that good designers and engineers use cycles of discovery to come up, first of all, with a clear understanding of the problem to be solved, and secondly, insight into the simplest, most effective solution. If the problem is not well structured, the practice of starting with a complete list of detailed requirements is, almost by definition, bound to lead to a suboptimal solution.

Outsourcing

One of the most common ways to separate design from implementation is outsourcing software development. There are good reasons for having software developed outside of a company, but cost reduction isn't one of them. If you don't have enough qualified people available, if you have a global market presence and want local savvy for every market, if the skill you need is not something your company does well—then absolutely seek a sourcing partner. But don't separate design from implementation—if you have an outside development team, give it the whole problem to solve.

Sending a long list of so-called "requirements" to a remote team and expecting delivery of exactly what you had in mind just doesn't work, and no amount of wishful thinking will change that. Those things that we have come to call requirements are actually design—and design of a complex software intensive system is an ill-structured technical problem that requires deep experience both with the technology and the domain, as well as cycles of learning between the technology and the domain.

If you are considering outsourcing solely for the purpose of cost reduction—or worse, if you have a mandate to outsource a percentage of your work because of someone else's mistaken idea that this will lower cost—recognize that this approach to cost reduction has a very poor track record. The first step is to improve efficiency the way Standard Life did. First, stop spending time on work that does not add value. Second, connect development team members directly with the people who will derive value from the system. And third, develop an architecture and processes that support small projects, rapid deployment, and constant learning.

Flow

If you want to learn a lot about a software development organization very quickly, there are a few simple questions you might ask. You might find out if the organization focuses on projects or products. You might look into what development process it uses. But perhaps most the revealing question is this: How far apart are the software releases?

It is rare that new software is developed from scratch; typically, existing software is expanded and modified, usually on a regular basis. As a result, most software development shops that we run into are focused on the next release, and most of the time releases are spaced out at regular intervals. We have discovered that a significant differentiator between development organizations is the length of that interval—the length of the software release cycle.

Organizations with release cycles of six months to a year (or more) tend to work like this: before a release cycle begins, time is spent deciding what will be delivered in the next release. Estimates are made. Managers commit. Promises are made to customers. And then the development team is left to make good on all of those promises. As the code complete date gets closer, emergencies arise, and changes have to be made, and yet, those initial promises are difficult to ignore. Pressure increases.

If all goes according to plan, about two-thirds of the way through the release cycle, code will be frozen for system integration testing and user acceptance testing (UAT). Then the fun begins, because no one really knows what sort of unintended interactions will be exposed or how serious the consequences of those interactions will be. It goes without saying that there will be defects. The real question is whether all of the critical defects can be found and fixed before the promised release date.

Releases are so time-consuming and risky that organizations tend to extend the length of their release cycle so as not to have to deal with this pain too often. Extending the release cycle invariably increases the pain, but at least the pain occurs less frequently. Counteracting the tendency to extend release cycles is the rapid pace of change in business environments that depend on software, because the longer release cycles become a constraint on business flexibility. This clash of cadences results in an intense pressure to cram as many features as possible into each release. As lengthy release cycles progress, pressure mounts to add more features, and yet the development organization is expected to meet the release date at all costs.

Into this intensely difficult environment a counterintuitive idea is sometimes suggested: Why not shorten the release cycle rather than lengthen it? This could be an excellent way to break the death spiral, but it isn't as simple as it seems. The problem, as Kent Beck points out in his talk "Software G Forces: The Effects of Acceleration"[5] is that shorter release cycles demand different processes, different sales strategies, different behavior on the part of customers, and different governance systems. These kinds of changes are notoriously difficult to implement.

Quick and Dirty Value Stream Map

I'm standing in front of a large audience. I ask the question: "Who here has a release cycle longer than three months?" Many hands go up. I ask someone whose hand is up, "How long is your release cycle?" She may answer, "Six months."

"Let me guess how much time you reserve for final integration, testing, hardening, and UAT," I say. "Maybe two months?" If she had said a year, I would have guessed four months. If she had said eighteen months, I would have guessed six months. And so far, every time, my guesses have been very close. It seems quite acceptable to spend two-thirds of a release cycle building buggy software and the last third of the cycle finding and fixing as many of those bugs as possible.

The next question I ask is the following: When do you decide what features should go into the release? Invariably when the release cycle is six months or longer, the answer is "just before we start the cycle." Think about a six-month release cycle: for the half year prior to the start of the cycle, demand for new or changed features has been accumulating—presumably at a steady pace. So the average wait of a feature to even be considered for development is three months—half of the six-month cycle time. Thus, if there is no accumulated backlog of work, an average feature spends three months waiting before the cycle begins, plus six months of being in development and testing before that feature is released to customers—nine months in all. If there is a backlog, then an average feature will have to wait much longer to get developed.

Finally I ask, "About how many features might you develop during a six-month release cycle?" Answers to this vary widely from one domain to another, but let's say I am told that about twenty-five features are developed in a six-month release, which averages out to about one feature per week.

This leaves us with a quick and dirty vision of the value stream: a feature takes a week to develop and in best-case scenario takes nine months (thirty-eight weeks) to make it through the system. So the process efficiency is 1/38, or approximately 2.6%. Much of this low efficiency can be attributed to batching up twenty-five features in a single release. A lot more can be attributed to the fact that only four months of the nine total months are actually spent developing software—the rest of the time is spent waiting for a release cycle to start or waiting for integration testing to finish.

Why Not Quarterly Releases?

With such dismal process efficiency, let's revisit the brilliant idea of shortening release cycles. The first problem we encounter is that at a six-month cadence, integration testing generally takes about two months; if releases are annual, integration testing probably takes three or four months. This makes quarterly releases quite a challenge.

For starters, the bulk of the integration testing is going to have to be automated. However, most people rapidly discover that their code base is very difficult to test automatically because it wasn't designed or written to be tested automatically. If this sounds like your situation, I recommend that you read Gojko Adzic's book *Specification by Example.*[6] You will learn to think of automated tests as executable specifications that become living documentation. You will not be surprised to discover that automating integration tests is technically challenging, but the detailed case studies of successful teams will give you guidance on both the benefits and the pitfalls of creating a well-architected integration test harness.

Once you have the beginnings of an automated integration test harness in place, you may as well start using it frequently because its real value is to expose problems as soon as possible. But you will find that code needs to get "done" in order to be tested in this harness—otherwise you will get a lot of false negatives. Thus, all teams contributing to the release would do well to work in two-to-four-week iterations and bring their code to a state that can be checked by the integration test harness at the end of every iteration. Once you can reasonably begin early, frequent integration testing, you will greatly reduce final integration time, making quarterly releases practical.

Be careful, however, not to move to quarterly releases without thinking through all of the implications. As Beck noted in his "Software G Forces" talk, sales and support models at many companies are based on annual maintenance releases. If you move from an annual to a quarterly release, your support model will have to change for two reasons: (1) Customers will not want to purchase a new release every quarter, and (2) you will not be able to support every single release over a long period of time. You might consider quarterly private releases with a single annual public (or corporation-wide) release, or you might want to move to a subscription model for software support. In either case, you would be wise not to guarantee long-term support for more than one release per year, or support will rapidly become very expensive. This is true whether you are supporting a system that has been sold by your company or an internal system with a tightly coupled architecture.

From Quarterly to Monthly Releases

Organizations that have adjusted their processes, architectures, and business models to deal with a quarterly release cycle begin to see the advantages of shorter release cycles. They see more stability, more predictability, and less pressure, and they can be more responsive to their customers. The question then becomes whether to increase the pace and release monthly. Organizations quickly discover that an additional level of process and business change will be necessary to achieve the faster cycle time because four weeks—twenty days—from design to deployment is not much time.

At this cadence, there isn't time for a lot of information to move back and forth between different departments; you need a development team that includes analysts, testers, developers, and build specialists—and the team needs to remain together over time so that the members don't have to take time out to learn how to work effectively with each other. This cross-functional team synchronizes via short daily meetings and visualization techniques such as cards and charts on the wall—because there simply isn't time for paper-based communication. The team adopts processes to ensure that the code base always remains defect-free because there isn't time to insert defects and then remove them later. Both test-driven development and specification by example become essential disciplines.

From a business standpoint, monthly releases tend to work best with software as a service (SaaS). Pushing monthly releases to users for them to install creates huge support headaches and takes far too much time. Another advantage of SaaS is the ease with which a company can do A-B testing. A new version of a service can be deployed to a select set of customers; then behaviors such as usage or changes in buying patterns can be measured. This gives the development team immediate and valuable feedback on what works and what doesn't. This, of course, requires effective configuration management and operations automation.

Weekly/Daily Releases

There are many organizations that consider monthly releases a glacial pace, so they adopt weekly or even daily releases. At a weekly or daily cadence, iterations become largely irrelevant, as does estimating and commitment.

Instead, a flow approach is used; features flow from design to done without pause, and at the end of the day or week, everything that is ready to be deployed is pushed to production. This rapid deployment is supported by end-to-end automation and requires a great deal of discipline, and it is usually limited to internal or SaaS environments.

There are several companies doing daily releases; for example, one of our customers with a very large web-based business has been doing daily releases for five years. The developers at this company don't really relate to the concept of iterations. They work on something, push it to systems test, and if it passes, it is automatically deployed at the end of the day. Features that are not complete are hidden from view until a keystone is put in place to expose the feature, but code is deployed daily as it is written. Occasionally a roll-back is necessary, but this is becoming increasingly rare as the test suites improve. Managers at the company cannot imagine working at a slower cadence; they believe that speed to market is a key competitive advantage and that daily deployment increases predictability, stability, and responsiveness—all at the same time.

Continuous Delivery

In the introduction of their book *Continuous Delivery,*[7] Jez Humble and David Farley state: "Mary and Tom Poppendieck asked 'how long would it take your organization to deploy a change that involves a single line of code? Do you think this is a repeatable, reliable process?' " Humble and Farley wrote *Continuous Delivery* to show how development and operations teams can collaborate to make this time as short as possible.

Two fundamental principles underlie continuous delivery. First, the later you find and fix a problem, the more expensive it becomes, often by two or more orders of magnitude. So clearly you need work practices that detect problems as early as possible and a policy to repair them immediately while the cost is low. Second, one of the most important strategies in Lean manufacturing is to attack setup time. Setup time is whatever motivates you to work in big batches, and for software this is the effort to do final integration, test, and deployment. Many companies attack these issues by developing software in small batches, a few features at a time. To do this they have to employ low-dependency architectures amenable to incremental change and strive to minimize their technical debt.

However, just because a feature is ready to deploy does not mean it should be deployed. Any new deployment could pose risks to stable processes, and with large batch releases, almost every new deployment created some kind of instability, not to mention the training and support necessary for the new features. In large companies, tightly coupled existing systems that operate on a global basis add significant complications to any release. Thus, in many companies, frequent releases seem foolhardy.

As counterintuitive as it seems, frequent releases can go a long way toward increasing stability, because changes are small, training is minimal, and the impact of small changes is much easier to both predict and contain. In addition, when a deployment team gets used to doing something frequently, it invariably gets better and better at doing it well. But getting to the point of safe, frequent releases isn't easy. For starters, it involves significant investment in designing a new deployment process, testing it, and automating every step of the process with scripts—development and production environment setup, configuration management, unit testing, feature testing, system integration testing, UAT, appropriate approval gates, and finally, deployment. This requires ongoing close cooperation on the part of many parties—development, testing, operations, support, database, and so on.

But the benefits of a steady flow of new features into production can be substantial. And once your organization has mastered the discipline necessary to do (semi)continuous deployment, you can be sure the people will never want to return to the bad old days of big batch deployments.

Every step of your software delivery process should operate at the same cadence. For example, with continuous delivery, cumbersome portfolio management processes become a thing of the past; instead, people make frequent decisions about what should be done next. Continuous design is necessary to keep pace with the downstream development, validation, and verification flow. And finally, measurements of the "success" of software development are based on delivered value and improved business performance, because there is nothing else left to measure.

Notes

1. Pete Swabey, "Agility Applied at Standard Life," *Information Age*, October 18, 2007.
2. From *Field Manual 5-0: The Operations Process*, Headquarters, U.S. Army, March 26, 2010. This document is in the public domain and has been approved for public release and unlimited distribution.
3. Fred Brooks, *The Design of Design* (Upper Saddle River, NJ: Pearson Education, 2010), 176–177.

4. Tom Gilb, "Value-Driven Development Principles and Values," *Agile Record*, no. 3 (July 2010), http://www.AgileRecord.com. Used with permission.
5. See http://www.youtube.com/watch?v=KIkUWG5ACFY&feature=youtu.be.
6. Gojko Adzic, *Specification by Example* (Greenwich, CT: Manning Publications, June 2011).
7. Jez Humble and David Farley, *Continuous Delivery* (Boston: Addison-Wesley Professional, 2010).

Chapter 14

Lean Data Management
*The Invisible Dimension
Supporting the Flow of Value*

John Schmidt

Traditional data management techniques that work well at a departmental or system level are incomplete and insufficient for addressing enterprise data management needs. Lean principles and techniques, which have matured over many years in other process areas, can be combined with traditional practices to form Lean data management. As a result organizations can become data-driven—where data is an asset that serves as a competitive differentiator.

The Enterprise Context for Data Management

Is your enterprise data an asset or a liability? The question is not about financial accounting because data generally does not show up on the balance sheet (except occasionally in the context of a corporate acquisition). The question is whether your data significantly contributes to enterprise value and growth or if it is viewed as a cost to be minimized.

When data is an asset, it contributes to bottom-line results by being trustworthy, valuable, and timely:

- Trustworthy data is predictable and produces consistent, correct, and auditable business results across functional lines, across regions, and throughout the entire information lifecycle. There is consistency across different application systems, and only those people that are allowed to use the data are able to do so.

■ Valuable data is complete, accurate, and delivers the desired outcomes in the context of a business decision, process, or transaction. Valuable data is meaningful and understandable by the people using it.

■ Timely data is available to management, staff, customers, and partners precisely when they need them throughout the entire Value Stream.

When data is a liability, it looks very different:

■ Data is inconsistent across systems, with each system owner claiming his or her version is the right one. Wrong decisions, contradictory decisions, or no decisions are being made.

■ Data is not understandable with each database having different definitions for the same data elements and no easy way to map them to a common view. Business users keep the "real" data in spreadsheets on their desktop and spend significant effort reconciling conflicting reports.

■ The data needed for a decision or process exception is not available without launching an information (IT) project, which takes too long and costs too much.

■ Production systems are burdened with inactive historical data, which slows down end-of-period jobs, affects online transaction response time, and drives up the cost of operations and application upgrades.

■ Legacy applications that are no longer needed cannot be turned off, and there are no policies, processes, or tools to systematically archive the data that must be retained and eventually deleted when it is no longer required. Legacy data stores and structures are carried forward and restrict new system design.

■ Data security is weak or—worse—undefined, with a high potential for data loss or noncompliance. Copies of production data are used in nonproduction processes such as software development and testing without formal access controls.

In short, the enterprise is essentially a Tower of Babel with data spread across a collection of unmanaged silos and a high risk of negatively affecting the organization. More data can mean more information, but having more data is not an unambiguous good. If the sheer volume of data makes it harder to find the information, or if the cost of managing that data exceeds the value of the information, more data can be a serious liability. Many organizations are drowning in their own data.

If you view data as an asset, then you will manage it diligently, keep it safe, apply formal governance policies to maximize its use, and continue to invest in new data assets as opportunities arise. If you see data as a liability, then you will find tactical solutions to close the most critical gaps to stop the bleeding and not invest time and resources on strategic capabilities.

Most organizations are somewhere in the middle of the asset ←→ liability spectrum. The reality is that organizations are pressured to grow revenue, increase customer loyalty, expand their product portfolio, reduce time to market, optimize procurement, and comply with government regulations, which is simply not possible without a minimum level of information technology. As a result, executives are driving their organizations to implement new business strategies that rely on cross line-of-business processes to drive global growth. Steve Schuckenbrock of Dell sums up the rationale nicely:

> CEO's, CFO's and CIO's all recognize there is zero separation between business strategy and IT execution today. There is pretty much nothing you can do, from cutting costs or growth without the enablement of IT in one way, shape or form.*

The vast majority of executives want to be in the data asset camp. Unfortunately, they are finding that global business processes are complex to implement because lines of business grew over time as independent silos, which have gradually led to inconsistent, incomplete, and incompatible information across value streams. Enterprise information is locked in fragmented business applications and in desktop business analytical tools and is unreliable in supporting global business processes. What's needed is a mechanism to unlock that information and turn it into trusted, valuable, and timely data so it can be relied upon to improve value stream performance and ensure the success of business strategies.

The Difference between Data Management and Lean Data Management

Data management is defined by the Data Management Association (DAMA International) as "the development and execution of architectures, policies, practices and procedures that properly manage the full data lifecycle

---

* Steve Schuckenbrock, president, Dell Large Enterprise Business, *Financial Times* special report, October 27, 2010.

needs of an enterprise."* But what does it mean to *properly manage* data? Furthermore, it seems we need to worry about the *full data lifecycle* from initial creation of data to its ultimate demise. We also apparently can't manage data for just one application system or one business domain; we have to meet the needs of the entire *enterprise.*

This is where Lean comes in. But first, let's take a step back to the birth of data management practices to understand what has changed and why Lean techniques and IT value streams should be adopted now.

Data management first emerged in the 1980s as computer systems evolved from sequential processing of data (cards and tapes) to direct random-access disk storage. This new technology made it theoretically possible to store a data fact in just one place and allow anyone that needed it to access it directly. That's not how it turned out, of course, and today it is common for large enterprises to have the same customer information stored in fifty or more different databases, and virtually every one of them has a different format and structure. For an even more shocking example, a large U.S. financial institution, as part of a security and compliance improvement program, conducted a survey to find all the places where employee social security numbers were stored. They found them in over 1,000 databases.

There is one underlying driver for the proliferation and variation of data—the growth of complexity, which drives the trend to proliferation and variation combined with the lack of a disciplined approach. As organizations grow in size and complexity in terms of products, channels, markets, and customers, it becomes increasingly difficult to meet all the needs with a single monolithic system. Data management for a single department within a business function such as sales, manufacturing, accounting, or distribution, while complex, is still a relatively tractable problem; a team of analysts and developers working under an IT architect can build an application system that combines processes and data in a tightly integrated and highly cohesive fashion. In the 1980s, application systems were generally stand-alone systems that met the needs of functional groups. The interfaces between functions were generally quite simple and were addressed through manual, paper-based processes. In the 1980s there were few organizations that felt they had an "enterprise" data management problem. Rather, we had a series of departmental data management challenges that were sufficiently simple in that a single individual could understand each one well enough to design and manage a cohesive system.

---

* The Data Management Association, http://www.dfwdama.org/aboutUs.asp, June 20, 2011.

Fast-forward to present day. Enterprises are now much larger. Walmart, the largest company in the world by revenue, is about the same size as the entire Fortune 500 was forty years ago. Businesses, even relatively small ones in today's terms, are global and need to address multicurrency, multilanguage, multichannel, and multibrand needs. Legal and regulatory compliance requirements have added yet more complexity. And with the growth of social media, cloud computing and the constant stream of location, context, and behavior-specific "big data" being generated by various mobile and other Internet-aware devices, volumes are growing exponentially and are becoming increasingly distributed and fragmented. Furthermore, technology continues to change at an increasing rate, adding yet more complications in keeping legacy systems operational while taking advantage of new opportunities. The net result is mind-boggling complexity and a system of systems at the enterprise level that is impossible for one person to understand at a level of detail necessary to build a cohesive data and process solution.

This is not to be confused with applications such as Google's search engine. It certainly is an extremely sophisticated and complex system and can serve up an amazing array of information—yet it is just one system. Behind the scenes, Google is like many other enterprises with different systems supporting the wide range of corporate functions such as accounting, sales, marketing, and so on. If Google's corporate IT application portfolio is simpler and more rationalized than other enterprises of similar size, it is largely due to the fact that it has been in business for only fifteen years and as a result doesn't have as large of a legacy problem. Give Google another fifteen years of growth and acquisitions, and its IT infrastructure could be just as complex as any other large corporation (unless, of course, it adopts Lean IT value stream practices ☺).

In response to this growing complexity over the past thirty years, IT professionals did what humans have been doing for thousands of years when faced with unmanageable intricacy—break the problem into small pieces, solve each part independently, and worry about integration later. A term that is frequently used in data management circles to describe each piece is "data silo." Just as a farm may have multiple silos, which are separate stores of different grains and animal feed, modern enterprises have multiple independent silos of data.

How can we call these data silos independent in cases where all the enterprise systems are under the control of a single management structure reporting to the chief information officer (CIO)? The reality is that the hundreds, or thousands, of application systems in a modern enterprise were designed and developed by separate teams (or external software companies) with limited or no cross-team communications, and thus are based on incompatible data models and possibly different technologies, and they continue to evolve independently.

Data management practices have continued to evolve since the 1980s in an effort to address the *full-data lifecycle needs of an enterprise.* The data management body of knowledge* provides a framework of ten topic areas, each of which contains multiple practices.

1. Data governance—planning, supervision, and control over data management and use
2. Data architecture management—as an integral part of the enterprise architecture
3. Data development—analysis, design, building, testing, deployment, and maintenance
4. Database operations management—support for structured physical data assets
5. Data security management—ensuring privacy, confidentiality, and appropriate access
6. Reference and master data management—managing golden versions and replicas
7. Data warehousing and business intelligence management—enabling access to decision-support data for reporting and analysis
8. Document and content management—storing, protecting, indexing, and enabling access to data found in unstructured sources (electronic files and physical records)
9. Metadata management—integrating, controlling, and delivering metadata[†]
10. Data quality management—defining, monitoring, and improving data quality

With such a comprehensive list of practice areas, why do we still need Lean? If we add Lean practices to the mix, doesn't that complicate an already comprehensive collection of best practices? First, we should keep in mind that just because something is a "best practice" it doesn't

---

[*] Data Management International, "The DAMA Guide to the Data Management Body of Knowledge," http://www.dama.org/i4a/pages/index.cfm?pageid=3364, April 5, 2009.

[†] Metadata is "data about data or data processes." It provides structured information that describes, explains, locates, or otherwise makes it easier to retrieve, use, or manage an information resource.

necessarily mean that it's any good for a particular situation. Many data governance programs fail to realize any business results, and just about every enterprise struggles to achieve "one version of the truth" for key performance metrics and to keep pace with growing data volumes and the accelerating rate of change.

Lean data management is a sustainable approach to treating data as an asset across the enterprise. It is a method of applying Lean principles of waste elimination, automation, continuous improvement, and staff empowerment to data management and data governance processes. The end result is a data-driven organization with increased organizational agility to innovate and react to opportunities faster than the competition.

Traditional approaches have focused on leveraging the value of data from a functional perspective or at a point in time. If marketing needed to improve the effectiveness of a direct-mail campaign, it could collect data from internal and external databases and analyze them to create a more targeted campaign to raise the sales conversion rate. If operations needed to improve the order-to-cash process, it could launch a project to drive the needed changes. If accounting was required to implement tighter controls in response to new government regulations, it would implement a system with a database to satisfy the need. I refer to these techniques as "ad hoc data management"; there is no enterprise master plan, so when a data problem or opportunity arises, it is addressed with a custom point solution.

In non-Lean organizations, these data management activities are independent initiatives. Lean data management by contrast shows how marketing, sales, finance, customer service, manufacturing, research and development, and operations can work together to derive value from a wide spectrum of information value streams across the enterprise. In other words, getting value from data at a point in time or from a single functional (silo) perspective is relatively easy with many well-defined and mature practices upon which to rely. Deriving value across organizational groups that are independently managed and that evolve at different rates is much harder. Techniques that work at a departmental or single-system level do not necessarily scale to be effective at the enterprise level.

Furthermore, Lean data management is sustainable while many traditional ad hoc approaches are not. Lean principles of continuous improvement and waste elimination help to ensure that the data management processes continue to improve and remain cost-effective and competitive over time.

Applying Lean Principles to Data Management

Although there are indeed technical challenges related to the data life-cycle, the fundamental reason for enterprise initiatives failing to achieve the desired results is not technical. Enterprise data management is fundamentally an agreement problem, not a technical problem. Lean techniques, such as value stream analysis, are particularly effective at gaining agreement and facilitating change across independent teams that need to coordinate their work to satisfy the end customer. Manufacturers have used Lean techniques to re-engineer entire supply chains, all the stakeholders of which are independent companies, around just-in-time manufacturing processes thereby reducing work-in-process inventory, shortening delivery times, and providing customized solutions for each customer. Healthcare delivery organizations have used Lean techniques to gain agreement across independent surgeons for a common set of operating room processes and instruments, thereby reducing setup time, improving throughput, and cutting costs.

Lean principles can accomplish the same thing for data management activities. IT value streams are complex structures that include independent internal groups (often only coupled by a common brand and rolled-up financials—but still managed separately) as well as external suppliers, partners, and customers. In our book *Lean Integration,*[*] David Lyle and I discuss seven Lean principles in the context of enterprise systems and data integration. The book includes fourteen case studies that demonstrate the power of these techniques in delivering tangible business value.

Enterprise data management is also an integration problem, and as such, the examples and case studies in Lean integration are applicable. Although I won't repeat here what has already been published, I am hoping it will be helpful for you to internalize a few of the principles with some specific examples of how they could apply to data management. Specifically, I will elaborate on three of the principles: waste elimination, automation, and staff empowerment.

Waste Elimination

Lean is a management system that considers the expenditure of resources for any goal other than the creation of value for the end customer to be

---

[*] John G. Schmidt and David Lyle, *Lean Integration: An Integration Factory Approach to Business Agility* (Boston: Addison-Wesley, 2010).

wasteful and thus a target for elimination. Lean may also be used to improve the productivity of value-added activities, but the principles of waste elimination put the emphasis on identifying and eliminating nonvalue-added activities.

For example, data that is in production systems but not being used is waste. However, despite the fact that most of the data accumulating in these systems is dormant (up to 80% according to some industry estimates), you can't just get rid of the data, which puts it in the nonvalue-added but required category. Purging data warehouses and applications as well as decommissioning redundant or obsolete applications is difficult because of competing pressures. Business leaders want to keep everything because the data might be useful at a future date, and eDiscovery* requirements mandate that you hold onto the data for ever-longer periods of time. Yet practical cost pressures and some regulatory requirements demand that data be destroyed.

To make matters worse, the number of nonproduction copies you're maintaining acts as a multiplier effect—larger applications and data warehouses mean larger backups and larger copies for development, testing, and training. The proliferation of these copies also increases your risk as you have more sensitive data scattered throughout your enterprise or being given to outsourcing and offshore partners.

The cost associated with this data proliferation surfaces in both dramatic and subtle ways. Left unchecked, you'll certainly need to buy substantially more database licenses and more storage to land the data on, but you'll also need to be prepared for slower query performance, backups that can't complete overnight, upgrades that can't complete over a weekend, and more time and budget spent tuning—only to find in six months that you're back where you started. In addition, you'll need to have your lawyers and public relations team ready for the increasing number of "data spills" that will inevitably occur.

Lean data management, when applied to data archiving, removes dormant data from operational applications and data warehouses, shrinks and secures nonproduction copies, and retires redundant or obsolete

---

* eDiscovery refers to the use of electronic data in civil litigation. Data is identified by attorneys as relevant and placed on legal hold. Electronic information is considered different from paper information because of its intangible form and persistence. Electronic information is usually accompanied by metadata that is not found in paper documents and can play an important part as evidence. (For example, the date and time a document was written could be useful in a copyright case.) The preservation of metadata from electronic documents creates special challenges.

applications. IT can dramatically lower cost, improve service level agreements, and ensure proper compliance by proactively managing retention of structured data. Lean thinking helps IT align the value of information with the cost associated with managing it and articulate the business value through meaningful key performance indicators.

Automation

Many (most?) activities performed by IT staff are manual. For evidence of this, check out Forrester's cost of IT studies,* which shows that in most industries, as organizations get larger, the IT budget consumes a larger (not smaller) percentage of the enterprise budget. This is counterintuitive: Where are the economies of scale for IT as organizations grow? This is an indication of heavily manual processes and diseconomies of scale. E-mail, MS Word, Visio, and Excel are not automation—they are simply electronic versions of traditional manually created unstructured paper documents. Writing code in Java or any other language is also not automation.

To test this assertion, try this exercise. Take an IT process that you are familiar with and double the demand. How many additional staff members are required? If doubling throughput requires doubling staff, or even increasing staff by 50%, then you have a manual process. On the other hand, if you can double throughput with just a 10% increase in staff (or ideally with no increase), then you have a highly automated process that has eliminated scale factors.

The answer is to turn as much of the IT code, frameworks, database schemas, and infrastructure into data—data-about-data (or metadata) to be more accurate. To borrow a quote from Brian Foote and Joseph Yoder's *Big Ball of Mud*,† "Metadata allows systems to adapt more quickly to changing requirements by pushing power into the data, and out onto users." In this case, the user of the metadata is IT staff members who are enabled with tools that facilitate seamless handoffs between team members in an IT value stream.

If this sounds too technical and esoteric, let's take a look at how another process, order-to-cash, has evolved. Years ago, if you wanted

---

* Andrew Bartels and Craig Symons, "US IT Spending Benchmarks for 2008, More Options for CIOs to Find the Best IT Budget Benchmark," Forrester Research, December 23, 2008.
† Brian Foote and Joseph Yoder, *Big Ball of Mud* (Addison-Wesley Software Patterns Series, 2000).

to buy some hiking boots from a mail-order catalog, you would phone the company up, order the item, they would ship it to you along with an invoice, and you would mail in your check, which eventually cleared through your bank account. The entire process from order to cash from the supplier's perspective could easily be one month or more. In today's world, with one click of the mouse, Amazon has made the order-to-cash cycle instantaneous; you order the hiking boots, and Amazon has your money immediately. How is this possible? There are three things they had to do: standardize the process (including preapproval of one-click terms and conditions), enable it with technology (the Internet, easy-to-use interfaces and payment services), and make it data-driven (software algorithms with a supporting database). In other words, they turned paper into data and automated the manual steps.

We can do the same thing with IT value stream processes. There is no reason why we can't automate current manual IT processes such as creating a new business intelligence report, adding a table to a data warehouse, or building a data quality scorecard. Of course, you need more than just metadata; you must also provide access through self-service portals. When you do this in a sustained and systematic manner, then IT begins to move at the speed of data—at least to a large degree from the business users' perspective. Under the covers, the infrastructure and frameworks still move slowly, but the users can serve themselves quickly for much of their information and processing needs.

For example, data quality management is a critical element of an enterprise data governance program. Metadata, along with appropriate integrated tools, could provide data-quality dashboard views to business executives and data governance committee members.

The same metadata could provide a different view through a browser to data stewards, including detailed metrics, fact table analytics, reference data, and business glossary definitions. This provides data stewards with direct access to the underlying data structures and transformation processes so that they can quickly research and resolve data quality issues without the usual lengthy process of tracking down paper-based documentation or waiting weeks to schedule a meeting with the people that have the knowledge in their heads.

The same metadata could provide yet a different view to a software engineer's thick-client integrated development environment that shows end-to-end data lineage and program source code for data transformations. As a result, project teams can estimate projects many times faster because they have a good visual map of the environment, and they make fewer mistakes because they have impact analysis, which helps prevent errors due to cross-dependencies.

Furthermore, metadata allows all team members in the data quality value stream to communicate with each other by passing notes, comments, and even screen shots to each other within the same integrated and automated environment.

Staff Empowerment

Lean integration provides a case study from a multinational pharmaceutical company that used Lean principles to not only get their data clean but to empower staff to keep it clean. In a nutshell, they identified the top fifty data attributes across the enterprise, defined what "quality" means for each of them, measured the quality of all attributes in each system that used them, and reported the results publicly, including trends over time. The Lean principle at work is visual controls.

The effect of this simple principle was amazing. System owners whose quality metrics didn't improve as fast as others became publicly embarrassed—peer pressure changed their focus. Frontline staff saw the charts and learned how their data entry activities could affect the numbers—as the metrics improved month over month the staff could see how their new behavior affected the quality. Senior business executives saw the improvements in quality and how they affected operations and bottom-line results, so they became motivated to participate in an enterprise data governance program.

Other Examples

Lean Data Management can take many forms. Following are a few more examples of how Lean principles can be applied to applications, data warehouses, and portfolio management:

Lean applications
- Achieve zero production data growth in online transaction processing applications by defining business rules to systematically archive closed transactions on a regular basis.

- Cost-effectively manage long-term retention and eDiscovery of structured data through an online, optimized archive store rather than keeping dormant data in your more expensive transaction processing systems.
- Shrink and secure nonproduction online transaction processing environments by provisioning dramatically smaller, functionally intact, but completely obfuscated copies of production for use in development, testing, and training.
- Prevent the creation of duplicate data at creation time by checking data entries against a trustworthy master version of the data (i.e., the Lean principle of build quality in at the source).
- Cleanse data at creation time to standardize elements into a form that is compatible with downstream processes.

Lean data warehouses
- Analyze usage of production data warehouse to determine what end users are actually querying and systematically remove data or reports that are no longer of use.
- Keep aggregates and frequently accessed transaction data in the data warehouse. Purge data and eliminate loading information that is not being used at all and that has no value for compliance purposes.
- For infrequently used data that has some long-term analytic value, or where retention is required for compliance purposes, move it to lower-cost storage.

Lean application portfolios
- Evaluate the entire application portfolio, removing obsolete or redundant applications to eliminate complexity and reduce costs.
- Archive legacy data into an optimized archive store before decommissioning the associated applications. This ensures ongoing, online access to the legacy application data for reporting and compliance purposes.
- Establish retention management policies to ensure eligible data is destroyed in accordance with company policies, industry regulations, and sovereign laws.

A Data Governance Program for Lean Data Management

Let me start this section with an assertion. My hope is that in the next few pages you will agree that this statement is justified and worthy of consideration:

If we use Lean insights and techniques that have matured over many years in a wide range of Value Streams and apply them to the relatively new and emerging discipline of data governance, then we can increase the value of, and reduce the implementation risks of, an enterprise data management program.

Data governance, for many people, is a vague and unfocused concept. For some it appears to be a theoretical, and impractical, approach to managing data as an asset. For others it conjures up images of bureaucratic processes and committees debating whether a data element should be called a "customer," "prospect," or "party." Others perceive it as a somewhat academic or technical activity with talk about metadata and semantics.

Yet there are organizations that have formal data governance programs and are leveraging information across the enterprise to generate revenue, manage risk and compliance, and control costs. These organizations view data governance as the process of managing information across the corporate enterprise. How do they do it? How did they get past the theoretical, academic, bureaucratic, and technical issues and turn data governance into reality and deliver tangible results to the business bottom line?

An in-depth data governance benchmarking study* was conducted in 2010 to seek answers to these questions. The object of the survey was to gather data from organizations with active data governance initiatives and to drill into the detail of these initiatives to see exactly what they are doing, how broad their scope might be, and how effective they are. The survey was targeted at senior business and IT leaders worldwide, primarily from organizations larger than US$1 billion in annual revenues.

In summary, the study found that organizations that considered themselves to have a quite successful data governance program had the following:

1. A data governance mission statement
2. A clear and documented process for resolving disputes
3. Good policies for controlling access to business data
4. An active risk register[†]

---

* Data Governance Benchmarking Survey 2010, The Information Difference Company Ltd., November 2010.

† A risk register is a formal element of a data governance program in which the business risks associated with poor data quality and/or inconsistent data are recorded along with steps to mitigate them.

5. Effective logical models for key business data domains
6. Either business processes defined at a high level or fully documented at several levels and available for data governance
7. Data quality assessments that were undertaken on a regular basis
8. A documented business case
9. A link between program objectives and team or personal objectives
10. A comprehensive training program
11. A website alongside a broader range of communication methods

This collection of data governance practices is not theory. The list is empirically collected and provides a foundation of techniques that have been demonstrated to be effective in the real world. So how then can we correlate these techniques with the knowledge from years of practicing Lean? How can we bring the IT and business organizations together in an efficient data management value stream that eliminates waste, continuously improves, and is responsive to customer needs?

While preparing for this chapter, Steve Bell shared six key principles of Lean value streams that I found useful. Table 14.1 correlates the data governance practices from the survey with these Lean principles (shown in the columns). For example, a mission statement supports the Lean principle of simplicity by providing a clear articulation of the reason for the data governance program that everyone can understand. Teams from the entire data management value stream can use the mission statement as a guide to making decisions that simplify the process. The mission statement is also a reflection of the systems-thinking principle—it represents an enterprise-wide view of the value stream and not just one function or team. Finally, the mission statement represents the voice of the customer since it provides a statement of the intended value of the data governance program from a customer perspective.

In short, each checkmark in this table represents an opportunity to use proven Lean techniques to improve the emerging data governance practices. For example, to improve your data policy practice, you could adopt the following Lean principles:

- *Simplicity*: Establish a framework that categorizes policies in a way that makes sense for the enterprise, provide a high-level description of each, and publish the results in employee or customer portals.
- *Quality at the source*: Embed data policies in enterprise applications and web portals such that data is captured correctly the first time they are entered into a system.

Table 14.1 Data Governance Practices versus Lean Value Stream Principles

Data Governance Survey Practices	Lean Value Stream Principles					
	Simplicity	Quality at the Source	Respect for the Individual	Systems Thinking	Voice of the Customer	Problem Solving, Management Systems, and Knowledge Sharing
Mission statement	√			√	√	√
Clear dispute resolution	√		√			√
Good (effective) data policies	√	√			√	√
Active risk register				√	√	√
Effective models of business data	√	√		√		√
Business processes defined	√	√		√		√
Regular data quality assessments		√				√
Documented business case					√	
Link program and team objectives			√	√	√	
A comprehensive training program		√	√			√
Broad communication methods			√			√

- *Voice of the customer*: Once you have a clear picture of the "customer" of the data governance program (there may be several, but nonetheless a finite and specific list), ensure that data policies reflect their true needs and not just policies drawn from a textbook.
- *Problem solving, management systems, and knowledge sharing*: Establish organizational roles such as data stewards and data owners with clear responsibilities, provide them with the tools to measure and monitor data quality and compliance exceptions, and use visual controls such as dashboards and control charts to publicize the results to everyone in the value stream.

Hopefully, the message is clear. Data governance is a relatively immature and emerging discipline, yet there is solid evidence of common success patterns. Lean principles and practices are well established and proven for bringing disparate teams and individuals together to better satisfy customer needs. By combining the insights from both of these domains, we can achieve improved enterprise data management.

Chapter 15

Lean Business Intelligence
Listening to the Virtual
Voice of the Customer

Steve Bell

With the convergence of many technological advancements, we have reached a new level in our ability to learn from the digital world around us, a tipping point where new things are not only possible and practical but required if the enterprise is to remain competitive. According to Erik Brynjjolkfsson, director of the MIT Center for Digital Business, "Most great revolutions in science are preceded by revolutions in measurement. We have had a revolution in measurement, over the past few years, that has allowed businesses to understand because in much more detail what their customers are doing, what their processes are doing, what their employees are doing. That tremendous improvement in measurement is creating new opportunities to manage things differently."[1]

There is no doubt that the tools and techniques for data gathering, measurement, and analysis are evolving rapidly, but perhaps even more important is the exponential growth of data in many forms: structured data in application databases, unstructured documents in countless repositories, and the vast ocean of digital information, public and private, flowing across the Internet every second. Is this all just technology flotsam, or is it possible that we can harness that information to help deliver more value to our customers?

When thinking Lean, every action, transaction, and interaction is an experiment; we compare what we expected to happen with what did happen. Every time we achieve the expected outcome, we learn something. And every time something unexpected happens, we also learn. We are continuously learning and adapting to our environment through *feedback*. This is fundamentally the purpose of business intelligence (BI), the C in the PDCA (plan-do-check-act) cycle of our daily work.

BI is a topic of great interest to many business stakeholders, and not surprisingly, to the CIO. In 2011, IBM conducted a face-to-face survey of over 3,000 CIOs in the hopes of learning how their corporate mandates translated into initiatives. For those who strive to *transform* the business, a top mandate is "leveraging better data with strong analytics to create insights and take action."[2]

In order to learn how to take advantage of these emerging technology-enabled capabilities for learning and continuous improvement, let's start by exploring the common problems and challenges. Then we'll explore how Lean thinking can help to overcome them and the possibilities that await those who can.

Business Intelligence Anti-Patterns

Not surprisingly, BI project failure is an all-too-common problem. According to BI specialist Stephen Dine, "While the exact reasons for failure are often debated, most agree that a lack of business involvement, long delivery cycles and poor data quality lead the list."[3] Here are the top three BI anti-patterns[*] that I witness most often.

BI Anti-Pattern 1: A Technical Solution Searching for a Problem

Clearly this misguided approach isn't confined to BI, but it may be particularly acute here, because the domain of business intelligence contains an array of fascinating technologies that produce mesmerizing visuals. BI tools and techniques include data warehousing, data mining, multidimensional analysis, statistical analysis, data visualization, natural language, machine learning, predictive analytics, and artificial intelligence.

When you visit The Data Warehouse Institute[†] (TDWI) website, you will find a community gathering spot for a collection of sophisticated

---

[*] *Anti-pattern* is a term used in software engineering to describe a common but ineffective approach to a problem.

[†] TDWI is a for-profit membership organization that provides education, research, professional certification, networking, and events. See http://www.tdwi.org.

engineering disciplines. You will see an intense focus on the technical aspects of business intelligence, with less explicit emphasis on the purpose of business intelligence: to solve business problems and make well-informed decisions. This is not a criticism as much as the recognition of a reality—one would expect any highly technical discipline to have a gathering spot for learning and knowledge sharing.

But such an intensely technical discipline, blended with a sense of artistry and magic, can have predictable consequences and may result in technology for its own sake. Performance management specialist Bill Henderson advises clients "not to worry about hiring people with the right technology experience." Rather, he argues, "hire people with the right mindset, business understanding, and judgment. Too often organizations have large investments in very technical staff and sophisticated BI software but lack people who can work with business leaders to understand strategy and measure performance on executing that strategy."[4]

This is the very issue that Lean thinking tackles head on; the disciplined A3 problem-solving process begins with two simple questions: (1) *Why is this important?*, and (2) *What is the problem we are trying to solve?* Starting with these very fundamental questions helps technically oriented people gain insight into the underlying business problem and the value that is sought.

BI Anti-Pattern 2: A Problem We Don't Understand and Hope Technology Will Solve for Us

Whereas anti-pattern 1 describes technologists not gaining a full appreciation for the underlying business issues, anti-pattern 2 describes the opposite. This is a common disconnect where business colleagues do not fully understand the technical issues necessary to properly utilize BI capabilities, which is often characterized by tossing poorly defined requirements over the wall to BI specialists to sort things out and try to deliver something useful. Success with a BI project requires a keen understanding of the process that is being measured, the drivers for success, and the events and transactions that require attention. This, in turn, requires a deep understanding of how these events are represented in the data model, which often spans several systems that are rolled up into a single source repository or data warehouse. While business people may understand the first aspect (although not as often as they may think), the second usually requires a close partnership with technologists. And this is where BI projects often break down: the business and IT value stream partnership does not materialize.

In one case, a retail CIO had all the best intentions of bringing in a BI solution. But because the business and IT staff were so busy keeping the ship afloat, he cut some corners. This CIO asked about a few of their hot-buttons in a focus group. Coming away from the focus group, he had a few ideas, but mostly based on marketing buzz-words. He subsequently began conversations with BI vendors. The process was painful for all involved, delivering nothing in the short term (not even a pilot) because each vendor and retail segment had a different understanding of the problems it was trying to solve. Trying to "save the business hassle" by not involving business colleagues in the discussions, in the end, this effort took much longer than both the CIO and the business leaders intended, creating more frustration and distrust.

Solving problems requires close collaboration as teams strive to understand the problem and develop an appropriate response. PDCA problem solving is a discipline to which we must hold ourselves and our teammates accountable; otherwise we fall back on our normal pattern and joust at symptoms, coming up with quick and dirty "solutions" while seldom getting to the root cause. When we do this, the same problems keep coming back, and all the effort and investment (including BI) we put into pursuing them are wasted.

BI Anti-Pattern 3: Underestimating the Complexity

Teams often start down the path of a BI project only to find the quality and fragmentation of their data to be a significant impediment. Worse yet, teams may invest in BI solutions and act on their outcomes without realizing the data they are using is of questionable integrity.

Because the primary role of ERP and other commercial off-the-shelf (COTS) software is standardization and automation of business processes, they naturally become the repository of core transactional data for the enterprise. Most of these systems come with a rich library of built-in reporting capabilities, usually accompanied by sophisticated add-on modules and/or partner products that provide integrated decision support capabilities that are designed to work with the system with only a limited degree of modification.

But the need to aggregate and present information usually stretches beyond the native data within the COTS software, incorporating data from a variety of other sources to provide a standardized view to the flow of work across extended value streams. This is where customized solutions are involved, and they typically require considerable design, integration, and development effort.

Data is typically fragmented across multiple enterprise systems; it's usually not normalized (meaning that the structures of the various data sources don't line up well); they generally provide an incomplete view of the entire value stream; and data quality is often low. Moreover, the business stakeholders who want the information to support decision making may not understand the underlying complexities and so do not know what to ask for or how to judge the quality of what they receive from a BI project.

Every enterprise, no matter how large or small, would benefit from an assessment of its data architecture to identify its strengths to leverage and weaknesses to improve upon in order to realize the most value from their data assets. Such an assessment should include structured and unstructured data generated and gathered internally, as well as various data sources available in the public domain (which we'll explore shortly). Understanding the underlying data and business relationships will help guide stakeholders in simplification and rationalization efforts. Certainly a well-crafted data aggregation and warehousing intervention may temporarily overcome many of the structural inadequacies, but until an enterprise develops a master data management strategy, BI investments will never realize their full potential. For more on this topic see Chapters 12 and 14.

Because of the complexity of BI projects in general, there is now gathering interest around the adoption of Lean-Agile software development practices: engaging business stakeholders and technical specialists in defining purpose and requirements, encouraging rapid and iterative experiments to design, prototype, test, deploy, and realize measurable value from BI capabilities. The PDCA approach plays well in the complex environment of BI, where emergent solutions must be discovered through cycles of experimentation and learning.

Going Beyond the "Voice" of the Customer

There are two Lean perspectives on business intelligence: Lean for BI and BI for Lean. The first, which we have just explored, relates to the application of Lean-Agile practices in the design and development of BI solutions. The second, BI for Lean, addresses how quality information, presented in the right format, to the right stakeholders, at the right time, can help make informed decisions to improve enterprise performance and customer value.

So let's turn from the *what* and *how* of Lean BI to the most important question, which justifies all investment and effort: *Why* is business intelligence important?

Existing information systems are often aligned with specific organizational functions, covering some but not all parts of a value stream. And even when a broad COTS system is used, it is often integrated with several applications, each with a separate database. A properly designed BI systems may be able to assemble an end-to-end perspective, bridging these information silos to present useful *value stream views* of the enterprise. Furthermore, a properly designed operational decision-support framework ensures that each stakeholder is dealing with the appropriate granularity of information, presented as visually as possible, at the right time, to support the flow and cadence of the Lean management system:

- Executives should have access to summary views (scorecards and dashboards) that present key performance indicators, strategic targets, trends, and important exceptions to monitor.
- Managers should have access to tactical views (scorecards, dashboards, and event and exception notifications, with drilldown to detailed performance and trend analyses), so that they can respond quickly to emerging problems and opportunities and provide their teams with focused support.
- Frontline workers should have access to line-of-sight value stream views, which helps them see what is flowing, what is not flowing, and how what they are doing adds value to the customer. Information should be presented to facilitate daily huddles, instant ad hoc problem identification, swarming, and solving while still monitoring important trends and "watch list" issues.*

Going beyond operational excellence, from a customer-facing perspective, views of transactional data can also be useful. For example, many retailers have developed sophisticated transactional systems that provide real-time visibility into customer purchase trends, which has helped them fine-tune their supply chains. Some have learned to leverage loyalty programs to track

---

* In earlier chapters of this book, I encouraged readers to create manual visual management systems whenever possible, because the visual, tactile, and interactive characteristics of a pen on whiteboard are so engaging. However, there are many reasons why electronic BI systems, dashboards, scorecards, and sophisticated analytics may also be useful.

customer purchases and precisely target promotions; next time you're in the grocery store, examine the coupons that print with your receipt and see if they provide you with promotions that match your purchasing patterns.*

For years, companies have been using transactional data as a proxy to grasp customer behaviors and trends in order to make more informed decisions. But now, with mature Web 2.0† applications reaching into virtually all aspects of consumer behavior and preferences, this leads to an important question: Is there a new "voice of the customer" we should be paying closer attention to?

Let's return to the foundation of Lean thinking: adding value to the customer through value streams. And how do we know what the customer values? We may think we know, but until we go to *gemba* we are only working on assumptions. To truly understand what our customer wants and needs, we need to observe their behavior.

We should visit the physical *gemba* whenever possible, where we can observe and interact with real people while observing their strengths and weaknesses, their triumphs and frustrations, the subtle environmental influences, and their unspoken and often unconscious behavior when confronted with the realities of daily life. But visiting the physical *gemba* may not always be practical, so we may supplement it with other techniques such as interviews and surveys to gather information on what the customer wants. But that method has its limitations. Behavioral scientists have long known that most people are not able articulate what they do and don't want, especially when it's a significant departure from the status quo. So how, then, can we learn what our customers will value?

For example, Microsoft has invested heavily in usability research to better understand how its customers realize more value from its products. Years ago, they evaluated new designs by having users experiment with the software and then complete a survey. But the responses were often vague and not very helpful. So Microsoft began recording keystrokes and, with subject permission, simultaneously videotaping what turned out to be a wide range of customer reactions (grimaces, hesitations, etc.).[5]

---

* See the *Information Week* 500 case study on Catalina Marketing for an example of how big data analytics create value for the end consumer. Without data driven analysis, redemption rates for coupons printed at time of checkout are approximately 1%. With basic targeting, redemption rates rise to 6% to 10%. See http://www.netezza.com/81127.pdf.
† Web 2.0 describes the second generation of the Internet: collaborative platforms; interoperable, service-oriented, customizable, user-centered design; and dynamic content, where all elements interact and add value to all other elements in real time.

They also learned that there is more to software utility and value than just a pleasing user experience. According to Microsoft:

> Likeability is always a desirable trait in a product. If people like the product, they are more likely to use it and to recommend it to others. [But] people often like a product for reasons unrelated to utility and usability. They may be attracted to its styling and flash, or to the status they believe the product confers upon them. People tend to like highly usable products, but you should not assume that means a well-liked product is usable.
>
> Usability can be broken down into three elements: Discovery involves looking for, and finding, a product's feature in response to a particular need. Learning refers to the process by which the user figures out how to use a discovered feature to complete the task at hand. Efficiency refers to the point at which the user has mastered the feature and uses it without requiring further learning.[6]

There's a great deal of subtlety involved when determining degrees of utility and satisfaction in any product or service. In determining customer preferences, we're often going beyond what the customer consciously knows and articulates. We must rely on keen observation to unlock the secrets of what customers really want, particularly when they don't know it themselves. This is not new—from Henry Ford's famously repeated "If I had asked them what they wanted, they would have said faster horses" to the market-creating vision of Steve Jobs, there will always be some who seem to have insights into what customers really want, not just what they tell you.* The question is how do you become one of them?

Virtual *Gemba*

We are now entering the field of behavioral science—business anthropology and ethnography—where we must engage our powers of scientific observation and quantitative and qualitative analysis in order to develop better products, services, and processes to serve our customers. *InformationWeek*

---

* There is an endless debate in innovative circles: Do we ask customers what they want and try to give it to them, or do we try to give them something new, something they would have no concept of until they saw it? This is one of the distinctions between sustaining (incremental) and disruptive innovation. Ask yourself why you can't strive for both.

recently declared that "Web-enabled mobile devices and applications are the biggest game changers since the PC."[7] And perhaps they're right. Look around you. Everywhere it seems people are using their mobile devices to interact in real-time with the world around them. If our customers are using these devices to interact with us and the products and services we offer, what can we learn by watching their behavior carefully?

The power of the Internet may help us listen to our customers, but emerging BI capabilities are needed to help us glean relevant conclusions about their behaviors and preferences, both collectively as markets and communities and individually as highly targeted customers. I like to call this new domain *virtual gemba*: a new way of observing what our customers and prospective customers are doing and saying in the virtual realm. There are two significant aspects of virtual *gemba*: social media and big data.

Social Media Listening

Many feel that the single most important measure of customer satisfaction is the *Net Promoter Score*, which is a response to the simple, and some say the "ultimate" question:

> On a zero to ten scale, how likely is it that you would recommend us to a friend or colleague?[8]

Sophisticated surveys and analytics aside, doesn't it really come down to this? Would you really recommend this company, product, or service to your friend? To your best customer? To your *mother*?

And how enthusiastically do you want to share this recommendation? Do you just passively recommend a product or service when asked, such as a nearby restaurant recommendation? Or do you eagerly share news about a great book, a trustworthy auto mechanic, or a good dentist with a sincere desire to improve someone's life experience in a meaningful way?

A nine or ten response on the Net Promoter Score suggests that you are enthusiastic and will actively promote this product or service, and we can learn a lot from you about how we delivered such great value. A seven or eight is not particularly excited, but at least you are satisfied, and perhaps you're willing to share more with us about how we can better serve you. And if you answered six or below, then we have a problem—you may be dissatisfied or even angry. And we all know that angry people are, in general, more vocal than satisfied people. However, when customers are disappointed, they are often not inclined to say anything. It is usually too late when you learn your customers have moved on. We can learn the most from disappointed customers if we can identify them before they leave and in time to prevent the damage.

So where can we go to find people openly expressing their likes and dislikes every day? Clearly, the emerging phenomenon of social media and networking is prime territory for exploration.

If people really "like" us, it takes just a few keystrokes for them to say so, and they often end up identifying themselves with us at an emotional level. If we're really lucky, they may naturally organize and segment themselves into affinity groups and communities where we can monitor and learn how they are using our products or services in distinct ways. Alternately, when someone really "dislikes" us, then look out—they can broadcast their feelings in just a few keystrokes, and occasionally such messages can go viral around the globe in a matter of hours.

In *The Tipping Point*, Malcolm Gladwell examines what causes things (ideas, trends, social behaviors, products, companies) to "tip"—and suddenly spread like wildfire. "There are plenty of advertising executives who think that precisely because of the sheer ubiquity of marketing efforts these days, word-of-mouth appeals have become the only kind of persuasion that most of us respond to anymore."[9] Clearly, many of us don't trust mass marketing and are searching for a more intimate connection. Gladwell calls those who are natural communicators and influencers "connectors," people who have naturally large networks and who seem compelled to communicate with and influence the opinions of others—in some cases very large numbers.

In the past, these people built networks the old-fashioned way, writing letters, making phone calls, meeting in person. But now there is a new generation of connectors, people who enthusiastically spread their opinions and influence very quickly through virtual channels of communications and online communities. Many enterprises are now investing in brand development through popular social media channels while monitoring messaging traffic to spot everything from key influencers, to innovative uses of their products and services, to negative customer comments, and to competitive moves and emerging trends. But is it effective? Where's the ROI?

John Wanamaker, a department store tycoon who is considered by many to be the father of modern advertising, once said, "Half the money I spend on advertising is wasted. The trouble is I don't know which half." It's quite possible that, for many, "wasted" spending on emerging social networking could be equally significant, but the opportunity to develop new and intimate relationships and precisely target customers through their trusted social connections creates a new world of marketing opportunity that is too appealing to pass up. Keep in mind that each experiment doesn't need to be large or expensive; experiments can be very small and highly targeted. For example, recent tests have shown that a button that says LEARN MORE is much more effective in gathering respondent e-mail addresses than a button that says SIGN UP NOW.[10,*] Such "split testing" can be very effective if we are able to use real-time market feedback to plan media investments and instantly measure the response directly in consumer sentiment, behavior, and transactions.

For example, Waggener Edstrom Worldwide is a pioneer in digital media public relations and the 2011 recipient of the prestigious Digital PR firm of the year award. According to Jason Moriber, director of their Innovation Strategies Lab, social media listening has created an entirely new foundation for effective research and development.

> The "fire hose" of available social data has created a new foundational first step for a PR or communications program; a "deep listening." It used to be that a team would gather in a room, and work towards the big idea without this data. Now, we can create a specific, powerful momentum towards creating a big idea that is infused with social intelligence. We can use the wealth of social data, the conversations, the keyword, the influentials, and the influence multipliers, to empower and right-set our thinking.[11]

This new field of *automated sentiment analysis* marks the convergence of business intelligence and social intelligence; it uses machine learning, natural language processing, and statistical analysis techniques to mine vast quantities of online opinions to identify important conversations and trends. In its simplest form, sentiment analysis begins by attempting to classify and quantify conversations in terms of positive, neutral, and negative. It also attempts to identify key influencers, those whose opinions seem to matter more, and are watched carefully by others. It can also spot sudden events, such as when a negative comment quickly spreads; some tools will help you identify the origin, so you can take appropriate steps—whether that's

---

* *The Lean Startup: How Today's Entrepreneurs Use Continuous Innovation to Create Radically Successful Businesses* by Eric Ries (New York: Crown Business, 2011) describes an extensive example of "split testing" with the Grockit case study.

quickly identifying and responding to a malicious threat or discovering the need to offer a humble apology to a global audience.

Many enterprises are investing in experiments to learn how social media outbound communication and inbound listening tools and techniques can help them better understand what their customers want now, locate spontaneously self-organizing communities, and spot trends that might indicate what new innovations would be valuable. This may very well be the source of your next big idea.*

While some may scoff at social media, others are taking this very seriously, because this is how the new, always connected, crowd-sourcing world is learning and communicating. And the more your customers (and those who influence your customers) engage in this space, the better you'll need to become at learning how to listen carefully for those precious needles in this enormous virtual haystack that may help you better understand what people are thinking, saying, blogging, tweeting, and posting about you and your competitors.

Big Data

Consider the rapid growth of Internet-enabled, context-sensitive, location-aware devices, from smartphones and online weather stations and traffic monitors to smart power grid devices that optimize power consumption—even my dog wears a GPS collar that transmits his location! We are increasingly living in a world where much of what we do is creating an endless stream of data that enterprises may use to track behavior and drive innovation. "Data exhaust"—the trail of clicks that Internet users leave behind from which value can be extracted—is becoming a mainstay of the Internet economy. Hal Varian, Google's chief economist, predicts that the job of statistician will become the "sexiest" around. Data, he explains, are widely available; what is scarce is the ability to extract wisdom from them.[12]

---

* Online communities can be a powerful source of new ideas. Bill Joy, cofounder of Sun Microsystems, once said, "No matter who you are, most of the smartest people work for someone else." The trick with an *open innovation* strategy is to tap into the knowledge and creativity and collaborative energy that exist outside your enterprise boundaries. The motivation to participate can be for-profit, such as with Proctor and Gamble, where more than 50% of their product initiatives now involve significant collaboration with outside innovators (see http://www.pgconnectdevelop.com). Motivation can also be altruistic; consider Wikipedia and the open source software movement.

This is the realm of "big data analytics," defined by TDWI as "[e]xploring the granular details of business operations and customer interactions that seldom find their way into a data warehouse or standard report, including unstructured data coming from sensors, devices, third parties, Web applications, and social media—much of it sourced in real time on a large scale. Using advanced analytics techniques such as predictive analytics, data mining, statistics, and natural language processing, businesses can study big data to understand the current state of the business and track evolving aspects such as customer behavior."[13]

For ethnographers (many of whom now work in marketing departments of corporations) virtual *gemba* can be viewed and analyzed through this new real-time, data-enabled stream of event, transactional, and behavioral data that we can use to better serve our customers. For example, consider how Google observes its customers. On a daily basis, they release software without telling anyone. And then they observe user behavior. They look for how quickly a new feature is discovered, how much it is used, and how it spreads. And from these behaviors they learn how to design better software that gets noticed and gets used.

Another example of gathering and utilizing vast amounts of transactional data is the recently introduced Boeing 787 Dreamliner. Its extensive onboard systems self-monitor and report maintenance requirements to ground-based computer systems. This will help keep the planes safer, with more hours in the air and less time sitting on the ground due to unscheduled maintenance. And the system helps Boeing gather enormous volumes of performance data on every aircraft across all operating conditions to inform continuous improvement and innovation of its designs.

Finally, consider emerging technology from Care Innovations (a joint venture of Intel and GE) aimed at helping healthcare practitioners monitor patients from home. With this technology, patients at home can measure their own vital signs such as blood pressure, pulse, and weight and respond to questions specific to their diseases on a daily basis, with all data reviewed by the clinical care team working with their primary care provider.[14]

Another research project underway at Care Innovations includes the application of remote monitoring sensors and predictive analytics to help improve quality of independent life for those with declining health and mobility. When such a system notices a deviation (such as not getting out of bed at a certain time, increased trips to the bathroom, changes in patterns of contact with outsiders, or atypical behavior in the kitchen), it may automatically trigger a notification to the family or caregiver.[15]

These examples of performance and behavior monitoring transcend the traditional "rearview mirror BI" and offer the potential to help us better understand and serve our customers on a daily basis. When asked what characterizes truly advanced analytics, compared to ordinary business intelligence, Jim Goodnight, founder of analytics pioneer SAS, said, "Unless you can drill down through the data and come up with a probability that a customer is going to leave you next month, you're not really in the advanced-analytics business."[16]

Can you envision an opportunity for big data in your enterprise? Can you afford it? That is a concern especially for the small enterprise with limited resources. But you may be surprised at the statistics-savvy people you already have working with you, people who naturally think analytically and can, with the right approach (PDCA) and some inexpensive and reasonably accessible analytics tools, start looking deeply inside your business problems and opportunities. Remember to keep your experiments small, fast, iterative, and highly targeted, and always with a clear focus on the business purpose, and you may quickly find your way to new realizations that unlock significant value.

Go ahead, the necessary tools may already be there waiting for someone to assemble in a new way, and you may already have access to valuable data in your own internal systems and in the public domain. Your customers and prospects may be willing to share even more useful data with you if it's in their best interest (and if they trust you). While there are certainly many concerns over privacy, there are also many opportunities to learn how to understand such behavior and help deliver new value, which may in turn fund new (and perhaps more sophisticated) experiments.

It's up to business stakeholders, who have a vision for creating new value for their customers, to work in close partnership with their technical counterparts to explore new possibilities. The world of Lean BI presents many new skills and tools that must be learned experimentally—and together. According to Eric Brynjolfsson from MIT:

> A lot of companies think they're using data, and you often see bar charts and pie charts and numbers in management presentations. But, historically, that kind of data was used more to confirm and support decisions that had already been made, rather than to learn new things and to discover the right answer. The cultural change is for managers to be willing to say, "You know, that's an interesting problem, an interesting question. Let's set up an experiment to discover the answer."[17]

How to Begin Your Lean Business Intelligence Journey

There is no single prescription for Lean BI. Where to begin depends on where you are now and the problems you need to solve. That said, here are a few general suggestions to consider as you assess your current condition and chart a course for the future.

- *Establish a BI Center of Excellence*: By taking a formalized approach to BI education and standardization, creating a clearinghouse for communication and collaboration, you can help to guide and accelerate the cycles of experimentation, learning, and value realization. Even a small company on a small budget can engage in Lean BI by asking some fundamental questions about problems it needs to solve and exploring the available data that might provide insights.

- *Invest in skills development*: These include the soft skills of collaborative learning, knowledge management, and problem solving, and the hard skills of statistical analysis, data visualization, and other disciplines that may be necessary to succeed in this new scientific/social domain.

- *Assess your current condition*: Catalog your current data sources and identify gaps and overlaps and potential new sources of useful information. Determine where you need to invest in improving quality and filling in the gaps. This is a lifelong journey, but it starts by understanding where you are today.

- *Consider your policies on data security and privacy*: The Lean principle of "respect for people" should extend to your customers; so in order to maintain a trusting relationship with your customers, establish a respectful and trustworthy position on privacy matters.

- *Encourage a fact-based culture*: Intuition is wonderful—and essential. But intuitions and assumptions should be tested using facts; this is the PDCA approach. Don't just look at the data as events and transactions; search for the underlying behaviors, motivations, and patterns.

- *Apply the A3 problem-solving thought process*: Whenever you start a new BI development effort, ask: *Why is this important, and what is the problem we're trying to solve?* In some cases, you'll learn that a BI investment won't solve the problem, and you'll avert an expensive disappointment. And when it does help, the solution will be very precise, and it will support specific countermeasures and target outcomes for further experimentation. Start small, move fast.

Notes

1. "Competing through Data: Three Experts Offer Their Game Plans," *McKinsey Quarterly* (October 2011).
2. IBM, "The Essential CIO," 2011.
3. Stephen Dine, interview, October 20, 2011.
4. Bill Henderson, Perkins Consulting, interview, January 5, 2012.
5. Michael George, James Works, and Kimberly Watson-Hemphill, *Fast Innovation* (New York: McGraw Hill, 2005), 43.
6. "Usability in Software Design, Microsoft Corporation," 2000, http://msdn.microsoft.com/en-us/library/ms997577.aspx.
7. Chris Murphy, "Innovation Atrophy," *InformationWeek*, May 30, 2011, 23.
8. Fred Reichheld and Rob Markey, *The Ultimate Question 2.0* (Boston: Harvard Business Review Press, 2011), 4.
9. Malcolm Gladwell, *The Tipping Point* (New York: Little Brown and Company, 2000), 32.
10. "Boffins Wanted," *The Economist*, February 11, 2012, 35.
11. Jason Moriber, interview, January 19, 2012.
12. "Data, Data, Everywhere," *The Economist*, February 25, 2010.
13. The Data Warehouse Institute, http://tdwi.org/portals/big-data-analytics.aspx.
14. "GE Healthcare, Intel and Mayo Clinic Explore New Models of Health Care Delivery," Mayo Clinic, http://www.mayoclinic.org/news2010-rst/5657.html, February 22, 2010.
15. Eric Dishman, "Technological Innovation and the Future of Aging," http://www.pdxcityclub.org/content/future-aging-through-technological-innovation, March 25, 2011.
16. Rich Karlgaard and Jim Goodnight, "King of Analytics," *Forbes*, August 22, 2011.
17. "Competing through Data: Three Experts Offer Their Game Plans," *McKinsey Quarterly* (October 2011).

Appendix A

What Is Lean IT?
A Working Definition

Steve Bell

Fundamentally, Lean is the practice of collaborative learning, continuous improvement, and innovation. One learns by asking questions. So to address the question "What is Lean IT?" we begin by asking "What is Lean?"

In his opening address to the first Lean IT Summit, held in Paris in October 2011, Dan Jones offered this definition of Lean:

> My current hypothesis is this, and I choose my words very carefully: Lean is a journey. Lean is the practice (not theory but derived from experience) of using the scientific method (PDCA, hypotheses and testing) in order to gain insights into how we can intervene in a dynamic system to make it improve.

Why does he refer to this as his "current hypothesis"? After all, in 1990, Dan, along with Jim Womack and Daniel Roos, introduced the term *Lean*, and he has coauthored several influential books on the subject. So why, after more than two decades, is the definition still a hypothesis?

This is the whole point: Lean isn't a "thing" to be figured out. It's not a tool. It's a dynamic, experiential practice based on a set of fundamental principles, most notably the scientific method of learning through problem solving (plan-do-check-act), and of respect for the intelligence and creativity of the individual. In our rapidly changing world, the value of any particular "solution" at one point in time, although perhaps momentarily useful, is often short-lived. The only lasting value is the organizational capability to quickly learn and adapt to constant change.

Lean practice has evolved beyond manufacturing into virtually every industry. While IT itself may be considered a distinct industry (enterprises producing or providing software, hardware, communications, or IT services), quality information, effective information systems, and technology-enabled products and services are a vital part of *every* industry and *every* enterprise. This leads us to the next important question we should ask: "What is IT?"

This question proves to be surprisingly difficult to answer. IT can be defined as a set of capabilities, a collection of assets (human, intellectual, physical, and virtual), a compilation of technology and process-related products and services, and a diverse community of technology specialists. No single definition is likely to satisfy everyone, so rather than try to define IT as a noun, I will define IT by the capabilities it delivers:

1. Quality information and effective information systems that enable business processes to serve customers
2. Information gathering and analysis to manage process performance and to develop a clearer vision of customer needs and wants
3. Technology-enabled features and functionality that add value to the products and services the enterprise delivers to its customers
4. A medium for information exchange, communication, and collaboration among the enterprise, its customers, and the larger marketplace

So having postulated a current definition for "Lean" and for "IT," we arrive at the original question: What is Lean IT? This is the definition published in 2010 in *Lean IT*:

> Lean IT engages people, using a framework of Lean principles, systems, and tools, to integrate, align, and synchronize the IT organization with the business to provide quality information and effective information systems, enabling and sustaining the continuous improvement and innovation of processes. Lean IT has two aspects: outward-facing, supporting the continuous improvement of business processes, and inward-facing, improving the performance of IT processes and services.

Although it is less than two years old at this writing, there are several aspects of this definition I now feel are inadequate.

First, I believe the dichotomy of *inward-facing* and *outward-facing* perpetuates the artificial separation between business and technical colleagues. Teams can utilize IT capabilities to support Lean practice throughout the enterprise by improving business processes, products, and services. Teams can also apply Lean principles to achieve IT operational excellence. But these efforts should not be treated separately or be undertaken without a view of the entire flow of value. To do so will result in local optimization and a failure to deliver value to the end customer. (For an example, see the discussion of Lean software development and governance in Chapter 5.) To optimize enterprise performance, all specialties and disciplines must work closely together *with a shared purpose* to create value for the customer. This means eliminating cultural and organizational barriers wherever they are found and changing the language that reinforces them.

Furthermore, this 2010 definition emphasized enabling business processes but disregarded the innovative product development aspects of IT; technology capabilities are embedded within, bundled with, or support most products and services offered today.

Finally, this definition disregarded the dynamic, interactive, and often instant collaborative relationships that we now share with many of our partners and customers.

Does this mean the 2010 definition was wrong? No, it indicates that my understanding and the context itself (with the rapid changes in the Internet, cloud computing, consumerization of IT, and so on) continue to evolve.

So my current definition, my latest hypothesis, is this:

> *Lean IT is the practice of adaptive learning through collaboration and experimentation among business stakeholders, technical specialists, suppliers, and customers to continuously improve and innovate the use of information, information systems, and technology-enabled products and services to add value for the end customer.*

This definition may continue to evolve, hopefully becoming simpler and richer over time. I encourage you to conduct your own inquiries and experiments to determine what Lean IT means for you.

Appendix B

Additional Lean Resources

Steve Bell

Here is my personal short list of favorite resources.

Lean IT Strategies – http://www.LeanITStrategies.com
Here you'll find a list of my upcoming workshops, public presentations, webinars, articles, and other publications.

Lean Enterprise Institute – http://www.lean.org
LEI offers access to a vast global community of Lean practitioners, resources, newsletters, webinars, and events.

***Gemba Walks* – Jim Womack**
This is the first book I recommend for executives and managers who want to understand what it means to "think Lean" in a transformative way. Easy to read and digest, *Gemba Walks* can be read one chapter at a time in any order and is an ideal choice for book clubs and discussion groups.

***Managing to Learn* – John Shook**
Helps you experience the A3 problem-solving journey through parallel stories of a mentor and his mentee.

***Toyota Kata* – Mike Rother**
Goes to the heart of the learning culture of a Lean enterprise. The *kata* approach emphasizes that you can't "implement" something where continuous learning is required. Offers great insights into the hidden value of *kanban* as a learning tool.

The Toyota Way to Lean Leadership: Achieving and Sustaining Excellence through Leadership Development – **Jeffrey Liker and Gary Convis**

Provides an in-depth, inside look at how Toyota creates a sustaining culture of lifetime learning. Looks beyond popular "Lean" tools and techniques to see what makes Toyota's culture truly unique, with insights on how you can do this with your own company.

The Lean Startup – **Eric Ries**

Demonstrates through many interesting stories how Lean thinking can be applied in conditions of extreme uncertainty; this book is not just for small startups but for anyone who wants to pursue breakthrough innovation.

Getting the Right Things Done – **Pascal Dennis**

Illustrates the journey of strategy deployment and how an organization learns to align continuous improvement efforts with its true north enterprise strategy.

Drive: The Surprising Truth about What Motivates Us – **Daniel Pink**

Inspiring. Learn why autonomy, mastery, and purpose are essential to any high-performance team or organization.

Appendix C

Case Study: Ci&T
Doing the Right Things

Bruno Guicardi

Ci&T employs Agile methodologies and Lean principles to deliver application outsourcing, software product engineering, and digital marketing services from development centers in Brazil (headquarters), Argentina, and China to customers in North and Latin America, Europe, and Asia Pacific. A strong commitment to innovation has put Ci&T at the forefront of exploring how Lean thinking eliminates waste and delivers value to help clients reduce costs and improve quality, speed, and business agility.

Established in 1995 by three friends studying computer science at the University of Campinas, Brazil, the company has prioritized investments in operational excellence through the use of benchmark methodologies and maturity models. The company was a Brazilian pioneer in adopting RUP® and in achieving high maturity levels in software development (e.g., CMMI Level 4 in 2006 and Level 5 in 2007). As a consequence, it achieved a high level of predictability in schedule, cost, and quality, as 98% of the projects were being completed on time and 95% of them completed within budget; in addition, the postproduction defect rate was below 0.1 def/KLOC (compared to an average of 0.4 def/KLOC in other CMMI Level 5 companies).

While this performance seemed like a great achievement according to industry benchmarks, more often than its executives would like to admit, business users' feedback on the final product indicated a disconnect between the business problem and the capabilities delivered by the system, along with complaints about the inflexibility of the process and the inability to handle change. Postmortem analyses often pointed to a common sentiment from the development team: "We did our job delivering on budget and on schedule. The problem is that business people don't know what they want, and it keeps changing."

In 2007, several development teams started using Agile methods. After the first projects, customers were happier with the greater level of flexibility and control of the process, and it was possible to maintain similar results in terms of predictability and quality. Encouraged by the results, the company started to gradually roll out Agile to other teams while the senior management began to study the model, its sources, and its principles. This investigation led to Lean, with its more comprehensive set of principles and tools.

Although project teams were following the traditional practice of gathering customer stories, and while a great deal of flexibility was added to the process through shorter cycles of delivery, there was surprisingly little change in the "business doesn't know what they want" issue. So it was clear that under these conditions Agile methods would only help on the "do it right" part of the problem, not on the "do the right things" issue. We suspected this was partly because, as an external contractor, we weren't invited inside the business as deeply as we needed to be in order to maximize customer value. A new approach to help business customers make better decisions was needed, so Ci&T created a framework for asking the right questions, to guide decisions in an objective, data-driven way.

Ci&T adapted a technique created in World War II by GE and extensively used in the automotive industry called *value engineering*. This approach quickly proved to be a complement to Agile methods. Value engineering made it possible to establish a value-based dialogue between information technology (IT) and business areas. The discussion over whether a feature/component should be incorporated into the product is now based on its contribution and its value to the expected business goals of the project.

But to understand real value, projects had to start differently. Instead of asking business users about their requirements, technical teams had to work alongside business users to understand the purpose of the investment, what business goals they wanted to achieve, and how they expected to realize a return on their investment. Only when the business purpose was well understood among all stakeholders would the project team start to gather requirements. We quickly realized that this was the Lean A3 thinking process: understanding the business problem and asking why (A3 left side) before jumping to the solution (right side). In this way, value engineering techniques can be viewed as an objective linkage between left side (business drivers) and right side (solution components).

The main steps of the value engineering technique introduced by Ci&T are as follows:

- *Value drivers definition*: Based on the understanding of the business context and goals, a few business drivers are elicited (usually two or three) and assigned weights based on their quantitative contribution to achieve the business goals. If quantitative data are unavailable, weighting is assigned by business users based on consensus. In either case, it is necessary to develop a precise understanding of how value is realized. In one case, a car insurance company wanted to redesign its sales tool used by noncaptive brokers to increase success rate of proposals by a target of 1% to 3%. After the problem analysis, two value drivers were identified as the main means to increase the success rate: pricing definition responsiveness (prices took too long to respond to competitors' strategies and risk factors as regional claim ratio) and a simplified and friendly system interface (some brokers reported they did not quote with the company because of the very complex system interface). The team assigned appropriate weighting factors to these two drivers to guide decision making.
- *Solution definition as a set of value components*: The solution is broken down into value components—each one an aggregation of the system features. Each of these components must be meaningful from a business point of view and can be individually validated. A component map or a process diagram is used as a visual management tool so the team has a clear understanding of the big picture.
- *Features definition, ranking and prioritization*: At project initiation, all components are identified and described at a high level, with a preliminary estimate of effort. Value-based features are the unit of control for effort and cost management during the project. The contribution of every feature to every business driver is agreed upon among business users and organized as a matrix, in a way that the most "valuable" features are assigned the highest weights. The attributed weight is not absolute but relative; after all items have been attributed, the matrix is reweighted to ensure consistency and comparability across the whole matrix.

  Figure C.1 shows this prioritized list of features in a burn-down format, which is helpful for the development team and the customer to monitor progress and make informed tradeoff decisions when necessary.

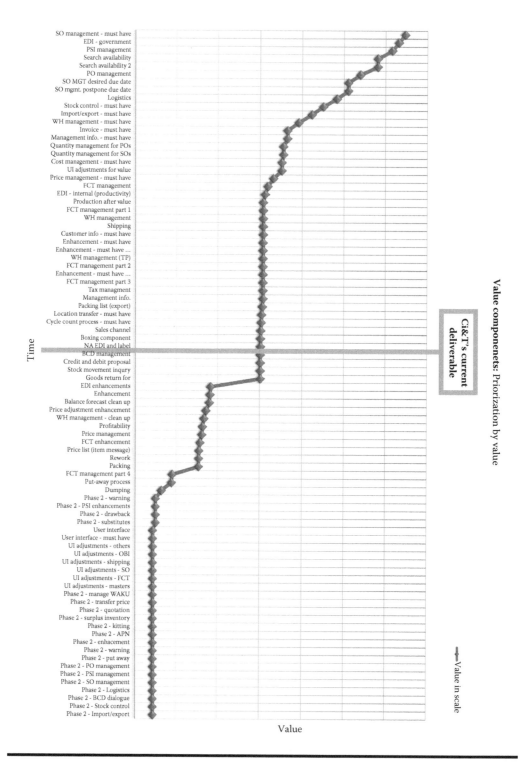

Figure C.1 Value components: prioritization by value.

- *Project roadmap definition*: Once all features are prioritized, a visual project roadmap is produced containing all major product milestones (Figure C.2), so that it is clear to the whole team when each part of the product will be ready for user validation or moved to production. This is important to plan other related activities, such as marketing plans, change management, and so forth.

Ci&T's experience with value engineering has clearly demonstrated that the most valuable solutions that emerge from the creative process are often not the original ideas the business customers had in mind. After a value-driven reflection and a deeper understanding of the business problem, the approach for the solution can change the technical and/or functional requirements to a large extent. In a typical scenario, 40% of the features delivered in the final solution were not present in the initial list of features requested by business areas. They end up replacing features of equal effort that, if added to the final product, would add little or no value to the business drivers. This is much in line with some studies that show that only 40% to 50% of features are actually used and generate value to the business.

Ci&T has learned that exercising Lean thinking discipline, focusing on the problem domain before jumping to the solution domain, is much easier said than done. IT specialists are not used to asking the value of a project, and business users are not used to answering these kinds of questions,

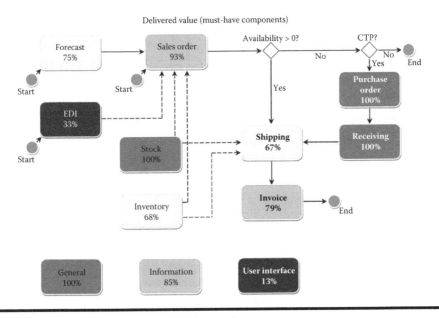

Figure C.2   Product components: roadmap view.

particularly from external contractors! However, Ci&T teams have used this approach during the last three years in more than one hundred projects, and we have learned that, in almost every case, key business users (called "product owners" in Agile) do not have a clear idea of the business drivers and expected value of the projects they are responsible for. Of course, most know the business goals, but usually on a very high level ("to streamline employee productivity," "enhance collaboration," "provide for better decision making," etc.). But there is rarely a deep understanding of the cause and effect, about how the many possible drivers contribute to the desired outcomes in a measurable way.

Once the team starts asking these types of questions and key users escalate the questions up the leadership chain looking for answers, the project runs into two common scenarios. The first and easiest one occurs when these questions meet a leader who can provide the team with the vision it needs. The information is there somewhere, sometimes clearly stated in a business case approved in an executive committee, but which nobody in the project had access to. Or sometimes it is hidden in a bulky report also approved by the board, while at other times the justification is implicit in the minds and strategies of key executives. But they are there, and only need to be structured, shared, and aligned with the project team.

The second and more challenging scenario occurs when, after navigating the full leadership chain, the teams' questions get no clear answers. This means that although everyone in the organization may agree on the high-level objectives and expected outcomes, there is no clear vision of the "hows" (specific drivers and strategy) that will lead to those outcomes.

When projects get to this point, Ci&T assigns senior staff members to engage with customer teams to grasp a deeper understanding of the business problem, in a process that is rather unpredictable and can take from days to many weeks of problem solving to arrive at a consensus. In these cases, Ci&T has experienced a wide range of outcomes: projects that have turned into big programs with a much more comprehensive scope encompassing additional business functions other than IT; projects that are cancelled as no reasonable payback was discovered; and projects that end up with a solution involving only process revision and user training with no IT-related work at all. In fact, this is the outcome one might expect when taking a rigorous problem-solving approach during the launch of any new project, program, or product.

The results of this approach to Lean problem solving and value definition at the beginning of each project have been tremendous, and the enthusiasm is shared by customers such as NSK, a bearings manufacturer, that has hired Ci&T to build from scratch a new version of its commercial system for the Americas: a project that started with a list of 311 features in the backlog, approximately 35 people working full time, and whose deadline was a natural constraint to the implementation of the full 311 items.

Because the business users group was large and distributed across six different countries, the value engineering framework played a key role in making the discussions over priorities more transparent, objective, and value-driven. "Very early in the process the team had a clear understanding of what was crucial for the business, and the resulting solution has simplified our processes considerably. And we did it together with many business areas from a number of different countries, and it just ran smoothly," reports Randy Pomerville, NSK Americas chief information officer. The success was such that NSK started to roll out the value engineering approach to other projects: "The Lean thinking is something we've started introducing into our own business as a result, and is one of the greatest legacies Ci&T has brought to us."

Appendix D

Case Study: ING Bank Netherlands
Our Lean IT Transformation Journey

David Bogaerts and Jael Schuyer

ING is a global financial institution of Dutch origin that offers a range of banking and insurance services in more than fifty countries with many millions of private, corporate, and institutional customers in Europe, North and Latin America, Asia, and Australia. ING has more than 100,000 employees worldwide. In the Netherlands, ING Bank has approximately 28,000 employees, of whom 12,000 are working in operations and information technology (IT), the department in which the back office and IT processes of the bank are executed. Operations and IT's mission is to provide ING with a strategic advantage via efficient and effective employment of people, processes, and technology. Our strategy is as follows:

- To strengthen our workforce to have capable and engaged employees
- To ensure agile and efficient processes within the bank's risk appetite
- To simplify our technology landscape and further improve user experience while maintaining reliability

In response to this strategy, innovation, time to market, and agility are important drivers for us.

Our Lean journey began in the operations and IT department with improving the administrative office processes (e.g., mortgages, savings, lending processes). Like many companies, we started adopting Lean practices without fully understanding the underlying Lean principles. As a result, our Lean coaches didn't succeed in guiding management toward employee engagement and empowerment; focus was on (simply) producing results. We succeeded in creating transparency by introducing fact-based management supported by visual controls and structural process performance dialogues with operational teams. In several departments, however, this emphasis on performance and transparency without engagement and empowerment caused friction between management and employees and, therefore, with the working counsel.* Employees felt pushed beyond their limits; they didn't understand the purpose of Lean.

We quickly learned that a top-heavy focus on waste elimination and process improvement, without enough focus on establishing team ownership, wasn't working. So our Lean department developed† a training program called the "Lean Operational Management Course" that was offered to all first-line managers who were working with the Lean transformation. The training program (spread over eight months) covered soft skills required for Lean, such as how to facilitate a *kaizen* event (servant leadership) and team standup meetings.

The training was well received and reduced the tension between management and employees; however, we are still recovering from our initial focus on control instead of empowerment. The outcome of this training program was measured not just in hard results—quality, speed, and increased productivity improvement—but also in employee satisfaction. Our results so far are significant; our data shows an average efficiency gain of >30%, with cycle time improvement of 25% to 75% in processes such as payment processing, mortgages, and business lending.

Until 2009, our Lean efforts were focused in our office operations; then we turned our attention to IT operations and performed our first pilot. Having learned that we needed to focus first on helping people understand the purpose, we made "winning the hearts and minds of our employees" an explicit focus of our Lean transformation. Although we had good experience with our Lean operational management course, we were looking for more managerial focus right from the start, and we wanted to touch not only the first line but also the middle managers.

---

* Every Dutch company or organization that employs more than fifty employees has to have a workers' council. The council is elected by the employees. The council has several rights and responsibilities: on some subjects such as working hours, management has to ask the council for commitment; on other subjects the council has to be informed and can give advice.
† Together with VergouwenOverduin, a professional training company.

So our Lean department* developed a special manager training program, a "Lean Boot Camp" of five consecutive days, which was used when introducing Lean into a new department. This program addresses management behaviors necessary to encourage the adoption of Lean tools and techniques.

During this weeklong training we discuss the impact Lean has on processes, operational management, and most of all on the mindset and behavior of both managers and employees. The Lean boot camp starts with a discussion with senior management about the goal of the Lean transformation. During this session participants are asked to reflect on a satisfying team effort in which they have been involved. This reflection is used as a foundation for discussing underlying Lean principles and the need for a clear purpose and full engagement of everyone involved. It leads to effective and nonthreatening discussions about roles and responsibilities and the relationship of management and self-directing teams.

After this initial Lean boot camp for management, we developed a three-day process improvement course for employees. This course helps employees to act on an improvement idea in a structured way using the plan-do-check-act (PDCA) process. This training also helps to align employee engagement and problem-solving activities with the new management behaviors.

During the Lean IT transformation, we have been building on our existing ITIL framework for our IT maintenance processes. Lean helped us bring daily choices on how these processes should be executed and improved back to the "IT operations shop floor." By taking this approach, we were using the knowledge and skills of many of our employees—our experts who perform these processes every day—instead of using the minds of a few managers. What we learned is that Lean and ITIL support each other: ITIL provides an initial framework for best practices, while Lean encourages

---

* ING Netherlands established a "Lean IT department" consisting of dedicated Lean coaches organized in a staff department of operations and IT banking. This team reports to the chief financial officer of operations and IT, who in his turn reports to ING's chief information officer. At the moment we have twenty-five Lean coaches working in the field of IT. We approach Lean as a joint journey of management, employees, and coaches. We are asked by management to help everyone in the organization with the transformation, but we are pulled by request rather than pushing our assistance on anyone. Requests for coaching can come from every level: operational, middle management, and senior management. However, before we offer structured coaching, commitment from all layers must be there, and the contribution of the improvement effort to the strategic direction of our company must be clear. Lean initiatives and results are not owned by the Lean department but by the managers and employees doing the daily work.

users to engage, adopt, measure, and continuously improve upon them in a way that blends with their existing culture and practices. We saw that in the domains where we have been applying Lean. In this way our IT operations process performance has improved (e.g., a lower number of incidents) compared to other domains, while at the same time major efficiency gains, in some areas 30% or more, have been realized.

Until this time, our Lean IT efforts had been focused on departments and functions, but we hadn't shifted our focus to cross-functional value stream management. While we had a good start on our Lean transformation, little did we know what was just ahead in our journey. We decided to take what we had learned from Lean IT operations and move into application development. Considering the growing importance of rapid and innovative application delivery within the financial services sector, and specifically to our company strategy, focusing our Lean effort in this area seemed the sensible thing to do. And we were right.

We first performed a pilot in 2010 to try to adopt conventional Lean practices in an application development environment. While everyone thought it was a worthwhile learning experience, we were struggling to get satisfying results. Then two first-line managers came up with the idea to start using Scrum, an Agile technique for managing development projects. One of these two managers had been one of the first to work with Lean in our office transition, so she understood the subtle but important differences. Having convinced senior management to give it a try, they invited us on their journey, and we started to learn together.

Until that point we had focused on building a strong group of internal Lean coaches, selecting individuals because of their natural talent as facilitators and leaders and not so much on their subject matter knowledge and expertise. We believed that if the talent is there, the knowledge and expertise can be acquired, but not the other way around (or to put it in Buckingham's words, "you cannot put in what has been left out"*). But now it seemed necessary to bring in outsiders with special expertise, and we were right. External Agile/Scrum coaches brought special knowledge and expertise that our internal Lean coaches didn't have. Working together, we extended our own capabilities (our Lean coaches are quickly becoming Agile coaches now) while together helping development teams quickly improve their speed and effectiveness.

---

* M. Buckingham and Curt Coffman, "First, Break All the Rules," The Gallup Organization (1999).

However, we learned early on that Scrum and Agile tend to leave management out of the equation. With the scale of our internal development efforts, this was not a feasible approach. Going from zero to forty Scrum teams within a year, potentially going up to sixty to eighty in the year to come (with more expansion possible), we definitely needed a management structure that could guide and coordinate the transition. We returned to our Lean roots and the training we had developed and created an Agile management boot camp that focused on the application development value stream. We defined the value stream pragmatically; in an organization of our size, you become paralyzed if you are trying to get the whole end-to-end value stream on board at the start. The scale just becomes too large, and we have learned that it is very difficult to align everyone up front. We know how to focus on the IT value stream, bringing in IT operations, the immediate business partner, and, of course, the development chain (developers, testers, analysts). We are just beginning experiments with DevOps integration techniques.

In addition to the Agile management boot camp training, we launched another management initiative. Middle managers, together with their senior managers, were invited to work together on solving enterprise impediments using the PDCA approach. A working room (like an *Obeya* room, although we call it the "sprint room") was created with visual tracking of progress and standups twice a week. This *Obeya* room is for the senior managers with middle management. They work on the impediments that have an impact on all Scrum teams and are too difficult to solve for teams and lower management levels. Although we are still early in this effort, employees and management alike feel this has already stimulated many improvements in management problems that had lingered for years.

Now that we are past the initial learning curve, the Lean Agile transformation in application development is moving quickly. Our time to market acceleration in domains where Lean Agile is applied successfully is up 37%, while the first indications are that development costs are decreasing as well. Our working council, of course, always very interested in what is right for the employees, announced in 2012 that Lean is being applied successfully in operations and IT banking. Yes, we really can see the inspiration it gives to employees. And our customers feel it!

Appendix E

Case Study: Netsis
An ERP Publisher's Lean IT Journey

Murat Ihlamur

Netsis (http://www.netsis.com.tr) is an enterprise software producer (ERP, CRM, SCM) based in Turkey, founded in 1991, with a presence in ten countries in Eastern Europe, the Middle East, and Africa. We are the first Turkish company to offer an ERP SaaS product.

As our company grew, departments, regions, and countries expanded, and Netsis management became more institutionalized and departmentalized. The software development team no longer heard the voice of the customer as before. Product development started taking too long. There were signs of erosion in customer satisfaction and employee morale. Meanwhile, SAP was accelerating its penetration in our market, and other multinational ERP competitors were moving in, motivated by the growth potential of the currently small software sector as Turkey became one of the largest emerging economies in the world.

As a result of these challenges to our continued success, in 2008, the top management of Netsis, aware of Lean concepts through our experience providing MRP, ERP, and business-to-business to subsidiaries of large multinationals such as Ford, Henkel, and Opel, asked the Lean Institute of Turkey to provide Lean workshops with a clear goal: learn to eliminate aspects of Netsis processes, products, and services that do not add value to the customer. Lean thinking as a philosophy deeply affected top management, as it became clear that it addressed most of our critical strategic and tactical concerns. We wanted Netsis to be much faster and more flexible than the large foreign multinationals, using our ability to adapt to local conditions, and to be more efficient and sophisticated than the local competitors, always being the first to innovate and deliver state-of-the-art products and services.

After the initial workshops, Netsis started its Lean journey with a relatively simple function: the sales call center. This is where the voice of the customer is first heard, and our performance with this important first impression was not always good. The potential customer had to talk to a call-center employee, a sales manager, a sales expert, and, finally, a distributor, in that order, to set up a meeting, which usually took approximately three days. The Lean solution was much more simple and direct. The call-center employee was trained to engage with customers on the phone, providing them with basic information along with a sense of confidence in the company, and set up the meeting at once. Now the whole process takes less than a few hours instead of three days.

Despite the fact that the call-center staff members' formal education levels were not high, the combination of the product experience and training, coupled with *Gemba* visits, enhanced their ability to assist the customer, which not only accelerated the sales process but also motivated them to offer better service. Most new Netsis employees are now invited to accompany the sales team on sales meetings to gain an appreciation for the customer experience, observe detailed product presentations, and listen to customer questions and concerns.

In most software companies, the call center is not a popular place to work, and it is often used as a stepping stone in the career development of employees. But as a result of the Lean effort, staff members' salaries were raised as their experience grew and as their contribution became more significant. Now, when a customer calls, a motivated employee who understands the business answers and reacts rapidly, as opposed to the old system in which the person answered with a memorized discourse or reading a text.

Product Development

After the initial success in the sales call center, when everyone could see the positive impact on customer responsiveness and call-center employee morale, Lean thinking began to be embraced throughout the organization. Product development is critical to our success and thus became a primary focus in our comprehensive adoption of Lean thinking across our enterprise value streams.

In the past, there were often large development backlogs along with the typical story of disjointed activity; work did not flow. System analysts got involved in the analysis when a new subject was received. They visited the customer, evaluated the products from the competition, and developed the analysis. Then the subject was transferred to a software developer, and the system analyst moved on to another subject. Coding started, and then the testing teams got involved. At the end, document teams wrote the documentation and notified the system analysts that the product was ready to begin the approval process. But as the system analysts were working on multiple projects, sometimes long waiting periods occurred.

Meanwhile, the developers started another project, as the existing software was considered complete, and handed over the task to the implementers, who started the last part of the existing project at the customer site. The implementation required a couple of months on average to realize. When a problem arose, it took awhile for the developers to focus on the old project again, and they were frequently unable to react or address issues properly. As a result, there were delays in product development and implementation, customer satisfaction levels in new products declined, development of the knowledge and skills of the software team slowed down, and the software team became isolated and frustrated—working harder but with less satisfaction.

With our Lean approach, now each product group manages the whole process as a distinct value stream: SaaS ERP, Win.ERP, CRM, HRM, and MRP. The entire product lifecycle, including the analysis of the product, coding, testing, documenting, and delivery to the customer, is done by the same team. Each has its own management, system analyst, developer, tester, and implementer, who all remain focused on one product at a time. Netsis has separated its resources as much as possible into value streams, both in product groups and in support, to avoid task switching, interruptions, and conflicts, matching demand with capacity more efficiently.

All product managers are responsible for the daily management of their product's value stream and the overall performance, while the vice presidents (VPs) act as the executive sponsors for these product teams, helping to monitor the overall value streams and coordinate activity among them. The close cooperation of the product managers with the VPs ensures the alignment of the shorter-term plans with the goals of the company. Our intent is to gradually transfer more responsibility from the VPs to the product managers.

As a result of this value stream approach, customer response time is much faster, at least by 50% with new products. New development and enhancement are usually initiated as the outcome of an analysis by the development team or by a request coming directly from a customer, often a large institutional organization. The product team analyzes the problem in focus groups with customers and quickly develops new solutions tailored to their needs. Once proven useful, these solutions are adapted as a general-purpose packaged solution, serving all customers.

As our teams have become more familiar with the customers and how they use our products, they have become more innovative. Product refactoring is now ten times faster, as it takes less than three months to complete compared to the old system, where it took a few years to do the same thing. Customers like the new versions and the new products very much because they are far more functional.

Product development and project follow up are supported by visual management. There is an *Obeya* room in our primary development center where teams keep the quarterly and monthly plans for all projects. They update these plans every month and post them on the wall. Teams prioritize and solve problems with the help of upper management, who is teaching *kaizen* to the rest of the employees. Each product group has a meeting every week, where group members write the advances, developments, problems, and risks on post-it notes. They place the new post-it over the old one as the new month's plan. A similar process is applied to customer ERP implementation projects, where an *Obeya* room is established at the customer's site.

Obeya gatherings are standup meetings, where each product group meets for fifteen minutes per week. These meetings involve every member of the group and strictly focus on the plan. If there is a need for a more comprehensive meeting or problem-solving *kaizen*, the members meet separately. *Obeya* was the first visual management tool adopted by Netsis; the rest continues electronically for now. Nonetheless, there are plans to widen the use of visual management. One of the ideas is to have widescreen monitors on the walls, where daily requests and numbers of errors would be displayed, and positive or negative trends would be seen.

Product Maintenance and Support

For several reasons it often took months to reply to customer enhancement requests before adopting the Lean approach. Managers could not focus on one subject because they were in charge of different products and areas. Additionally, employees were reluctant to reject a request even if it was not practical to do it.

Netsis now replies to these requests within one week and explains whether the request can be addressed. Disciplined root cause analysis is used to solve problems. Before there was no time limit to solve customer problems, whereas now each request is classified initially into two groups: problems that can be solved within two weeks and problems that can be solved within two months. Separate support teams are now dedicated to each product, and these teams are not involved in new product development. When necessary, support team members can escalate an issue, asking the product development team for help with difficult root cause analysis, but this does not happen often, and when it does it happens very quickly.

The most stressful task of the support department is phone support, where no one wants to work for more than two to three years. Therefore, we ask our solution partners to send their younger employees to this team for periods of six months to a year, and we pay their salaries during that time. More experienced Netsis experts receive fewer calls, which come mostly from institutional clients, and so they can offer more education and mentoring to these young employees, who answer most of the calls received by the solution partners, balancing the workload on the latter. The end result is motivated young workers who know both the product and the employees of Netsis.

Partner Channel

The Lean journey of Netsis includes its partner ecosystem, and we are trying to encourage them all to adopt Lean thinking. With respect to the distribution and consulting partner channel, our aim is to work with fewer solution partners that have higher commitment and integration with Netsis. Before our Lean transformation, our solution partners were already well acquainted with the company, many being former employees. Now they are invited to attend management meetings to align their strategies with that of Netsis. The knowledge and skill levels of their teams are improving as a result of their participation in customer support and projects. Netsis also provides financial support in their recruitment, where warranted.

Management Style and Organization Structure

Before embracing Lean management principles, because of growth the once low-hierarchy organization structure of Netsis had turned into territories and silos, resulting in five layers of management. There was no team approach in software development. A large number of developers, each working on different products, reported to a single manager.

Now there are three levels of management: apprentice (formally associates and experts), headworker (formally chiefs and managers), and master (formally directors and VPs). There are still divisions of responsibility in the organization, although they are considered and treated as interrelated and overlapping (matrix). Our old approach to long management and project team meetings has changed. There are no regular meetings left except for the quarterly work planning, monthly *Obeya* control gatherings, and the weekly team standups.

The human resource strategy has always been to hire young and successful candidates from suitable schools through different programs. Netsis tries to hire state university graduates who are the best in their classes and who see Netsis as an important career opportunity. This profile has proved suitable for creating a team spirit with the principles of respect and humility. High-level managers directly do the interviews without creating many layers of meetings. The aim is to have a relatively low number of employees, offering good conditions, and using a cross-functional work concept. Salary changes with experience and skills. All employees are first trained in a technical area, even if they work in a field such as sales.

The more relaxed and Mediterranean atmosphere of Izmir (where Netsis is headquartered) and its more Western-oriented culture may be a positive factor in establishing a less hierarchical structure, as opposed to the main competitors, who are mostly based in Istanbul, a city with a millennium-long bureaucratic culture as the capital of both the Eastern Roman Empire and the Ottoman Empire. One example of the informal atmosphere is the fact that the VPs of Netsis are on a first-name basis with the chairman, which is rarely found in the Turkish business culture.

As we expected, the efforts to apply Lean thinking to software development met with some initial resistance. For example, a director who resisted the shift toward Lean thinking had to leave his position. He stayed in the organization as the leader of a product group. The company is sensitive to employee turnover. Turnover rate has declined from approximately 15% to 5% since the adoption of Lean thinking. Low hierarchy, modesty, respect for one another, and being proactive have become key principles, while self-confidence levels of the employees have increased notably. If someone wants to leave the company, a root cause analysis is done for each case, and then he or she is often encouraged to establish as solution partner or supplier or to work in another investment or firm of the Netsis Group.

Customers and the Community

Netsis intends to help customers and the rest of the community by promoting Lean thinking, recommending the Lean Institute, and using *Obeya* on the site of the customer for ERP implementation.

Netsis recommends Lean thinking in customer meetings, supports the workshops presented by the Lean Institute of Turkey, and sponsors the biennial Turkish national Lean summit. We often direct our customers to the Lean Institute to help them improve and simplify processes, especially when a complex software need arises. Our company's general strategy is based on the belief that if the customers use Lean thinking to simplify their processes first and understand their future state better, it makes for a more successful ERP implementation and a happier, more successful customer.

Lean Lessons Learned

One of the most important lessons Netsis leadership, managers, and staff have learned is how one can always find more waste in every activity in product development and projects, including the ones that seem to be value adding.

Another finding is that the savings originated from the small incremental improvements can often be equal to or more than the savings that come from the sudden initial breakthrough changes. Our employees are quick to realize that no matter how much one improves, there is always more room for improvement.

The improved customer satisfaction level was an expected outcome of embracing Lean thinking. One of the most surprising lessons so far has been the fact that employee satisfaction levels have also improved, which in turn is a key factor in satisfying our customers. Another surprise was the low cost of the adoption of Lean, compared to the benefits realized from it.

As Lean thinking is being expanded throughout the company (having just started in 2008), there are early signs of progress in customer and employee satisfaction levels, along with operational improvements in sales, software development, and customer support. Our ultimate goal is to become Lean throughout our enterprise, including the partner ecosystem. We hope to establish a culture of continuous improvement and nurture a true learning organization. Netsis upper management firmly believes that this is the only path toward the successful implementation of our strategic plan for sales and market share growth and the sustainable development of the company in a fast-paced economic and technological environment full of uncertainties.

Consistent with our true north, Netsis wishes to make a profit so that we can sustain business operations. In order to do this, we need to improve our people, processes, products, and services continuously and promote a successful partner channel, which in turn enables our end customers to develop Lean, sustainable business practices. For us, our customers' success comes first, and if that means simplifying and improving their processes so they need less software, then in the end we all win.

Finally, Netsis invests in development of Lean skills within our country, contributing to the creation of an active Lean-Agile software community that will help Turkey realize its economic and human development goals. A more productive, competitive, agile, sustainable, and Lean economy of a large emerging country such as Turkey is more relevant today than ever for the world.

Index